Text/Word Processing with Word

A visual guide for RSA Stage II

Part 1 and Part 2

Hilary Coombes

MACMILLAN

To my Mum and Dad
Thank you for your continual encouragement.

Acknowledgements

The author would like to thank the RSA for permission to reproduce examination requirements, and all the Macmillan staff who have been so helpful, especially John Winckler and Isobel Munday. I would also like to thank Victoria Coombes for hand-written scripts and Richard Coombes for the computer work undertaken. Last but not least I'd like to say a big thank you to my husband Keith for keeping the home running whilst I've been working at the computer non-stop.

First published 1997 by
MACMILLAN PRESS LTD
Houndmills, Basingstoke, Hampshire RG21 6XS
and London
Companies and representatives
throughout the world

ISBN 0–333–66968–1

A catalogue record for this book is available
from the British Library.

This book is printed on paper suitable for recycling and
made from fully managed and sustained forest sources.

10 9 8 7 6 5 4 3 2 1
06 05 04 03 02 01 00 99 98 97

Printed in Hong Kong

Contents

RSA TEXT PROCESSING II Part 1 WORK (LESSONS 1–8)

RSA WORD PROCESSING II Part 2 WORK (LESSON 9 onwards)

INTRODUCTION

WHO IS THIS BOOK FOR?

For you   –   if you already know a little about **Word** for Windows, but want to know more

For you   –   if you use **Word** software at work

For you   –   if you have taught yourself word processing (well done!) and would like to check that you are using the quickest methods. You will also expand your knowledge and learn a few shortcuts along the way

For you   –   if you wish to take the RSA Stage II Word and Text Processing examinations (there is a first book in this series which will take you to the Stage I examinations). It also covers the evidence required for NVQ Administration Level 2, 7.2, 13.1 and 13.2 plus Level I, Element 7.1 (but let's not be boring!)

For you   –   if you would like to learn with the very minimum of jargon

For you   –   if you would like to be able to check all your work against a model answer (they are all on the disk which accompanies this book)

For you   –   if you would like a comprehensive alphabetical reference guide (just print it off the disk). It gives you an instant step-by-step summary of 'how to do' something

HOW DO I USE THE BOOK

Well it's really up to you. You could work through it logically and cover everything in detail, or you could look up specific functions to practise.

Each new function is explained clearly (just look inside to check this out). There are also plenty of practise exercises and each one has a model answer on the disk provided with the book.

WHY SHOULD I CHOOSE THIS BOOK?

Because it's going to be fun to use ....

You are going to learn word processing the easy way, using interesting articles which will not allow you to become bored. Every step on the way is explained and when you have covered the book you will be well prepared for the RSA Stage II examinations should you wish to take them.

What have you got to lose?

DISK ACCOMPANYING THIS BOOK

The disk that accompanies this book contains a Summary of Instructions Reference Booklet for you to print out. This succinctly summarises the word processing functions contained in this book plus some extra ones for you to try. It also contains a model answer for every exercise in the book. It will be so easy to check that your printouts are correct.

If you have any problems obtaining this disk (ISBN 0–333–69567–4) please contact Macmillan Direct, Houndmills, Basingstoke, RG21 6XS (01256 329242).

LESSON 1	AMENDMENT AND CORRECTION SIGNS
	PRACTISE AMENDMENT/CORRECTION SIGNS
	ALSO USING UNDERLINE, EMBOLDEN AND LINE SPACING
	RETRIEVE AND AMEND TEXT
	WORKING WITH MORE THAN ONE DOCUMENT OPEN AT A TIME
	MOVING BETWEEN OPEN DOCUMENTS
	TO CLOSE MORE THAN ONE DOCUMENT FILE AND EXIT WORD
	CONSOLIDATION

If you are unsure how to carry out any of the basic word processing functions in this book refer to the QUICK REFERENCE section which can be printed out from the disk which accompanies this book. The basic functions are covered in detail in the first book in this series.

1) Switch on and load Word for Windows 6 software

2) Check that you are working on the correct disk drive. Your work should save on to your personal disk, usually in Drive A

3) Type in the following text as shown:

Exercise 1a

WHO NEEDS WORD PROCESSING?

The simple answer to that is that you do. You need it if you want to work in an office and obtain a well-paid, interesting job. You need it if you want to progress in your career. You need it to help you obtain professional looking documents. You may need it in your personal life – if you are the secretary of a club or society it will be invaluable to you. Writing letters, recording notes, etc will all be so much easier if you use your word processor. If you are a student you will save an immense amount of time if you can produce your own reports using a word processor.

You definitely need word processing skills if you want to take the RSA Word Processing examinations and the Text Processing examinations are much easier if you use a word processor (although you can use a typewriter for Text Processing examinations).

This book has been designed to enable you to consolidate and move on from the beginning stages of word and text processing. If you are wondering what the difference is between the 2, the latter usually covers text produced by typewriting or audio typewriting as well as by word processing, whereas the text produced by word processing can only be produced on a computer.

To succeed, it is important that you practise regularly and learn the functions covered. This book has been arranged logically and your knowledge will build up gradually if you work through the book in a step by step manner.

4) Carefully check your work and correct any mistakes found

5) Spell-check and save your file as **WORDPRO**. Clear the screen. You will use this document again later

AMENDMENT AND CORRECTION SIGNS

You may be familiar with some of the correction signs below. Note especially the last 2 signs, as they are new for Stage II.

[or //   New paragraph needed at this point. Press the return key twice.

Run on. The writer wants to join two separate paragraphs together.

Insert one or more words. The words to be inserted will be written either above the sign or in a balloon with an arrow.

Transpose items horizontally. Words or items need to change places.

Transpose items vertically. Words or items need to change places.

~~Change~~
(✓) ~~Exchange~~   One or more words may be crossed out and a new word/s written nearby. However on reflection the writer has decided she likes the first word/s better so the second word is also crossed out. The correct word to type would be the one with the dotted line underneath and the word 'stet' or a ✓ written in the margin.

Close up.

Leave a space.

PRACTISE AMENDMENT AND CORRECTION SIGNS

Exercise 1b

1)   Type in the following text and amend as indicated:

In the ~~workplace~~ *office* when people draft letters / *or reports* for their typist, they sometimes make mistakes or change their mind. When this happens they often cross out the incorrect work and write in an amendment nearby. [The Royal Society of Arts reflect this practice in their text processing and word processing examinations at Stage II.

The amendment signs used at Stage I are repeated at Stage II and 2 new ones are added. The first one is the 'close up' sign, when used the typist is required not to leave the space indicated. The second new sign is an instruction to leave a space - perhaps, in error, two words have been merged together .

2)   Carefully check your work against **model answer EX1B** which has been saved on the disk that accompanies this book

3)   Spell-check. Save your file as **AMEND**. You will recall this document again later in this lesson. Clear the screen

PRACTISE AMENDMENT/CORRECTION SIGNS ALSO USING UNDERLINE, EMBOLDEN AND LINE SPACING

Exercise 1c

1)   Type in the following text. Amend, underline, embolden and follow instructions as indicated

THE RETURN OF THE DEPARTMENT STORE *embolden + underline main heading.*

NEW RESEARCH *embolden*

Out-of-town shopping has been the ~~general~~ direction of the retail trade for some time now. It is surprising, therefore, to learn from an independent research document released ~~today~~ that department stores within city shopping centres are enjoying *much* better *this week* prospects than they have for many years. [The document published by a retail research group argues that demographic shifts, ~~including~~ the growth of 10% by the end of the *especially* decade in the number of people between the ages of 50 and 64, will favour department stores.

Typist. Please put first paragraph only in double-line spacing

2)   Carefully check your work against **model answer EX1C** which has been saved on the disk that accompanies this book

3)   Spell-check. Save your file as **STORE**. Clear the screen

Exercise 1d

1)   Type in the following text. Amend, underline, embolden and follow instructions as indicated

---

THE GEORGE INN ← *embolden heading*

The George Inn originated in the 16th century. It is thought to have been converted from a barn. The painted facade and the windows are topped by gently curved oak beams. Inside there are rambling rooms with low beamed ceilings and the stone slab floor is original. It is said that the Inn gained its name when King George III stayed there on his way to London

However, there is no evidence that the King actually stayed at the Inn.   ✓ *real*

↑ *underline*

---

2)   Carefully check your work against the copy above. Spell-check. Save your file as **GEORGE**

3)   Clear the screen

RETRIEVE AND AMEND TEXT

Exercise 1e

1)   Retrieve the following document previously saved as **AMEND**. Amend as shown

---

A M E N D M E N T S ← *bold + spaced caps*

In the office when people draft ~~letters or reports~~ work for their typist, they sometimes make mistakes or change their mind. When this happens they ~~often~~ usually cross out the incorrect work and write in an amendment nearby.

The Royal Society of Arts reflect this practice in their text processing and word processing examinations at Stage II. The amendment signs used at Stage I are repeated at Stage II and 2 new ones are added. ~~The first one~~ is the 'close up' sign, used when the typist is required not to leave the space indicated. The second new sign is an instruction to leave a space - perhaps, ~~in error,~~ two words have been merged together, by mistake.

1st paragraph in double line spacing add extra line space above + below this paragraph

The first new amendment sign

---

2)   Carefully check your work against **model answer EX1E** which has been saved on the disk that accompanies this book

3)   Spell-check. Save your file as **AMEND2**. You will now have your original document saved as AMEND and the updated version saved as AMEND2. Clear the screen

WORKING WITH MORE THAN ONE DOCUMENT OPEN AT A TIME

Until now when using **Word** you may have followed a pattern of:

   a)   Opening a document file

   b)   Keying in and saving the work (and perhaps printing)

   c)   Closing the document file

As you now have more word processing experience you might prefer not to close down individual document files. It is possible to leave several document files open so that they are placed one on top of another (just like paperwork on a desk). When you give **Word** the command it will close any open documents without exiting and at the same time it will prompt you to save any unsaved document files.

   This can be very useful. Perhaps you will need to extract information from one document to type into another, or you may need to transfer data between several document files. Leaving documents open also means that you can use them again later without having to go through the long process of opening them.

   By following the instructions below you will leave several document files open and close them automatically later. <u>If, having worked through these instructions, you prefer to close down each document file individually then that is quite all right</u>. It is important that you feel comfortable and happy with the functions you choose. However always be willing to try different ideas – you never know you might prefer them to the ones already tried and tested!

1)   Type in the following text:

Exercise 1f

MEMORANDUM ←(*centre*)

TO   Satheeta Whitcliffe
FROM   Simon Webb
DATE   Yesterday's date
REF   SW/MH

TRAINING OUTCOMES

As you may know I attended a word processing training day last Monday. I am at present writing a subsequent report but I heard that you were about to arrange external word processing training for the Legal Office.

I thought I ought to let you know that you might find it useful to read my report <u>before</u> organising training. Several topics in the report directly relate to future training. I will let you have the report as soon as possible

---

2)   Spell-check and proof-read your work

3)   Save as **INFORM** and <u>leave on screen</u>

4)   Open a new document file by clicking on the **New** icon on the standard toolbar

You will now have a new document page on screen ready to begin new work. Your previous document (saved as **INFORM**) is still open and if you think of the paperwork on the desk situation described on the previous page, you have now placed another sheet of paper on top of existing papers in order to start a new page.

5)   Type in the following text:

Exercise 1g

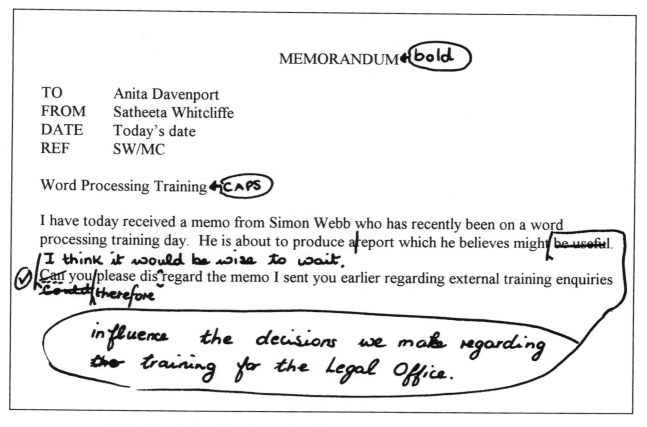

6)   Spell-check and proof-read your work

7)   Save as **NAME** and <u>leave on screen</u>

I N D E X

8)   Open a new document file by clicking on the **New** icon on the standard toolbar

9)   Type in the following text:

Exercise 1h

MEMORANDUM  (centre & bold)

TO   Kevin Hackman, Art Department
FROM   Satheeta Whitcliffe, Staff Development Officer
DATE   Today's date
REF   SW

TRAINING ADVERTISEMENT REPORT

Further to our talks yesterday, please stop the production of art work for the in-house training advertisement.

I'll be in touch again shortly. Sorry for any inconvenience caused.

10)   Spell-check and proof-read your work

11)   Save as **REPORT** and leave on screen

You have now produced 3 new documents, all of which have been saved. You did not 'close' any of the documents and you could now transfer data among them or work with more than one document at a time. It is also useful to leave documents open if you intend to use them again later. Follow the instructions on the next page

KEYBOARD SHORTCUTS

It is possible to use the keyboard instead of the mouse for many formatting functions. For example to change the size of the *font* you could either:

a)   Click on the downward arrow alongside the *font size* box on the **Formatting Toolbar** and choose the size required from the drop-down list

       or

b)   You could hold down the **Ctrl Shift** and **P** key and then type in the font size required

Choosing to use the keyboard in preference to the mouse is a matter of personal choice. One method is not better than the other – they are just different. On the whole 'touch typists' prefer to use the keyboard wherever possible as this enables them to keep their fingers in place on the keyboard and this in turn improves their typing speed.

A short list of keyboard shortcuts is given below. When you have tried these, why not use the **Help** facility to search for more? Start your search with the words 'Shortcut keys' and see where it leads ....

KEYBOARD SHORTCUT KEYS

IF YOU WISH TO USE THE KEYBOARD TO:	YOU NEED TO USE THESE KEYS:
Highlight text	CTRL + SHIFT + THE ARROW KEYS
Make one word bold	Place cursor in word. CTRL + SHIFT + B
Make one word Underlined	Place cursor in word. CTRL + SHIFT + U
Make more than one word bold or underlined	Highlight text. CTRL + SHIFT + B (or U)
Change the case of letters	Highlight text. SHIFT + F3 (the function key at the top of the keyboard)
Change the line spacing of a paragraph to double (and single)	Place cursor in paragraph. CTRL + 2 (CTRL + 1)
Centre a paragraph	Place cursor in paragraph. CTRL + E
Justify a paragraph	Place cursor in paragraph. CTRL + J
Left align a paragraph	Place cursor in paragraph. CTRL + L

MOVING BETWEEN OPEN DOCUMENTS

1)   With the **REPORT.DOC** still on screen click on **Window** on the **Menu Bar**

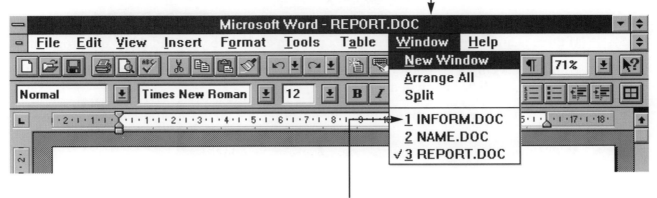

2)   Look at the drop-down menu. You will see the names of the files that you have open at present (ie the 3 files that you have just typed). Click on the file named **INFORM.DOC** in order to retrieve that file

3)   Add the following as a final paragraph to the **INFORM** document now on screen:

> In the meantime if you have any immediate queries that I can help you with, please do not hesitate to let me know.

4)   Quick save your document (see the first book in this series if unsure how to do this)

5)   With the **INFORM.DOC** still on screen click on **Window** on the **Menu Bar** again

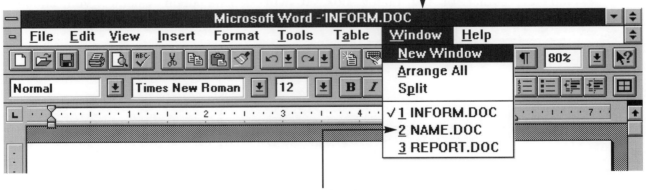

6)   Click on the document file named **NAME.DOC** in order to retrieve it. Add the following as a final paragraph to the **NAME.DOC** now on screen:

> Simon has expressed a willingness to answer any immediate queries if we contact him. If it would be helpful to you, do give him a ring.

3) A topical tip will appear for you to read

4) Look at the bottom right of the dialog box. Is there an ⊠ in the box?

5) If there is an ⊠ you should be shown a new tip each time you load the Word program.

If the box is empty ☐ point the arrow into the empty box and click the left mouse button once. The letter ⊠ will appear

6) If you would like to see more tips or the next tip click on the appropriate box

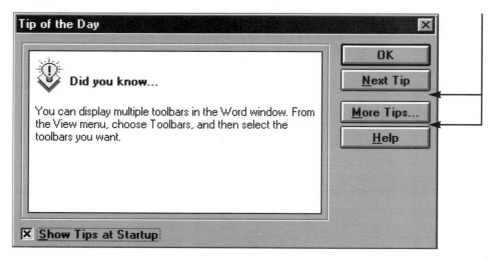

7) When you have finished with this topic either click 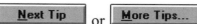 **OK** or double-click the top left corner of the dialog box. It will depend upon whether you choose

Next Tip or **More Tips...**

7)   Quick save your document

8)   With the **NAME.DOC** still on screen click on **Window** on the **Menu Bar** once again

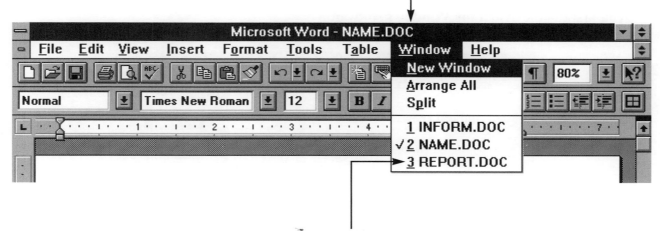

9)   Click on the document file named **REPORT.DOC** in order to retrieve it. Please amend the **REPORT.DOC** now on screen as shown below:

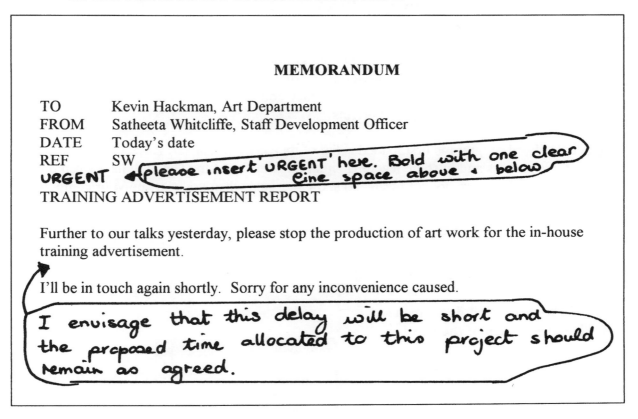

10)   Quick save your document

11)   It is possible to alter or add to an open document and then move to another document without saving the amendment/s. When you eventually close down all the open document files and exit **Word** the computer will remind you to save any updates or amendments. Follow the instructions on the next page to try this out

TIP OF THE DAY

You may have seen a "Tip of the Day" appear on your screen (similar to the one below) when you first run the **Word for Windows** software.

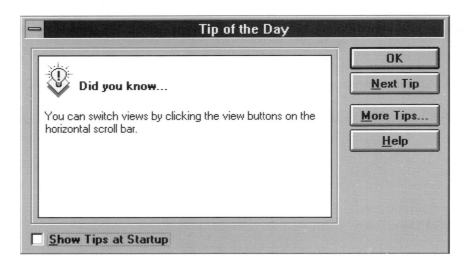

People who are new to word processing do not at first find these tips very helpful. If in the past you have been in this position do not worry, the more word processing experience you get, the more beneficial you will find these tips. In fact you will look forward to their appearance because they can teach you useful shortcuts.

When the Word program is first loaded a Tip of the Day will appear. However it is possible to disable this process and in some teaching situations the Tip of the Day will have been disabled so that new students are not confused. To show the Tips when you start-up your computer follow the instructions below:

1)   Click on **Help** on the **Menu Bar**

2)   From the drop-down menu
        click on **Tip of the Day**.

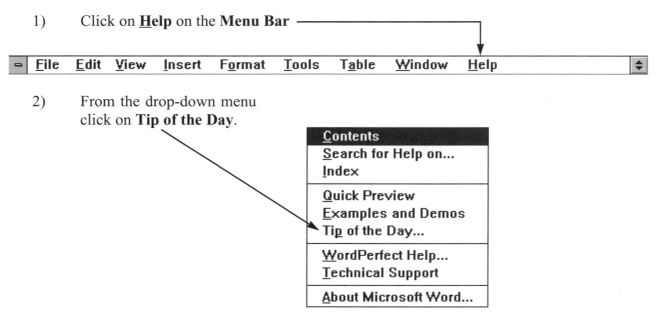

TO CLOSE MORE THAN ONE DOCUMENT FILE AND EXIT WORD

It is possible to leave more than one document open and when you have completely finished working close down all the documents and exit **Word** at the same time. If you have any unsaved work the computer will remind you to save it before you exit. Follow the instructions below:

1)   Open the document **NAME** and add your name bottom right. <u>Do not save or clear the screen</u>

2)   Open the document **INFORM** and add your name bottom right. <u>Do not save or clear the screen</u>

3)   Open the document **REPORT** and add your name bottom right. <u>Do not save or clear the screen</u>

4)   You now have 3 documents open. They have all been amended (by adding your name)

5)   Double click on the menu box with a short horizontal bar at the extreme left of the **Title Bar**

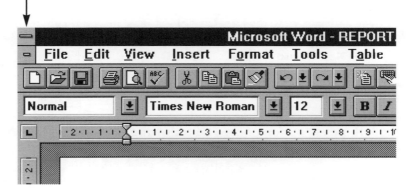

6)   The computer will prompt you to save each document before it is closed. After all documents have been saved you will exit **Word**

You can of course close and exit **Word** with only <u>one</u> document on screen if you wish to adopt this quicker way of exiting

---

Closing several documents when you have finished working or allowing Word to close them all for you when you exit is quicker. However, these short cuts are not obligatory. If you prefer to save and close each document as you work that is of course your choice.

This textbook will continue to instruct clearing the screen after each exercise – please ignore this instruction if you prefer to leave several documents open before eventually closing. However, it is advisable to adopt a pattern of closing documents occasionally, perhaps at the end of each Lesson. If a document is not saved and the computer should by any chance 'crash' you could lose your work.

USING THE 'CONTEXT SENSITIVE HELP' ICON ON SCREEN

Context Sensitive Help enables you to click on the ![help icon] icon on screen and point it to any part of the screen to get help on that particular topic.

You are going to use this facility in the first instance to request help with a familiar topic – aligning text to the left of the screen:

1)   Point the arrow to the **Context Sensitive Help** icon on the **Standard Toolbar** and click once

2)   The cursor point will no longer be a flashing **I** beam. It will look similar to the **Context Sensitive Help** icon itself – ![help cursor icon]

3)   Point to the **Align Left** icon on the **Formatting Toolbar**

4)   Click the left mouse button once. The following **How To** screen will appear:

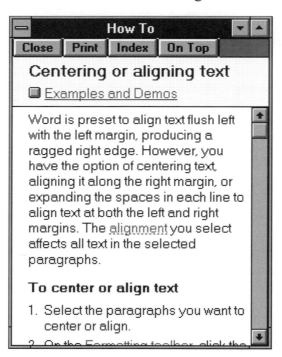

5)   You now have the same choices explained on pages 235 to 237. When you have finished with this **Help** topic return to a clear screen ready to look at the Tip of the Day feature which follows

CONSOLIDATION EXERCISE FOR LESSON 1

1)   Type in the following text:

Format this document to double line spacing

GETTING HELP ← *spaced CAPS + bold*

embolden *embolden*

If you forget how to use a Word command or other feature you can use Word's on-line **Help** to get info. about how the feature works. You can use this useful facility to search for info. on a feature that you have not yet learned. *covered*

The **Help** menu also includes the "Quick Preview and Examples and Demos" commands. Quick Preview gives you an overview of Word's *bold* features and E.............. and D...... gives you the opportunity of viewing a demonstration or example of how a feature is carried out. The "Tip of the Day" box will show you a useful tip or trick to make Word easier or quicker to use for you. *bold*

If you would prefer to see the tips rather than wait for them to come up at random you can click on "More tips" when you are in the Tip of the Day dialog box.

Your name aligned right →

---

2)   Carefully check your work on screen and correct any mistakes found

3)   Spell-check

4)   Save your file with a name of your choice (remember, not more than 8 characters)

5)   Print one copy

6)   Carefully check your work against **model answer CONSOL1** which has been saved on the disk that accompanies this book. If your copy does not have any further mistakes, well done!
If when checking your printed work against the correct copy you found mistakes, strive to check more thoroughly next time. The ability to check your work on screen is essential if you want to become an efficient word processor operator and pass examinations

---

The "On-line Help" facility described in the above document is covered in much more detail in the last lesson of this book. You can work through this lesson now if you prefer not to wait until you have completed the interim lessons.

12   iv) **CLOSE THE INFORMATION SCREEN COMPLETELY AND RETURN TO YOUR DOCUMENT**

It will depend upon where you are in the **Help** facilities as to how you close. There are several ways in which you could close screens and with practice you will soon discover the method you prefer. Experiment with the following:

a)   Look for a [Close] or a [Cancel] button and click on those. This should close down the dialog boxes individually

OR/AND

b)   Double-click the top left corner of the **Help** dialog boxes. This should close down individual dialog boxes or the complete **Help** procedure (depending upon which dialog box is on screen at the time)

> **You have only looked at a very small part of the Help facilities available with Word. Why not look for information on another topic using the Search facility.**
>
> **Alternatively click on 'Help' on the Menu Bar and spend time experimenting with the other useful facilities available to you. One of these items "Tip of the Day" is introduced after the next topic (USING THE HELP ICON ON SCREEN).**

LESSON 2	ABBREVIATIONS (as RSA performance criteria)
	EXPANDING ABBREVIATIONS
	PRACTISE AMENDMENT/CORRECTION SIGNS,
	UNDERLINE, EMBOLDEN, LINE SPACING
	AND EXPANDING ABBREVIATIONS
	SPELLING AND EXPANDING DERIVATIVES
	PRACTISE CORRECTING ERRORS IN SPELLING
	MORE SPELLING PRACTICE
	CONSOLIDATION

If you are unsure how to carry out any of the word processing functions in this book refer to the QUICK REFERENCE section. The basic functions are covered in more detail in the first book in this series.

ABBREVIATIONS (as RSA performance criteria)

The presentation of your work is important. Employers want their image to be reflected by a high standard of presentation and they would not expect you to use abbreviated words (for example approx. instead of approximately).

Sometimes abbreviated words will be followed by a full stop indicating the abbreviation. You are not meant to type the full stop unless, of course, it is the end of a sentence.

At Stage II the RSA expect you to be able to expand the following abbreviations.

ABBREVIATION	EXPAND TO	ABBREVIATION	EXPAND TO

The following are used for the Stage I qualification but are also used at Stage II

ABBREVIATION	EXPAND TO	ABBREVIATION	EXPAND TO
a/c(s)	account(s)	org	organisation
approx	approximate(ly)	poss	possible
cat(s)	catalogue(s)	ref(s)	reference(s)
co(s)	company/ies	ref(d)	refer(red)
dr	dear	sec(s)	secretary/ies
info	information	temp	temporary
misc	miscellaneous	sig(s)	signature(s)
necy	necessary	yr(s)	year(s)
opp(s)	opportunity/ies	yr(s)	your(s)

days of the week (eg Thurs, Fri)	Thursday, Friday, etc
months of the year (eg Jan, Feb)	January, February, etc
complimentary closes (ie ffly, sncly)	faithfully, sincerely
words in addresses (eg Rd, St, Ave, Dr, Sq, Cres, Pl, Pk), etc	

NB: Abbreviations in company names and commonly used abbreviations must be retained, for example: etc, eg, ie, NB, PS and plc, Ltd and & (in company names)

The following are new to the Stage II qualification

gntee(s)	guarantee(s)	mfr(s)	manufacturer(s)
immed	immediately(ly)		

10   ii) **WATCH A DEMONSTRATION OF HOW TO UNDERLINE**

a)   With the **How To** screen showing click the box   ▢ <u>Examples and Demos</u>

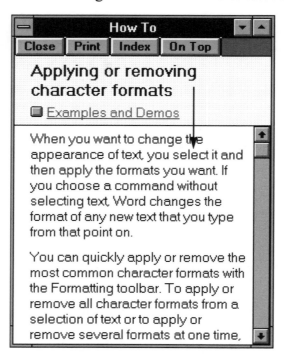

b)   Click on [**Demo**] and follow the screen prompts (instructions). When you no longer wish to watch the demonstration click on [Close]. You will return to the **How To** screen

c)   To close the **Help** screen completely see item number 12

11   iii) **KEEP THE HELP PROCEDURES VISIBLE WHILE YOU WORK**

If you want to follow the steps in a Word Help procedure while you work you can keep the **Help** procedures visible, or "on top", while you work. To do this:

a)   When the procedure you want appears on screen (in this case the **How To** screen on **"Applying or removing character formats"**), click the **On Top** button. The **How To** box will stay on top of the document as your work

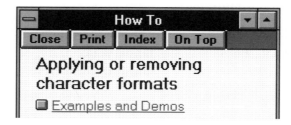

b)   When you no longer wish to see the **Help** screen click the **On Top** button again. If the **Help** screen does not disappear click on the word **Close**

c)   To close the **Help** screen completely see item number 12

EXPANDING ABBREVIATIONS

Exercise 2a

1) Key in the following text, expanding the abbreviations as you go. **Abbreviated words are sometimes shown with a full stop as indicated below. You are not meant to type the full stop as well as expand the word**

> **Notice 2 full stops, this indicates the end of a sentence**

MANAGEMENT RISKS

> *Typist Please expand Co. to Company in this last line, + company/ies elsewhere.*

The opp. to 'buyout' management has almost doubled in the past yr. according to a survey carried out by the local mfrs. Watchdog. The report which will be officially published on Feb. 12 has been refd. to by Andrew McKenzie in his paper entitled "Risk Management". He highlights org. problems involved in this area of business. //The news has prompted insurance cos. to issue a warning to all those considering the takeover of a co.. They warned any org. interested in a takeover to seek detailed info. on liabilities, which may not be apparent on first sight. The sorts of hidden risks a detailed check can uncover include those for environmental claims and other work-related injuries. They recommend immed. action be taken by consulting a Risk Management Co. before any serious consultations are entered into.

2) Save your work as **BUYOUT**. Spell-check and proof-read, then quick save your work **(the spell-checker will not always pick up all the abbreviations, it is not designed to expand words)**

3) Carefully check your work against **model answer EX2A** which has been saved on the disk that accompanies this book

4) Clear the screen. However, if you prefer to leave this file open please do so. (see Lesson 1)

Exercise 2b

1) Key in the following, but expand the missing abbreviations. Try to remember them but if you are having problems, look up the word on the previous page:

1) The a/cs. department saw the opp. of an imm. financial return on the cat.
2) The org. employs approx. 5 temp. secs. each yr..
3) Yr. ref. arrived on Wed. 20 Aug. The info. given was supportive.
4) He filed the files in the wrong order. He put the misc. file before the mfrs. file.
5) It is necy. for the co. to org. the event next Oct..
6) The sec. could not read the sig. It would be necy to ask the customer's name.
7) It is poss. that he missed the opp. last Fri of speaking to the boss.
8) The cat. was illustrated by a dr. little kitten on the front cover.
9) This org. can gntee. that you will receive the necy. info. by next Sat.
10) This co. cannot gntee. that this opp. will be repeated.

2) Carefully check your expanded abbreviations against the RSA list on page 12

3) Correct any mistakes made. Spell-check and save your file as **EXPAND**. Clear the screen

i) <u>TO PRINT THE HELP INFORMATION</u>

a)   Click on **Print**

b)   The following dialog box will appear:

When the information has been printed this box will disappear

c)   The screen will revert to the **How To** screen. Click on [Close]

d)   To close the **Help** screen completely see item number 12

PRACTISE AMENDMENT/CORRECTION SIGNS, UNDERLINE, EMBOLDEN, LINE SPACING AND EXPANDING ABBREVIATIONS

Exercise 2c

1) Retrieve in the following text which you saved as **WORDPRO**. Amend as indicated. If you are unsure how to move a block of text see the first book in this series or refer to the QUICK REFERENCE GUIDE on the disk that accompanies this book

---

DO YOU

~~WHO~~ NEEDS WORD PROCESSING? ← **bold**

The simple answer to that is that you do. You need it if ~~you want~~ *should you wish* to work in an office and obtain a well-paid, interesting job. You need it if you want to progress your career. You need it to help you obtain professional looking documents. You may need it in your personal life - if you are the secretary ~~of a club or society~~ it will be invaluable to you. Writing letters, recording notes, etc will all be so much easier if you use your word processor. If you are a student you will save an immense amount of time if you can produce your own reports using a word processor. ✓

You definitely need word processing skills if you want to take the RSA Word Processing examinations and the Text Processing examinations are much easier if you use a word processor (although you can use a typewriter for Text Processing examinations).

This book has been designed to enable you to consolidate and move on from the beginning stages of word and text processing. If you are wondering what the differences *is* are between the 2, the ~~letter~~ *former* usually covers text produced by typewriting or audio typewriting as well as by word processing, whereas the text produced by word processing can only be produced on a computer.

To succeed, it is important that you practise regularly and learn the functions covered. This book has been arranged logically and your knowledge will build up gradually if you work through the book in a step by step manner.

To summarise:

If you can use a word processor you will be able to work quicker

Amend work before printing *a* final copy

Change text easily when updating

Maximise yr. ○ opp. of obtaining a well paid office job.

} double line spacing for final paragraph

---

2) Carefully check your work and correct any mistakes found

3) Spell-check and save your file as **WORDPRO2**

4) Carefully check your work against **model answer EX2D** which has been saved on the disk that accompanies this book

5) Clear the screen if you wish (see Lesson 1)

8)   The following screen will appear:

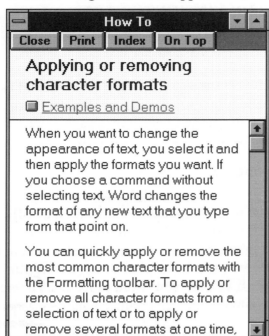

You can read the text that is at present off-screen by clicking on the maximise icon on the scroll bar

Alternatively double-click on the blue bar at the top of the screen – the text will then fill the screen width

9)   When you have read the information about underlining you have several options:

i)   You can print the help information for future use

ii)   You can watch a demonstration of how to underline

iii)   You can keep the **Help** procedures visible while you work

iv)   You can close the information screen completely and return to your document

Decide which you would like to do and follow through the appropriate instructions following:

SPELLING AND EXPANDING DERIVATIVES

The text processing examination will also test your spelling of the following words and their derivatives where marked * (eg plurals, -ed, -ing, -ment, -tion, -ly, -able, -ible):

In the examination it is likely that some of the words listed will be mis-spelt and some will also be circled to highlight the error.

Exercise 2d

1)   Type in the following text and carefully check work before printing one copy for future reference. Save as **SPELL**. Clear the screen.

---

* access accessed accessing accessible
* accommodate accommodated accommodating accommodation
* achieve achieved achieving achievement achievable
* acknowledge acknowledged acknowledging acknowledgment although
* apparent apparently
* appreciate appreciates appreciated appreciating appreciation
* believe believed believes believing believable
* business businesses
  client(s)
  colleague(s)
  committee(s)
  correspondence
* definite definitely
* develop develops developed development
* discuss discussed discussing discussion
  expense(s)
* experience(s) experienced experiencing
* financial financially
  foreign
  government(s)
* inconvenient inconvenience
  receipt(s)
* receive receives received receiving
* recommend recommends recommended recommending recommendation
* responsible responsibly
* separate separates separated separating separation separately
* sufficient sufficiently
* temporary temporarily
  through

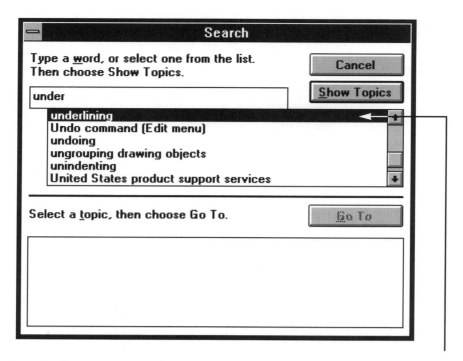

5)   There is an index entry named **underlining**. This is the information you want so click the left hand mouse button once on the word '**underlining**' and the name will appear in the box above

6)   Click on **Show Topics** The following screen will appear:

Word is offering you a choice of topics related to underlining

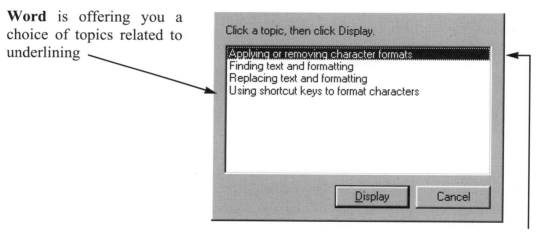

7)   The sentence '**Applying or removing character formats**' is highlighted in blue. This is the topic area that **Word** is offering you. Click on **Display** to accept

PRACTISE CORRECTING ERRORS IN SPELLING

Exercise 2e

1) Key in the following paragraph in double line-spacing. Amend all errors as you proceed. The spelling errors are circled

---

VOTING ON PAY ← bold

SHAREHOLDERS VOTE

The Comittee considering executive pay excperienced problems with the definition of the word 'executive'. Responsable documentation brought forward at the meeting encouraged discusion on what constitutes an executive. It was eventually recomended than an employee earning finanshull renumeration of more than £60,000 would be classed in this category. [The Committee aknowledged a seperate report from shareholders. After discussion they rejected the recomendation by Jacques Friedmann that shareholder be allowed acces to personal info. on employees. The decision caused the rejection of the idea that shareholders be permitted to vote on renumeration packages.

EXPENSES

Lynda Warmley raised the matter on executive expences and reoponsabilty for claims. The Chairman said he felt uncomfortable with the suggestion of 'opying' on busines colleages and recomended that no change be made to disclosure rules.

---

2) Carefully check your work and correct any mistakes found

3) Spell-check and save your file as **VOTE**

4) Print one copy and clear the screen

5) Carefully check your work against **model answer EX2E** which has been saved on the disk that accompanies this book

2)   From the drop-down menu

       Click once on

       Search for Help on .

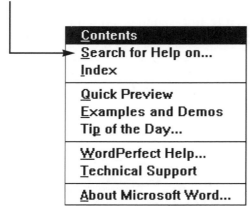

3)   A screen similar to the one below will appear:

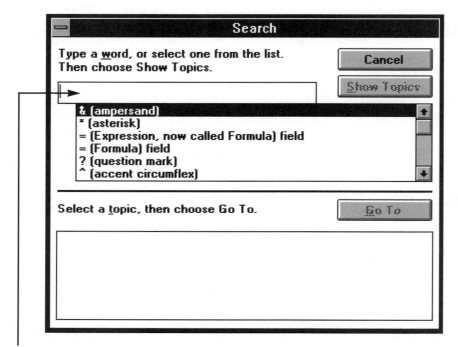

4)   Type the word UNDERLINE in the box indicated. As you do so notice that the index
       list is scrolling (moving). Before you have finished typing the word the list will show
       you the underline help items it contains:

MORE SPELLING PRACTICE

Exercise 2f

1) <u>All the words in the following list have been mis-spelt</u>. Key them in with the correct spelling. Do not immediately look up the words on page 12 or 15. If you are not sure how to spell a word, try to pronounce it aloud and make an attempt at typing it – check the word immediately afterwards. If you find a particular word very difficult, look it up, but make a mental note to write that word every day until it no longer causes you trouble.

accesed	acommodation
acknowledgement	apparantly
apprecation	acheive
altho	beleivable
bussiness	cliant
coleague	comitte
corespondence	defenate
developement	discusion
expensess	experiensing
financiall	foriegn
goverment	inconvenence
recept	recommendattion
responsable	recieved
suficient	temporararily
seperately	throug

2) When you have checked your work for spelling errors, repeat this exercise again but this time only attempt to spell those words that were incorrect the first time

3) Save your work as **ERROR**

4) Clear the screen if you wish (see Lesson 1)

LESSON 20	HELP FACILITY
	USING THE HELP ICON ON SCREEN
	TIP OF THE DAY
	KEYBOARD SHORTCUTS

Well done! you have mastered a great deal in the world of word processing. Working through this book means that you are well prepared to take the RSA Stage II examinations in text and word processing. Even if you do not wish to take examinations you can justly claim that you are now a proficient word processing operator. I am sure that you now feel much more confident about word processing and your ability to operate Word software.

It is time to take one more step forward and by taking this step you are beginning the process of becoming a word processing operator who uses the system efficiently and independently.

THE HELP FACILITY

Using the Help Search option

As you are no longer a beginner in word processing, you are in a good position to take advantage of the **Help** facility that **Word** offers. In order for you to see how useful the **Help** facility can be, you are going to search for information on something familiar to you – underlining text.

1)   Click on the word **Help** on the Menu Bar

| □ | File | Edit | View | Insert | Format | Tools | Table | Window | Help | | ◆ |

CONSOLIDATION EXERCISE FOR LESSON 2

Practise what you have covered so far by following through the instructions below.

1)   Type in the following text:

ATTITUDE CULT RECORDS ←centre 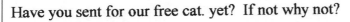 *Typist. Please leave the abbreviation SAE*

FREE CATALOGUE

Have you sent for our free cat. yet? If not why not?

We can offer you an amazing range of **VINYL** ~~still available~~ (including ~~foriegn~~ titles and our own specialist section). We also have a **FANTASTIC** range of ~~compact discs~~ *CD's*, cassettes, T-shirts, videos, etc.

This most comprehensive cat. is free. *completely* No ~~expence~~ has been spared in its preparation, if you contact us you will receive a brand new, full colour, up-to-date edition. It's yrs. for the price of a stamp (or a call).

We stock over 30,000 titles from the 60's, 70's, 80's and 90's. Yes! we have suficient stock to immed. meet 99% of requests. If you should be unlucky enough to choose a title that we haven't in stock, we will ~~acknoledge~~ your request and without delay seek a copy as soon as poss..

DISCOUNTS are given - why not make enquiries. Payment can be made by Visa, Access, Cheques etc. <u>BOTH UK AND EXPORT</u>.

EXPORT ENQUIRIES are ~~defanitely~~ welcome . Remember we gntee. there will be no VAT to pay on export orders.

absolutely There is no obligation, we are not a club, and we ~~apreciate~~ every one of our customers - you will be in good hands with us.

THE ABOVE REASONS SHOULD HAVE PERSUADED YOU. THERE'S NOTHING TO ⎤double line spacing⎦
LOSE BUT PLENTY TO GAIN. NO SAE NECY.

Remember the cat. is free. Fax us, phone us, or even write to us. Just contact us -
ATTITUDE CULT RECORDS, (Dept SS1), Buckingham Street, LONDON EC1.

TEL 01081 4674 1234   FAX 01081 4683 8895

---

2)   Carefully check your work and correct any mistakes found

3)   Spell-check and save your file as **RECORDS.** Print one copy

4)   Carefully check your work against **model answer CONSOL2** which has been saved
        on the disk that accompanies this book

Please key in the following document and insert the phrases as indicated.   Save and print one copy.

Our ref JH/HJH

Mr + Mrs U Johnson
Windsor House
Old Bath Road
BATH
BA1 3AU

Dear Mr and Mrs Johnson

We would like to take this opportunity of reminding you that The Friends Committee organise exciting social events throughout the year for boys and their parents.

(circled note: Check this from Document 1 and amend if necessary)

This month we are organising a "Musical Evening" that promises to be an interesting event which will encourage musical talent. (Insert PHRASE2 here) Tickets are still available for all evenings. Please see the enclosed leaflet for more details.

(Insert PHRASE4 here) You are very welcome to attend and if you wish you can bring along friends to make up your own team of 6. Your son will have been given an entry form.

The theatre production next month has been a popular choice of production. I am not sure whether the appearance of a live pony during the evening has something to do with this. (Insert PHRASE1 here) See the enclosed leaflet for more details.

In the springtime we are planning a Victorian Magic Lantern evening by candlelight. (Insert PHRASE3) Your son will be bringing home full details in due course.

We look forward to welcoming you to one of these events very soon.

Yours sincerely

(circled note: Top and 2 copies please. One file and one for The Headmaster. Indicate routing)

Angie Davies
Chairman of The Friends

LESSON 3	DISPLAY WORK AT STAGE II (CONCENTRATING ON REPORTS AND ARTICLES) including: Line spacing, following directions, distractions, style of presentation, single/double spacing, emboldening/underlining, initial capitals/all capitals, symbols etc, PROOF-READING EXERCISES – SPOT THE DIFFERENCE PRESENTATION STYLES TARGET TIMING CONSOLIDATION

Exercise 3a

1)   Type in the following text:

PEACE IN THE OFFICE!   ← *centre + bold*

Wouldn't life be nice if whenever we wanted peace and quiet we got it? Just imagine that you have finished your work day and you are waiting for the bus home. Instead of standing in a crowded, busy street in the rain, you are sitting in a park with the sun shining and the birds singing. You are no longer *waiting* for a crowded bus, with the likelihood of having to stand up most of the way home.   *jostle for a place*

No, your chauffeur is awaiting you. When you have finished enjoying the *sunshine* you will stroll ✓ across to your waiting Rolls-Royce and be driven home. Imagine you are in the work place and you have been given a complicated piece of work to type. You really enjoy the challenge of producing *accurate and well-displayed* text but you like peice and quiet in order to concentrate on the job in hand. You will be *extremely* lucky if you are able to sit ~~quietly~~ at the ✓ computer without interruption because most busy offices have telephones ringing, clients or colleagues talking, as well as the general noise and movement associated with the productive workplace.

We all know that life is not perfect and in the office we overcome interruptions and noise and get on with the job. The RSA Text Processing Stage II part 1 examination reflects the interruptions you are likely to encounter at work by requesting the examination invigilator to interrupt you during the examination and hand you a piece of text which must be incorporated into one of the documents you are asked to type.

Imagining a perfect world *is* nice sometimes, but living with reality can be a lot more] *embolden + in double line spacing* interesting - especially if you are prepared.

2)   Carefully check your work against **model answer EX3A** which has been saved on the disk that accompanies this book

3)   Save your file as **PEACE**. Clear the screen if you wish (see Lesson 1)

IMPORTANT NOTE

The following standard phrases have been saved on the disk that accompanies this book as phrase1, phrase2, phrase3 and phrase4. If you would prefer these standard phrases to be saved as auto-text files you are advised to key these in now before commencing the task 4 examination document.

---

phrase1

You might like to know that there are still several tickets available for the Friday evening performance.

phrase2

It will give you an opportunity to hear a variety of original work produced by composers from different years in the school.

phrase3

As you watch and listen to stories like "The Village Blacksmith" you will soon see how gripping a Victorian Magic Lantern evening can be.

phrase4

The much advertised quiz evening will be held on Friday of next week (..... typist please insert the date.....) at 7.00 pm in the Sports Hall.

PROOF-READING EXERCISES – SPOT THE DIFFERENCE

Exercise 3b

1   Proof-read the following text and follow instructions. **Do not start typing … READ the handwritten instructions first!**

Typist, There are 17 errors here. The copy at the bottom of the page is the correct version. Compare these 2 copies and find all the errors. When you have identified them, key in the correct copy and save as EGG. If you really cannot find all the errors there is a list on the next page, but don't cheat on yourself - look for the errors before turning the page.

ONE EGG SERVES 15

A breeding pair sells for $40,00 Canadian dollars. They grow 12 inches a month when young, in fact they grow so fast that by the age of 2 the average weight is 450 pounds. The entire bird is marketabel - the feathers make excellent cleaners of high-tech equipment and the hide makes high quality book leather. The eyes are used in medical research and in humna cornea transplat. Even the eeg scales and toe-nails are used to clear jewelry.   If omeleettes are liked by you then one egg will make 15 good size omelettes.

These are odd-looking birds, too big to fly but they can reach 40 mph in 2 seconds flat. It's big and goofy looking - have you guessed it's name yet? It's the ostrich, that roadrunner from Africa, and in Candada the bird is becoming every more popular as ostrich farms develop to meet the local supermarket and restuarant demand.

ONE EGG SERVES 15

A breeding pair sells for $40,000 Canadian dollars. They grow 12 inches a month when young, in fact they grow so fast that by the age of 2 the average weight is 450 pounds. The entire bird is marketable – the feathers make excellent cleaners of high-tech equipment and the hide makes high quality boot leather. The eyes are used in medical research and in human cornea transplants. Even the leg scales and toe-nails are used to clean jewels. If omelettes are liked then one egg will make 15 good sized omelettes.

These are odd-looking birds, too big to fly but they can reach 40 mph in 2 seconds flat. They are big and goofy looking – have you guessed their name yet? It's the ostrich, that roadrunner from Africa, and in Canada the bird is becoming ever more popular as ostrich farms develop to meet the local supermarket and restaurant demand.

(Key in the following table. Save and print one copy.)

SPORTING ACHIEVEMENTS

Congratulations are extended to all boys who have taken part in sporting competitions during the past year. To reach the final selections is something to be celebrated. Special mention must be made of the following boys who have played for county or country:

NAME	DETAILS OF COMPETITION	SPORT	POSITION/ OUTCOME
UPPER SCHOOL			
Morris, A	Five Counties	Rugby	Back line
Evans, C	Somerset U16	Cricket	Wicket keeper
Bale, A	Wales U16	Hockey	U16 unbeaten
Matiru, R	National ATC U17	Athletics	1.70m high jump (personal best)
MIDDLE SCHOOL			
Grout, S	England A's trial	Rugby	
Ivorra, P	Somerset U15	Swimming	1st freestyle B
White, J	Avon U15	Golf	4th
Arrow, B	Five Counties	Rugby	Scored 2 tries
Ellis, J	Region ATC	Athletics	Won 200 metres
LOWER SCHOOL			
Sudhakaran, S	Avon U12	Swimming	16.2 seconds off personal best
Day, R	Cathedral Cup	Gymnastics	Junior winner
Leventhal, K	Harriers Event	Cross-Country	5th
Gwyn, A	All Schools CC	Cross-country	36th in England

(Please sort into exact alphabetical order of name within each section)

(Please move SPORT column before DETAILS OF COMPETITION column)

(Please change order, so that LOWER SCHOOL is first followed by MIDDLE SCHOOL, with UPPER SCHOOL last.)

Did you find all of the errors in text on the previous page? Check below:

The heading should have been emboldened
The following words were incorrect

    $40,000

    marketable

    boot

    human

    transplants

    leg

    clean

    jewels

    sized

    omelettes

    by you

    They are

    their (did you also notice the apostrophe in the word "it's" should not be there?)

    Canada

    ever

    restaurant

2)   With the **EGG** document on screen make the following amendments:

ONE EGG SERVES 15 (centre)   ~~Double line spacing please~~

A breeding pair sells for $40,000 Canadian dollars. They grow 12 inches *each* month when ✓ young, in fact they grow so fast that by ~~the age of 2~~ *2 years of age* the average weight is 450 pounds. The entire bird is marketable - the feathers make excellent cleaners of high-tech equipment and the hide makes high quality boot leather. The eyes are used in medical research and in human cornea transplants. Even the leg scales and toe-nails are used to clean jewels. If omelettes are liked then one egg will make 15 good sized omelettes.

(rather) These are an odd-looking birds, too big to fly but they can reach 40 mph in 2 seconds flat. They are big and goofy looking - have you guessed their name yet? It's the ostrich, ~~that roadrunner from Africa,~~ and in Canada the bird is becoming ever more popular as ostrich farms develop to meet the local supermarket ~~and restaurant~~ demand.

---

3)   Carefully check your work against **model answer EX3B** which has been saved on the disk that accompanies this book

4)   Spell-check and quick save your file. Clear the screen if you wish (see Lesson 1)

EXAM DOCUMENT 2

Recall this document saved as EXAM2. Amend as shown. Print one copy.

BOARDING REPORT *(emphasise heading)*

— insert this section 13mm (½") from the left margin

At a recent psychiatrists conference the behavioural characteristics of the average troubled adolescent was defined as mad, bad, sick and thick! Although you will not find any such definition in any textbook, such forthright views do give an insight into the types of behaviour that have to be dealt with at various times in boarding schools.

As you sit comfortably at home occasionally confronting one or 2 (or ~~mabye~~ *maybe* three) tetchy teenagers spare a thought for those of us who oversee the growing-up traumas of 80 boys!

↕ leave at least 25mm (1") here   *(expand)*

Keeping boys active is halfway to keeping them away from the "M, B, S, and T" problems. We provide as many opportunities for letting off steam as possible. Listing just a few of those organised / *include:*

Soccer
Bowls
Cross-country
Rowing
Theatre (teamed up with the local girls' boarding school - always popular!)
Badminton and tennis
Cinema trips
Travel club
Chapel
Children in Need appeal work

← Sort this section into exact alphabetical order and centre

We have ventured into journalistic areas this past year. The boys have formed a 'House Committee' and with the help of Mr. MacGreggor, Head of English, and Mrs Wayne, Head of Computing, they are publishing a College Magazine. Further details will be announced in due course.

Simon Mitchell
BOARDING HOUSEMASTER

PROOF-READING – SPOT THE DIFFERENCES

Exercise 3c

1)   Proof-read the following text and follow instructions:

FOREWARD *Compare this printout with the correct one below. When you have found all the errors you can, Key in a correct copy and save as THEATRE.*

Welcome to the Summer theatre season. If you didn't see any of our Spring plays you will have missed a treat thisyear. As you will see from the critic reviews (snippets on page 4) that we played to packed houses and our new play "Forgettable - Wonderful" transferee to the West End on 1 May.

dON'T miss out this season. We're delighted to welcome Jilly Stockton and the Glasgo Theatre Company to open the season on on 20 May. The new play "A MONTH IN THE PARK" promises to be a delight. The Company have been playing to packed houses in the North East and this new comedy has been hailed as "a wonderfully funny limit less comic inventtion" by the Daily Mail. Fulldetails can be found on page 6.

Our resident Company will entertain you for the rest of the season and there is something for every one - from newly commissioned work to Chekhov's "Three Sisters". Take time to look through this brochuure and then come and enjoy an evening with us.

Brian Saver

FOREWORD

Welcome to the Summer theatre season. If you didn't see any of our Spring plays you will have missed a treat this year. As you will see from the critic reviews (snippets on page 5) we played to packed houses and our new play **"FORGETTABLE – WONDERFUL"** transferred to the West End on 2 May.

Do not miss out this season. We're delighted to welcome Jilly Stockton and the Glasgow Theatre Company to open the season on 20 May. The new play **"A MONTH IN THE PARK"** promises to be a delight. The Company have been playing to packed houses in the North East and this new comedy has been hailed as "wonderfully funny limitless comic invention" by the Daily Mail. Full details can be found on page 6.

Our resident Company will entertain you for the rest of the season and there is something for everyone – from newly commissioned work to Chekhov's "Three Sisters". Take time to look through this brochure and then come and enjoy an evening with us.

Brian Saver

leave this section in single

If our young are ever to lift their eyes to the hills, to see visions or to dream dreams, we must persuade them to look beyond the current ephemeral icons to great music, great literature, great poetry and great drama. We must direct them towards higher and more lasting values.

Copy this section to [A]

We strive for high standards not only in academic and sporting competitions but also in good order, good discipline, and good manners.

move this section to [B]

We are not a school of the mind and the body only - we are a 3-dimensional school which perhaps more importantly is also a school of the spirit. Education of the spirit is a difficult topic but one which must be taught if we are to direct our children towards higher and more lasting values. During the past year we have strived for excellence in the important values we hold dear.

Insert NEWS FROM COLLEGE SCHOOL as a header on every page

leave this section in single

Change school to college throughout this document

Did you find all of the errors in the text on the previous page? Check below:

The heading should have been emboldened and centred and spelt **FOREWORD**
The following words were incorrect
  this year (space between words needed)
  page 5
  that (after 'page 4') not used in correct copy
  FORGETTABLE – WONDERFUL (capitals, emboldened)
  transferred
  2 May
  Do not
  Glasgow
  A MONTH IN THE PARK (capitals, emboldened)
  limitless (no space within word)
  invention
  Full details (space between words needed)
  everyone (no space within word)
  brochure

1) Make the following amendments to your document **THEATRE**

Typist — Double line spacing except where indicated please.

Single line spacing

FOREWORD By ARTISTIC DIRECTOR ← initials Caps. for this sentence

Welcome to the Summer theatre season. If you didn't see any of our Spring plays you will have missed a treat this year. As you will see from the critic reviews (snippets on page 5) we played to packed houses and our new play "**FORGETTABLE - WONDERFUL**" transferred to the West End on 2 May. *At present it is playing to capacity audiences and looks as though it is set for a successful run.*

~~Do not miss out this season~~. We're delighted to welcome Jilly Stockton and the Glasgow Theatre Company to open the season on 20 ~~May~~ *June*. The new play "**A MONTH IN THE PARK**" promises to be a delight. The Company have been playing to packed houses in the North ~~East~~ and this new comedy has been hailed as "a wonderfully funny limitless comic invention" by the Daily Mail. Full details can be found on page 6. *^of this play*

Our resident Company will entertain you for the rest of the season and there is something for ~~everyone~~ *every member of the family* - from newly commissioned work to Chekhov's "Three Sisters". Take time to look through this brochuure and then come and enjoy an evening with us.

Brian Saver, *Artistic Director* ← bold ← bold

23

EXAM DOCUMENT 1 (to check your work against model answers for these mock exams, see WP-EXAM1, WP-EXAM2, WP-EXAM3 and WP-EXAM4 which have been saved on the disk that accompanies this book)

Please recall this document stored as EXAM1 and amend as shown. Change to double linespacing (except where indicated) + use a justified right margin. Adjust line length to either (a) 12.5cm (5") or (b) 50 characters. If proportional spacing is used please adjust line length to (a). Save and print one copy

THE HEADMASTER'S SPEECH

B

Last year I spoke of the need to provide new cafeteria facilities at the school and I am very pleased to let you know that during the course of the year we have completed a new sports wing which includes the promised new dining facilities. It is already difficult to remember our former more spartan and frugal arrangements.

I would like to
This year ~~we shall~~ turn our attention to the development of the area ~~vacated~~ *left* by Matron's ✓ Department. A number of ideas have emerged for this space and we shall need to look carefully at the claims of further technology, information technology, careers, reception area interview room and other worthy ideas. In any event, it is a large area to develop and will enable us to realise a number of ambitions for further first-rate facilities. **CLAIMS**

excellent
In the past year we again achieved ~~fine~~ results in public examinations. All fifth formers who joined us at 11-plus or 13-plus gained a minimum of 5 GCSE passes at grades A - C. At Advanced Level we again topped a 90% pass rate and 11 of our pupils gained 3 grades A each or better. Our curriculum continues to develop. We are doing more Design and Technology in junior groups and this year we shall see our first class taking Design and Technology GCSE. ~~We are also working in smaller groups with junior classes in music and this allows more appropriate work to be done as the department focuseson groups of similar ability.~~

A

Mr Binet left in the summer, after ~~10~~ 8 energetic years helping students achieve excellent language skills. He leaves us to be Head of Languages at Riseley High College. We wish him success and thank him for his loyal support to the school.

(the opportunity
Mrs Lucas's retirement (now replaced by Miss McCosh) provides us with ~~a cue~~ to thank her for her resourcefulness and cheerfulness - nothing was too much trouble for her.

We continue to be well supported by The Friends of the School Society who organise exciting events throughout the year. Last year's autumn event, culminating in the magnificent fireworks display in the yard, is, I am delighted to say to be repeated again this year.

The association with the school lasts, I am glad to say, for many years. 'Young' Old Boys return to give us news of their university courses or their life in the world of work. Old Boys (I count myself in this age group!) have given special support this year. The proceeds from their various fund-raising events and sports activities have enabled us to furnish our new sports hall. We cannot always publicise their kindness but it is extremely valuable; on occasion, even critical. *I would like to thank you sincerely.* *the school*

2)   Carefully check your work

3)   Spell-check

4)   Save your file as **THEATRE2**

5)   Leave the document on screen

6)   Add the following final paragraph to the document:

> We are lucky to have 6 Sunday Visitor Days this season. They range from local stand-up comedy acts, rehearsed poetry readings to an exciting new play written by a young, local Asian writer. We are also staging a Talent Contest for the Under 15's - so all you budding stars had better read page 10.

7)   The appearance of your text will change dramatically if you choose a difference *font*. To do this highlight the whole document. Change the *font* to Arial Narrow by clicking on the downward arrow alongside the existing font name (probably **Times New Roman)** on the **Formatting Toolbar**.

    From the drop-down menu click on the downward arrow key to find **Arial Narrow** and click on it. If you cannot find this *font* choose one for yourself. (Changing *fonts* was explained in detail in Book 1 of this series)

8)   Carefully check your work against **model answer EX3C** which has been saved on the disk that accompanies this book

9)   Quick save your work and print one copy

10)   Carefully check your printed work against the following correct copy. Clear the screen if you wish (see Lesson 1)

Exercise 19a

1) Retrieve the following document saved as **HINTS**. Format to a different font. Amend as indicated and use the auto-numbering facility to number sentences (see Lesson 7, page 76)

(Change to a font of your choice, size 12)

EXAMINATION HINTS ← *(bold + centre)*

(Adjust line length to either (a) 14 cm (5½") or (b) 55 characters. Justify right margin)

RSA WORD PROCESSING STAGE II PART 1 PAPER

GENERAL

The aim of this award is to assess candidates' word processing ability to produce a variety of documents which will include:

(Sort into exact alphabetical order)

notice for display
article
list of information
table
standard document which includes phrases to be inserted

The overall aim of the award ____ is to meet the requirements of *an* employer. *(document production)* *the* *(discerning)*

Four documents are produced within one and three quarters hours using a word processor. No more than 4 faults gives a candidate a distinction, no more than eleven would be a pass.

EXAMINERS' REPORTS

After each examination the RSA issues an overall report on the strengths and weakness of the scripts marked.

The following list gives an idea of common errors:

(Please put numbered list in double line spacing)

1) 2) Line length and justification not correctly carried out
2) 1) Inconsistent spacing between paragraphs
3) Failure to move paragraphs correctly
4) Paragraphs moved when should have been copied and vice-versa
5) Headings omitted
6) Ballooned instruction not carried out
7) *Failure to take an extra copy and indicate routing in* memo *or letter. the*

---

2) Carefully check your work against **model answer EX19A** which has been saved on the disk that accompanies this book. Save as **HINTS1**

3) Print one copy for future reference. Clear the screen

PRESENTATION STYLES

Exercise 3d

1)   Type in the following text in double line-spacing:

PRESENTATION OF WORK *Typist, Change paragraph headdings to initial caps, emboldened.*

ALL YOU NEED IS CARE

(✓) If you want to be ~~regarded~~ as an accurate typist, one who can be trusted to produce well

displayed, error-free work, then all you need is care and attention to detail. If you want to

pass the RSA Text Processing examination, then care and attention to detail will stand you in a

good position to ~~achieve~~ *(acheive)* the prize of 'distinction'.

PASS CRITERIA

in the criteria of assessment

The criteria for passing the RSA examinations are carefully laid down/ Whilst you are

producing the 3 examination documents, the examination board does not expect you to be

understand

perfect (however, they are delighted if you are!) They ~~know~~ that examination pressure puts

therefore, they allow   *some*

candidates under extra stress and, ~~they compensate for this by allowing~~ you to make/errors. If

/well deserved

throughout all the tasks, you make no more than 4 errors you will obtain a/Distinction

Certificate; if you make no more than 11 errors you will obtain a Pass Certificate. I'm afraid

that more than 11 errors will result in a feeling of depression because it means that you have

at another siting

not passed the exam - however you can have another go/

---

2)   Carefully check your work against **model answer EX3D** which has been saved on the
         disk that accompanies this book

3)   Spell-check and save your file as **EXAM**

4)   Leave the document on screen

PRACTISE INSERTING A SYMBOL

Exercise 18c

TARGET TIME 18 MINUTES

1) Change the *font size* to 12 and the *font* to Courier

2) Key in the following document in double line-spacing, except where indicated. Follow the presentation details (underline, embolden, etc) and insert a page number, centre bottom, on both pages. Remember to time yourself and fill in your target time sheet

---

BUILDING SOCIETIES ◄——— Typist, please embolden the heading

INSTANT ACCESS ACCOUNTS

Most building societies offer a premium account. This usually offers a high rate of interest, often on a tiered basis so that the more you invest, the more you earn. A monthly income facility is sometimes included.

Suitable for?
Lump sum investments   Typist, please put these 4 items in single line spacing
Irregular savings
Salary transfers
Day-to-day money management

◄——— Typist, please insert a page break here. The text should produce a 2-page document

Interest?
Variable. Rates are tiered so higher balances earn more.
Large sums earn 1¼ - 1¾ per cent more than smaller amounts.
If the balance drops below minimum level then the ordinary share rate is payable.

Open to?
Anyone. Children under 16 need their parents' signature.

---

3) Check your work. Spell-check and save as **INSTANT**. Check your work on screen with **model answer EX18C**. Amend if necessary

4) Print preview and print one copy. Check against the **model answer** once more. Clear the screen

5)   Insert the following text in single line-spacing at the end of your document:

What is a "word"

It is useful for you to know exactly what is regarded as an error but before listing them let's consider how the word "**word**" is defined by the examination board. The RSA regard a **word** as being:

(a)   any normally understandable word (hyphenated words count as one)

(b)   any series of symbols (including spaces where appropriate) which constitute a recognisable unit, eg postcode, initials or groups of initials, courtesy title, etc

(c)   including following or associated punctuation and spacing.

One fault errors

Faults or errors fall into 2 categories. The first category loses only one fault throughout the whole paper no matter how many times you repeat the error. For example if your left hand and/or top margin is less than ½″ on document one, then you will have gained one fault. If you repeat that error on document 2, no more faults will accrue. The following are a few of the errors that fall into this first category:

(a)   no clear line-space before and after items within a document (except listed or numbered items or items displayed against template or pre-printed headings)

(b)   failure to use emphasised text or emphasise text as instructed

(c)   work which is creased, torn or dirty

(d)   use of initial capitals/capitals/underlining not as presented in exam draft, or used inconsistently.

Inconsistent use of style, spelling or presentation is a mistake that can easily be overlooked in the stress of the examination situation. Always check that you have been consistent in your approach, for example if the sub-headings are requested in blocked capitals, make sure that you use block capitals throughout the task for all sub-headings.

---

6)   Carefully check your work and print one copy for future reference. Quick save the document and clear the screen if you wish (see Lesson 1)

9)   Save your document as **RECIPE**

10)   Add the following to the <u>beginning</u> of the document:

EASY THROW-IN COCONUT AND CHERRY DELIGHT

Mix dry ingredients together in a bowl. Rub in butter and milk to make soft dough. Gather into a ball and divide into 9 fairly equal portions. Lightly pat each into a round ¾ inch thick.

Place on greased baking tray and bake in a preheated medium oven for 25 minutes. Serve warm.

---

11)   Proof-read work and quick save

12)   Clear the screen

PRACTISE INSERTING A SPECIAL CHARACTER (OR SYMBOL)

Exercise 18b

TARGET TIME 15 MINUTES

---

1)   Key in the following text. Remember to time yourself and fill in your target time sheet

---

MICHELANGELO'S RISTORANTE

If you enjoy traditional Italian cuisine then you must visit the best restaurant in Carlsbad. We serve ¾ lb mouth watering veal steaks prepared with our special Sicilian style sauce. Pasta and Italian style bread are made fresh every day, and we have a special chicken piccata dish which is second to none!

Join us soon .... we're open ½ ten to midnight – 6½ days a week (we do open until 6 pm on Sundays). We're on the corner of State and Grand Street, ¼ mile from the harbour.

SPECIAL OFFER The first 10 customers who show this advertisement to us when they dine at MICHELANGELO'S will take home a ½ jar of our home made Presto sauce. It contains garlic, herbs, olive oil and capers and is a sumptuous souvenir of a fine meal.

---

2)   Check your work and save as **ITALY**. Clear the screen

TARGET TIMING

The performance criteria for the RSA Text Processing examination Stage II Part 1 states that 3 documents must be produced within $1\frac{1}{4}$ hours. If you do not COMPLETE ALL 3 documents you will fail the examination even if your attempted documents do not contain any errors.

It is essential, therefore, that you endeavour to complete work within a given time. From this point forward you will find some tasks have been given a TARGET TIME. Carefully time yourself whenever a target time is set for an exercise. Keep a record of your progress by filling in the details below. **Remember – you are aiming to increase speed without increasing mistakes. If necessary repeat the exercise twice in order to improve both speed and accuracy.** If after several attempts you cannot reach the target time, then you need to do more keyboard practice from Book 1.

DATE	PAGE NO	EXERCISE NO	TARGET TIME	ACTUAL TIME TAKEN	NO OF ERRORS
	29	Consolidation	20 minutes		
	29(2nd attempt)				
	31	Exercise 4a	20 minutes		
	31(2nd attempt)				

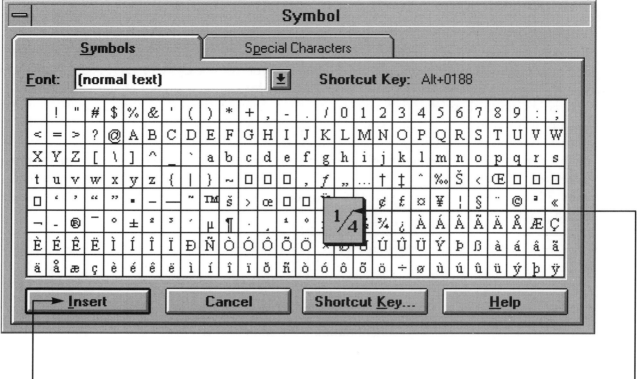

5)   Point to the ¼ character with the mouse and click the left mouse button. An enlarged view of the ¼ will appear

6)   Click on the **Insert** button

7)   Click on **Close** and you will return to your document with the ¼ on the screen

8)   Continue your document by keying in the following:

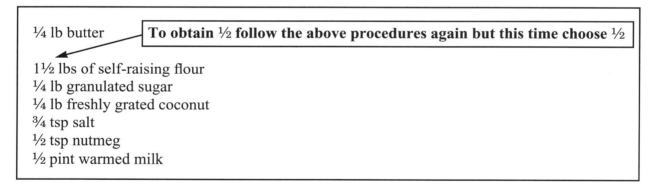

¼ lb butter

To obtain ½ follow the above procedures again but this time choose ½

1½ lbs of self-raising flour
¼ lb granulated sugar
¼ lb freshly grated coconut
¾ tsp salt
½ tsp nutmeg
½ pint warmed milk

TARGET TIMING – CONTINUATION SHEET

DATE	PAGE NO	EXERCISE NO	TARGET TIME	ACTUAL TIME TAKEN	NO OF ERRORS

The Symbol dialog box has **2** tab cards [Symbols and Special Characters]. It is easier for you to use the Symbol card.

If it is not displayed on top, click on the tab which contains the word Symbols at the top of the card and the **S**ymbols card will come to the front.

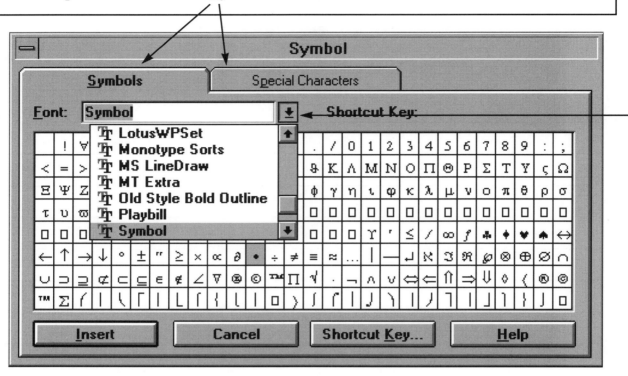

3)   Click on the downward arrow alongside the **Font** text box and a menu of available fonts will appear – the same selection you have for text

4)   Click on the upward arrow until the words [normal text] appear. Click once on [Normal Text] to choose it

CONSOLIDATION EXERCISE FOR LESSON 3

1) Change the *font* to **Century Schoolbook** size **12** **Do not commence typing .... read (2) below first –**

2) There are 5 differences between the text in <u>figure A</u> and the text in <u>figure B</u>. Can you spot them before you begin to type?

Figure A

Taking holidays abroad is becoming extremely popular with holiday makers. The importance of European trade has also steadily increased in recent years, consequently there are many reasons why it is useful to learn a foreign language

---

Figure B

Taking holidays abroad has become extremely popular with British holiday makers. The importance of European trade has also steadily increased in recent years. Consequently there are many reasons why it is useful and important to learn a foreign language.

---

3) Can you find the 5 differences? The answers are at the foot of the next page but do not look until you have tried to identify the differences for yourself.

4) Key in Figure B text above and save your document as **HOLIDAY**

5) Add the paragraph below as a final paragraph:

> Italian has always been the language of the arts - of opera and poetry. Many of the great masterpieces of world literature were written in Italian: Dante's "Divine Comedy" for example.

6) Click on the **Save** icon on the **Standard Toolbar**

> Because you have already saved your text once and given it a file name, when you click on the **Save** icon a second time the updated version is automatically saved with the same name.

LESSON 18   INSERTING A SPECIAL CHARACTER (OR SYMBOL)

INSERTING A SPECIAL CHARACTER (OR SYMBOL)

Exercise 18a

Sometimes it is useful to be able to use special characters or symbols in a document, for example ¼ ½ or ¾. Special characters can be inserted as you key in or afterwards.

1)   To insert a special character you need first to place the cursor at the point you wish it to appear.

You are going to insert the ¼ sign at the top of your document.

<u>With the cursor at the top of a new blank screen</u> click on the word **Insert** on the **Menu Bar**

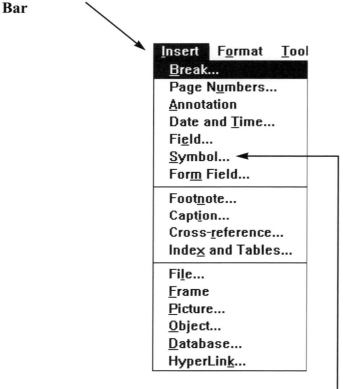

2)   From the drop-down menu click on the word **Symbol** and the following dialog box will appear:

7) Further amend the text as indicated below:

LANGUAGE ← bold + CAPS (Double line spacing for all text please)

Taking holidays abroad has become ~~extremely~~ popular with British holiday makers. The importance of ~~European~~ trade has also ~~steadily~~ increased in recent years. Consequently there are many reasons why it is useful ~~and important~~ to learn a foreign language. (Aparently) though the majority of people 'drop' languages as soon as ~~they leave~~ school. Some

Italian has ~~always~~ been the language of the arts - of opera and poetry. ~~Many~~ ✓ of the great masterpieces ~~of the world literature~~ were written in Italian: Dante's "Divine Comedy" for example.

I decided to learn Italian some years ago but I was ~~quickly~~ amazed at the strange sentences I was being forced to learn. "In this street there is a good hat shop" was not very useful to me, and "I want dancing shoes with thin soles and high heels" would not be helpful either! // I am afraid I eventually gave up.

---

8) Change the *font* to one of your choice. Quick save your work

9) Carefully check your work against **model answer CONSOL3** which has been saved on the disk that accompanies this book The *font* used was `Century Gothic` size `12`

10) Clear the screen. From this point forward this book will instruct you to 'clear the screen' after each exercise. If you would prefer to leave several document files open and close later that is, of course, your choice. See Lesson 1 for more information

---

The five differences between Figure A/Figure B (page 29)

is becoming/ has become (line 1)
holiday makers/ British holiday makers (line 1)
in recent years,/ in recent years. (line 3)
it is useful/ it is useful and important (line 3/4)
foreign language/ foreign language. (last line)

CONSOLIDATION EXERCISE FOR LESSON 17

Practise what you have learnt so far by following the instructions below.

TARGET TIME 20 MINUTES

1) Key in the following table. Remember to time yourself and fill in your target time sheet

EIGHTH HOCKEY TOURNAMENT ←(bold)

The Eighth Biennial Hockey tournament held in April broke new ground this year. For the first time all the matches were played on artificial turf circumventing the need for each team to play one or more games on shale or grass. This was regarded as a great improvement by all the participants.

HOCKEY MATCH RESULTS ←(bold) (Please move the RESULT column to become the first column before TEAM.)

TEAM	HOME TEAM	RESULT	COMMENTS
CUP GAMES			
West Country Youth	A (Combined)	4-1	Difficult game, playing the cream of players
Interleague	A (U18)	2-3	Played well
Under 15 County	A (U15)	0-1	Good, solid play
HOUSE MATCHES			
Cabot v. Carlisle	A, B and C (U13)	1-1, 1-2, 0-4	Challenging house rivalry
Cook v Carr	A, B and C (U13)	0-0, 5-2, 8-0	Strong play from Cook team
Cabot v Carlisle	A, B and C (U15)	1-6, 0-0, 8-2	Good to see the team spirit
INTER-SCHOOL			
Downside	B (U14)	2-2	Enthusiasm not lacking –good
Barnley	B (U15)	2-3	Equally matched sides
Cherub Road	A (U15)	4-4	An exhausting game, even to watch

(Please move HOUSE MATCHES below INTER-SCHOOL)

(Please sort TEAM column into exact alphabetical order within each section. Ensure all corresponding details are also re-arranged.)

2) Carefully check your work. Save your document with a name of your choice. Print one copy

3) Carefully check your work against **model answer CONSOL17** which has been saved on the disk that accompanies this book. Clear the screen

LESSON 4	PRINT PREVIEW
	PAGE NUMBERING (CONTINUATION SHEETS)
	PROBLEMS WITH PAGE NUMBERING – PAGE
	NUMBERS NOT SHOWING (OR PRINTING)
	PRACTISE PAGE NUMBERING
	PRACTISE SUPPRESSING PAGE NUMBERING ON
	FIRST PAGE
	WIDOWS AND ORPHANS
	CONSOLIDATION

PRINT PREVIEW

Exercise 4a

TARGET TIME 20 MINUTES (for keying in and checking)

1)   Key in the following text. Remember to time yourself and fill in your target time sheet

Double-line spacing unless instructed otherwise

LOOK BEFORE YOUR PRINT! bold

Leave at least 1.3cm (½") here

Even the experianced word processing operator finds it difficult to predict accurately how their work will print. To show the appearance of your printed document **Word** offers you the opp. of "viewing" your work before printing it.

bold

single line spacing

thumb nail

This feature makes it poss. for you to see anything from a bird's-eye view of mmmultiple pages an up to a bigger-than-life-size view of part of a single page.

larger

stet

require

It can help you acheive the display you want and avoid wasted time and effort on printing documents that do not produce the results you have in mind. If you wish to reduce the cost of your printing ink it is always neccessary to view your work through **Print Preview** before printing.

emphasize these words by emboldening them

Your name here ....

Today's date here ....

2)   Spell-check and save as **PREVIEW**

3)   Carefully check your work against **model answer EX4A** which has been saved on the disk that accompanies this book

MOVING COLUMNS WITHIN TABLES

Exercise 17m

It is likely that you will be required to move a column in the RSA Stage II Part 2 word processing examination. As the task containing columns will need to be keyed in and not retrieved you could decide to key in the required column in the correct position at the outset. You may prefer, however, to move the column using **Word** software after the document has been keyed in.

Moving columns was thoroughly covered in the first book in this series. You may wish to revise column moving with the document now on screen.

1)   You are going to move the DESCRIPTION column so that it becomes the first column in the table. Position the cursor on the dotted line above the DESCRIPTION column. When a small black downward arrow appears, click the left mouse button to highlight the column. Release the mouse button.

2)   Point the arrow head (<u>which will now have a small rectangular box beneath it</u>) into the highlighted area and drag it anywhere in the existing first column (ie NUMBER). Release the mouse button. Your table will look similar to the one below:

DESCRIPTION	NUMBER	ITEM	PRICE £
	Velour Range		
Fine tooth application	93	Lash comb	2.00
Washable, soft velour	103	Blusher puff	6.00

3)   Next move the 3 shoulder-headings **Velour Range**, **Exclusive Range and Simply Black Range** into the **DESCRIPTION** column. Do this by highlighting the text in each box and dragging it into the correct position in the **DESCRIPTION** column

4)   Carefully check your work. Quick save your document. Print preview and print one copy

5)   Carefully check your work against **model answer EX17M** which has been saved on the disk that accompanies this book. Clear the screen

PRINT PREVIEW (CONTINUED)

TARGET TIME 25 MINUTES (for keying in and checking)

1) Key in the following text. Remember to time yourself and fill in your target time sheet

[Handwritten: Typist/Double-line spacing please]

WHICH COMPUTER SHOULD I BUY? *[Handwritten: ← bold]* *[Handwritten: Full justification please]*

A computer is useful for both the office and the home. Modern computers can answer the telephone and take your voicemail messages - they can also send and recieve faxes. Add a modem to your computer and you will be connected to the telephone line and literally ~~an information world~~ *[Handwritten: a world of info.]* can be brought to your fingertips. The Internet, a network of millions of computers connected to the telephone system world wide, is bringing the world into the home. If you are considering buying a computer you should ask yourself first of all what you are planning to use a PC (personal computer) for. If the answer is that it is to be used for typing letters or short reports then what you require will be very different from an all dancing and singing system that answers the telephone, plays video games, uses CDs etc. The next dilemma to sort out is whether to buy a portable or a desktop computer. If mobility is important then a portable could posibly be ~~your~~ PC *[Handwritten: the] [for you,]* however, remember they are generally more expensife.

The brains of the computer is called the processor. If you want to use your computer for multimedia applications, ie using CD-ROMs, playing games, etc, then you need to look for the fastest processor that you can afford.

Memory *[Handwritten: clear line space below sub-headings]*
There are 2 types of memory both of which are measure in Megabytes (Mb). Hard-disk memory is the computer's permanent memory store - a little bit like a filing system. The more memory you have the better, but some compression software does allow you to double the space if necessary. *[Handwritten: ✓]* Random Access Memory (RAM) is a measure of how much information your computer can store. Modern software requires 16Mb of RAM to work efficiently, however you can in some instances get by with 8Mb

Software
Almost all PCs come with software pre-installed. This will include an operating system, such as Windows 3.1 or Windows 95 for PCs. You will find many packages such as word-processing, spreadsheets and personal finance come with your PC. These are all useful basic applications.

[Handwritten: Your name here]

2) Save as **COMPUTER**. Carefully check your work against **model answer EX4B** which has been saved on the disk that accompanies this book

PRACTISE SORTING WITHIN TABLES

Exercise 17l

TARGET TIME 25 MINUTES

1) Key in the following table. Remember to time yourself and fill in your target time sheet. Use the **Table Autoformat** function when your document is finished in order to achieve the best column widths. (**Table Autoformat** was fully covered in the first book in this series)

PROFESSIONAL LOOKS *(Please sort PRICE into exact price order within each section; all corresponding details should be arranged.)*

Professional make up artists have known for years that one of the secrets of a perfect look is using the right equipment. Our products have been made by one of Britain's finest brush manufacturers and are available exclusively to readers of LOOKS magazine.

NUMBER	ITEM	PRICE £	DESCRIPTION
Velour Range			
103	Blusher puff	6.00	Washable, soft velour
101	Shadow brush	7.50	Slanted head
124	Blender brush	8.75	Wide shaped head
93	Lash comb	2.00	Fine tooth application
Simply Black Range			
12	Sponge	1.05	Softly rounded
16	Lip brush	2.15	Tapered end
9	Brow comb	1.99	Straight broad head
20	Applicator	3.10	Glove-type foam applicator
Exclusive Range			
131	Shadow blender	7.00	Shaped head
132	Lip blender	6.50	Slanting narrow head
163	Powder brush	9.30	Large rounded head
100	Superlash	3.95	Fine brush

HINT TO TYPIST - You will need to highlight whole rows in order to sort

Please move Exclusive Range section above Simply Black section

---

2) Carefully check your work. Quick save your document. Print preview and print one copy

3) Carefully check your work against **model answer EX17L** which has been saved on the disk that accompanies this book. Leave your document on the screen

3)   Place the cursor at the beginning of the document. Click on the **Print Preview** icon on the standard toolbar. Wait for the screen to re-draw

4)   Your screen will look something like the one below. The text on the preview screen may or may not be readable depending on the font size and your computer set-up.

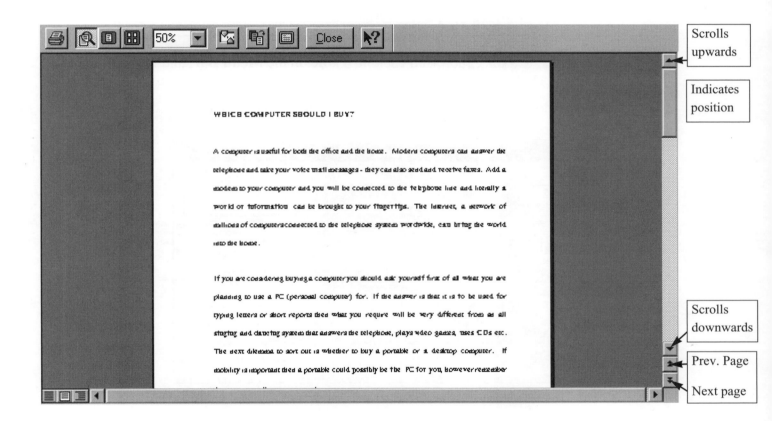

5)   Use the **Page Up** or **Page Down** keys on the keyboard to scroll up and down your pages. Alternatively you can scroll around text by clicking on the up or down arrow keys in the scroll bar. Experiment with these keys now, and move around your pages

6)   The **Print Preview** toolbar makes it easy to adjust your screen display

On the next page is a detailed look at the toolbar icons and their function. With the **COMPUTER** document on screen experiment with these icons

15) For our last sort with this document you are first going to instruct the computer to sort the DATE column in order and then request it to sort on a second column; that of VENUE. Recall your document saved as **SORT1**. To enable you to see the effectiveness of sorting 2 columns first amend the text on screen as shown below before you begin

<u>The West of England Area</u>

Bristol Cathedral	2 Feb	organ	Mark Holladay
St Mary Redcliffe	15 Feb	organ	Mark Holladay
Music School **2 Feb** ~~8 Mar~~		piano	Nyasha Ngozi
Music School **29 Mar** ~~12 Mar~~		piano	Michele Bardouille
St Mary Redcliffe	29 Mar	organ	Kate Williams
Bristol Cathedral **29 Mar** ~~1 Apr~~		organ	Mark Holladay

16) Highlight the text once more and click on **T**able on the **Menu Bar**, and from the drop-down menu click on **Sort**

17) Using the downward arrows alongside the options boxes choose the options shown below:

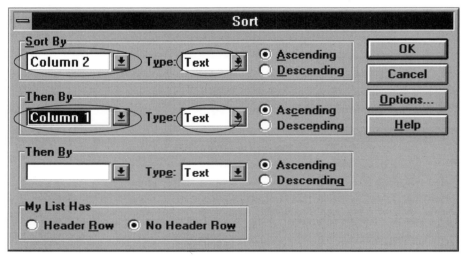

18) Click on **OK** and your columns should be sorted in the following order:

<u>The West of England Area</u>

Bristol Cathedral	2 Feb	organ	Mark Holladay
Music School	2 Feb	piano	Nyasha Ngozi
St Mary Redcliffe	15 Feb	organ	Mark Holladay
Bristol Cathedral	29 Mar	organ	Mark Holladay
Music School	29 Mar	piano	Michele Bardoukle
St Mary Redcliffe	29 Mar	organ	Kate Williams

19) **NOTE that the dates are sorted into date order first, but then the venues are sorted into alphabetical order AFTER they have been put into date order.** Save file as **SORT3** and clear the screen

Print icon

As with the print icon on the standard toolbar, you can click on this icon to print all of the current document

Magnifier

<u>Notice that this is automatically selected when **Print Preview** is actioned</u>. Click on the page near an area of text you would like to see magnified ..... and it is enlarged! Click once more to zoom out

Click on the **Magnifier icon** so that it is no longer selected or actioned (ie the icon will no longer look a slightly different shade and appear as though pressed down). You will be able to edit text in the normal way. However, note that you do not have your **Standard** and **Formatting Toolbars** in **Print Preview**. Your could use the keyboard shortcuts (see the end of the last lesson in this book)

One page

Clicking the **One page** icon will set the zoom setting to display a single page, normally with a 34% zoom setting

Multiple Pages

This icon enables you to see more than one page at a time. Click on the icon and you will see a drop-down grid:

Point to the first box on the grid, click and hold down the left mouse button. Drag across and down the grid and you will see that the grid will grow as you drag. Normally you will be able to see a maximum of 3 rows of 7 columns but this may vary depending upon your computer

Although you have highlighted all the pages you will only be presented with 2, the second of which will be blank. This is because your document only has 2 pages

You can zoom in and out on any page using the **magnifier** icon as described above

11)   The dialog box will appear once more:

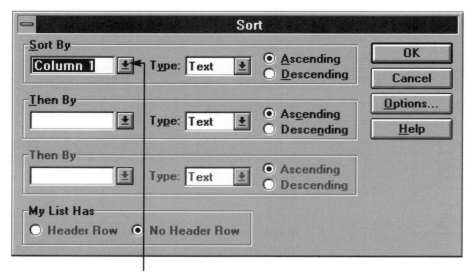

12)   Click on the downward arrow alongside **Column 1** and from the drop-down menu
       click on **Column 3** (because you wish to sort the INSTRUMENT column which is a
       text column and is in the third position)

3)   Click on [**OK**] and your columns should be sorted in the following order:

The West of England Area

Bristol Cathedral   2 Feb   organ   Mark Holladay
Bristol Cathedral   1 Apr   organ   Mark Holladay
St Mary Redcliffe   15 Feb   organ   Mark Holladay
St Mary Redcliffe   29 Mar   organ   Kate Williams
Music School   8 Mar   piano   Nyasha Ngozi
Music School   12 Mar   piano   Michele Bardouille

14)   Save as **SORT2** and clear the screen

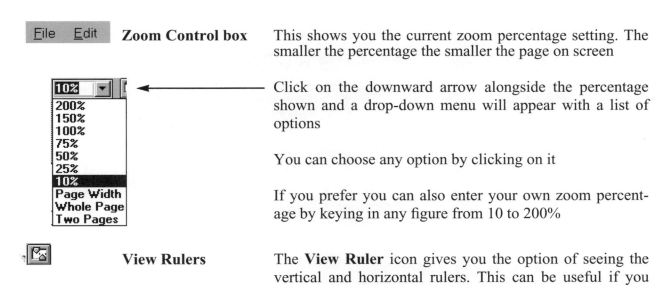

Zoom Control box

This shows you the current zoom percentage setting. The smaller the percentage the smaller the page on screen

Click on the downward arrow alongside the percentage shown and a drop-down menu will appear with a list of options

You can choose any option by clicking on it

If you prefer you can also enter your own zoom percentage by keying in any figure from 10 to 200%

View Rulers

The **View Ruler** icon gives you the option of seeing the vertical and horizontal rulers. This can be useful if you want to see or adjust the margins and measurements

On the first page of text, zoom to a 50% magnification so that your screen is similar to the one below. Click on the **View Rulers** icon. Notice the ruler bars that have appeared

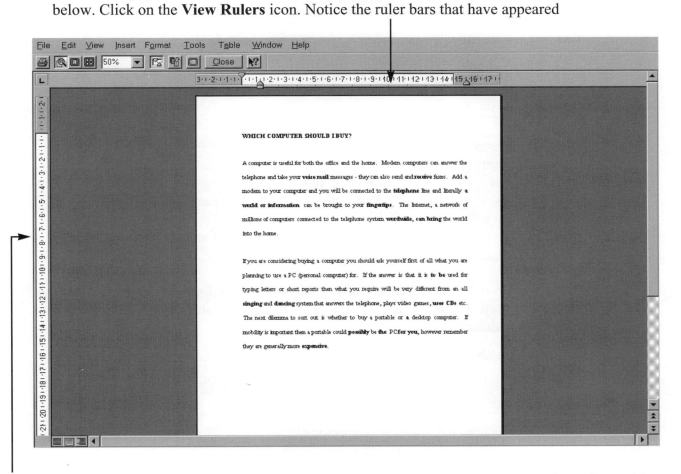

You can adjust the margins of your document whilst in this view. Point exactly to the position on the ruler bar where the white and grey area meets. When you see a double-headed black arrow, hold down the left mouse button – a dotted line will appear across the screen. Drag the mouse up or down the screen a little (the dotted line will move). When you release the mouse button the margin will move to that position

To remove the ruler bars click on the **View Ruler** icon once more

4)   The following dialog box will appear:

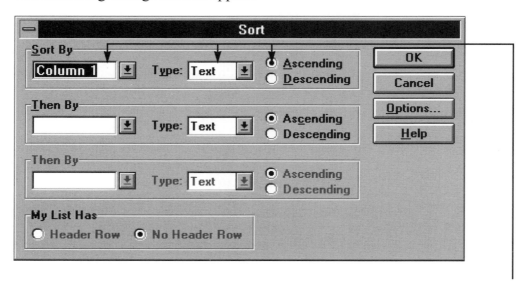

5)   You are going to sort the table so that it is in alphabetical order of VENUE. The default option you are offered is to sort **Column 1** as a **Text** column in **Ascending** order. This is exactly what you want, so press ⬛ **OK** ⬛

6)   Your columns should now be sorted in the following order:

The West of England Area

Bristol Cathedral	2 Feb	organ	Mark Holladay
Bristol Cathedral	1 Apr	organ	Mark Holladay
Music School	8 Mar	piano	Nyasha Ngozi
Music School	12 Mar	piano	Michele Bardouille
St Mary Redcliffe	15 Feb	organ	Mark Holladay
St Mary Redcliffe	29 Mar	organ	Kate Williams

NB   If you do not highlight the whole table before sorting, then only the column highlighted will be sorted – the text in the other columns will remain in the same position!

7)   Save your file as **SORT1** and leave on screen

8)   You are now going to sort the information in order of INSTRUMENT which is the third column

9)   Highlight the text once more (as shown in instruction 2)

10) Click on **Table** on the **Menu Bar** and from the drop-down menu click on **Sort**

Shrink to fit

If you had typed a document, only to discover that the last line of text would not fit onto the page it is possible to click on this icon and **Word** will automatically reduce the *font* size in an effort to fit the document on one page. Also you could adjust the bottom margin if you didn't want to reduce the font size (see **View Rulers** on the previous page)

 Full screen

This icon switches your text to a full screen view and hides everything else except the **Page Preview** toolbar. The point of full screen view is to display as much as possible of the page at one time

WARNING – YOU MUST USE THIS ICON CAREFULLY!

You can get yourself into a terrible tangle if you do not click on the Full screen icon to deselect it before closing the **Print Preview** screen.

If you should forget to deselect this icon before returning to **Normal** or **Page Layout View** you will discover that **Toolbars** will still be hidden as they were when you pressed the Full screen icon. If you should be in this unlucky position you may be able to return your screen to normal by pressing the **Esc** key on your keyboard. However, if the **Esc** key does not work for you, you will need to follow the instructions below:

All may not be lost!
Try the **Esc** key on the keyboard before carrying out these instructions –

a) Hold down the **Alt** key and press **F**

b) Click on Print Preview from the drop-down menu

c) Deselect the **Full screen** icon

d) Click on Close

e) You will still not have the Toolbar or Formatting Bar. Follow the instructions below to unhide the missing Toolbar and Formatting Bar

f) Click on **View** on the **Menu Bar**

g) Click on **Toolbar** and click in the box alongside the words **Standard** and **Formatting** and then click on OK

SORTING WITHIN TABLES

Information can be sorted in tables in a similar way to text not in a table. Work through the exercise below in order to practise this.

Exercise 17k

1)   Key in the following table:

RECITALS ORGANISED BY THE MUSIC DEPARTMENT			
VENUE	DATE	INSTRUMENT	ARTIST
The West of England Area			
Bristol Cathedral	2 Feb	organ	Mark Holladay
St Mary Redcliffe	15 Feb	organ	Mark Holladay
Music School	8 Mar	piano	Nyasha Ngozi
Music School	12 Mar	piano	Michele Bardouille
St Mary Redcliffe	29 Mar	organ	Kate Williams
Bristol Cathedral	1 Apr	organ	Mark Holladay

2)   Highlight the text shown below:

Bristol Cathedral	2 Feb	organ	Mark Holladay
St Marh Redcliffe	15 Feb	organ	Mark Holladay
Music School	8 Mar	piano	Nyasha Ngozi
Music School	12 Mar	piano	Michele Bardouille
St Mary Redcliffe	29 Mar	organ	Kate Williams
Bristol Cathedral	1 Apr	organ	Mark Holladay

3)   Click on **Table** on the **Menu Bar** and from the drop-down menu click on **Sort**

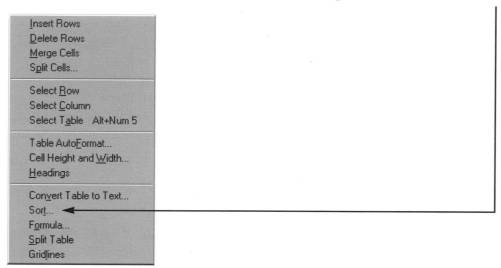

Unfortunately this displays the toolbars not only in **Normal** or **Page Layout View** but also in **Print Preview!**

You should return to print preview to remove them because they take up so much room on the screen. To do this:

a) Return to **Print Preview**

b) Point at any of the toolbars displayed at the top of the screen and click the **RIGHT** mouse button. The following quick menu appears: ───────

✔ Standard
✔ Formatting
Borders
Database
✔ Drawing
Forms
Microsoft
✔ Print Preview
Toolbars...
Customize...

c) Click on the word **Standard** to remove the tick and 'hide' the toolbar. This will only hide it in **Print Preview**, it will still appear in **Normal View**

d) Repeat step (b) above

e) This time click on the word **Formatting** to remove the tick and hide this toolbar

f) Close **Print Preview**. Upon returning to **Normal** or **Page Layout View** you will find that these toolbars are displayed although they are hidden in Print Preview

> **IT IS WORTH REPEATING HERE THAT IF YOU WANT TO AVOID CONFUSION – ALWAYS DESELECT THE FULL SCREEN COMMAND WHEN YOU HAVE FINISHED USING IT.**

Close If you click the **Close** icon **Word** will return you to the view your document was in before you chose the **Print Preview** command

Help This icon is discussed in full in the last Lesson in this book

When you have finished experimenting with these icons in **Print Preview**, return to **Normal**

or **Page Layout View** (whichever screen layout view you prefer) by clicking on [Close]. Clear the screen.

5)   The cell will split in 2 as it had been before you previously merged them to make one

Notice Accounts (number 121)			

6)   Highlight the text **(number 121)** and using the mouse button drag and drop it into the second half of the newly formed split cell. You will notice that the depth of the cell will revert to single spacing

Notice Accounts	(number 121)		

7)   Repeat this with the other 2 sub-headings, ie

<u>Tax Free Accounts</u> (number 120)
<u>Fixed Rate Accounts</u> (number 122)

All sub-headings should now be in 2 cells as the copy below:

Tax Free Accounts	(number 120)		
Child Bonus	3 years	minimum of £25 per month	
Index 12	5 years	minimum of £100	
43rd Tier	5 tears	maximum of £1,000	
Notice Accounts	(number 121)		
Classic	30 day	5.06	4.05
Direct	45 day	4.69	3.75
Union	50 day	4.88	3.90
National	90 day	5.36	4.29
Fixed Rate Accounts	(number 122)		
Pensioners' Bond	1 year	5.25	4.20
Option Bond	1 year	4.88	3.90
Capital Bond	2 years	4.99	3.99

8)   Quick save the document and clear the screen

PAGE NUMBERING (CONTINUATION SHEETS)

If you are producing more than one page of text it is useful to be able to add automatic page numbering to the document.

You will not be directly instructed in the examination to insert page numbering on each document. However in the "Notes for Candidates" printed on the front cover of the examination paper, you will be instructed to number continuation sheets.

> **ALWAYS NUMBER CONTINUATION SHEETS USING THE AUTOMATIC PAGE NUMBERING FACILITY IN THE EXAMINATION**

Exercise 4c

To add page numbers to the document **EXAM** which you saved in Lesson 3, follow through the instructions below:

1)   Retrieve the **EXAM** document

2)   Click on the word **Insert** on the menu bar

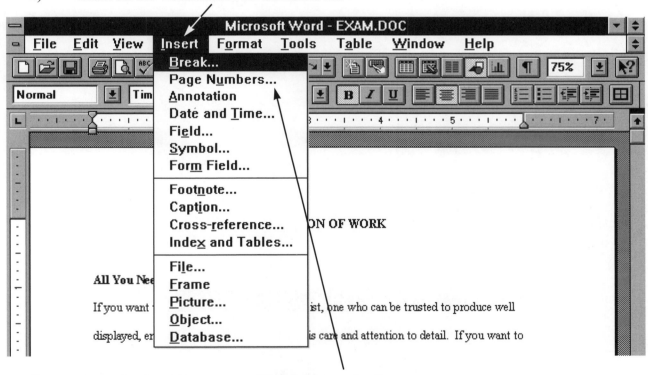

3)   From the drop-down menu click on **Page numbers**

SPLITTING CELLS WITHIN TABLES

You may wish to split cells previously merged – ie replace the cell wall back to its original position. You are going to use the **SAVER** document (*Exercise 17i*) which should still be on screen in order to practise splitting cells.

Exercise 17j

1)   With the **SAVER** document on screen, place the cursor in the cell
       Notice Accounts (number 121)

2)   Click on **Table** on the **Menu Bar** and from the drop-down menu click on **Split Cells**

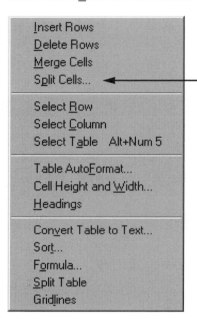

3)   The following dialog box will appear on screen:

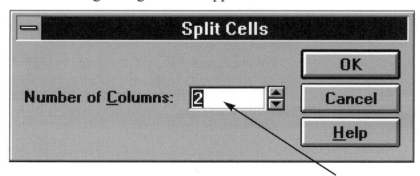

4)   You are going to split this merged cell back into its 2 original columns. If the **Number of Columns** is shown as **2** click on OK if not change to **2** and then click
     OK

4)   The following dialog box will appear on screen:

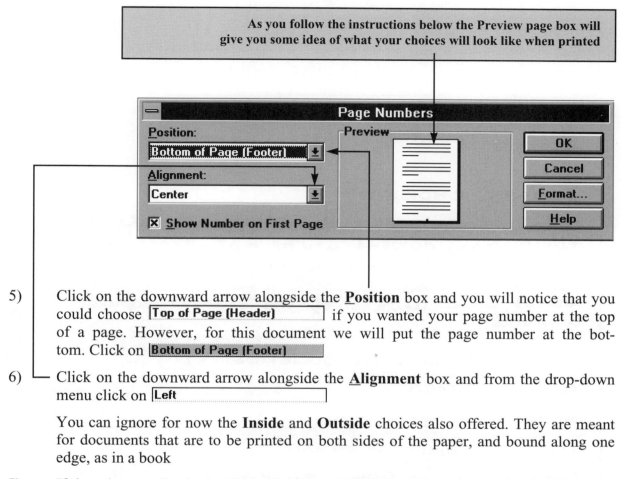

As you follow the instructions below the Preview page box will give you some idea of what your choices will look like when printed

5)   Click on the downward arrow alongside the **Position** box and you will notice that you could choose Top of Page (Header) if you wanted your page number at the top of a page. However, for this document we will put the page number at the bottom. Click on Bottom of Page (Footer)

6)   Click on the downward arrow alongside the **Alignment** box and from the drop-down menu click on Left

      You can ignore for now the **Inside** and **Outside** choices also offered. They are meant for documents that are to be printed on both sides of the paper, and bound along one edge, as in a book

7)   If there is a small **x** in the **Show Number of First Page** box, the number 1 will appear on the first page of your document. Click on the **x** and the box will become empty. When you print your document the first page will not be numbered

8)   Click on OK

9)   Quick save your document **EXAM**

Note – although you may now be able to see the page numbers on screen, you need to check the Print Preview screen (see next page) to ensure that the page numbers will actually print.

PRACTISE TABLES – MOVING TEXT AND MERGING CELLS

Exercise 17i

TARGET TIME 35 MINUTES

1) You will need a 4 × 15 row table to type in the following text as a table. Amend as shown

SAVERS' CHOICE

As the latest wave of interest rate cuts takes effect, many deposits with high street institutions are paying less interest than the minimum needed to keep up with inflation. The table below gives details of the 3 most popular accounts.

start your table at this point

BANKS AND BUILDING SOCIETIES

ACCOUNT DETAILS		25% TAX	40% TAX
NAME	TERM		
Notice Accounts (number 121)			
Classic	30 day	5.06	4.05
Direct	45 day	4.69	3.75
Union	50 day	4.88	3.90
National	90 day	5.36	4.29
Tax Free Accounts (number 120)			
Child Bonus	3 years	minimum of £25 per month	
Index 12	5 years	minimum of £100	
43rd Tier	5 years	maximum of £10,000	
Fixed Rate Accounts (number 122)			
Pensioners' Bond	1 year	5.25	4.20
Option Bond	1 year	4.88	3.90
Capital Bond	2 years	4.99	3.99

Display Tax Free Accounts before Notice Accounts

2) Carefully check your work and correct any mistakes found. Spell-check and save your file as **SAVER**. Print preview and print one copy

3) Carefully check your work against **model answer EX17(I)** which has been saved on the disk that accompanies this book. Leave this exercise on screen

10) Your document will be printed on two separate pages but <u>before you print</u> read the next paragraph.

The Print Preview screen shows you exactly what will be printed and this may differ from the normal document screen. It is especially important to check your work for correct layout before you print when you have more than one page of text. To do this follow the instructions below:

Click on the **Print Preview** icon on the standard toolbar. Wait for the screen to re-draw

11) Use the **Page Up** or **Page Down** keys on the keyboard to view the other page

12) If you are satisfied with the layout press the **print** icon, if not adjust the text layout. See the previous few pages if you are unsure about **Print Preview**

> **IF YOU ARE UNABLE TO SEE ANY PAGE NUMBERS, FOLLOW THE INSTRUCTIONS ON THE NEXT PAGE**

13) When you have successfully printed 2 pages, save the document and clear the screen.

Look through the next few pages before commencing page 43 – "PRACTISE PAGE NUMBERING"

11) Carefully check your work. Quick save your document

12) Print preview and print one copy

13) Carefully check your work against **model answer EX17H** which has been saved on the disk that accompanies this book

14) Amend if necessary before clearing the screen

You have used the 'drag and drop' method to move text within tables in this exercise. If you prefer to use the cut and paste method (covered in detail in the first book of this series) it works equally well.

The information given in this exercise informs you that you can, if you wish, use the keyboard to achieve certain character-formatting styles instead of the mouse. For example if you wish to underline text, you could highlight it in the normal way and then hold down the control [Cntrl] key on the keyboard and tap the [U] key, instead of using the mouse to click on the underline icon. If you would like more information on keyboard shortcuts look at the last lesson in this book.

PROBLEMS WITH PAGE NUMBERING – PAGE NUMBERS NOT SHOWING (OR PRINTING)

If, when you viewed your document the page numbers could not be seen or can only partially be seen, it is probably because the footer (or header) extends into the non-printing area of the page. This is not your fault and happens if the printer or computer has been set up in a certain way or if a certain size or type of font is selected. However you can change the 'Page Setup' so that the page numbers will print.

1) Check that you are in **Print Preview**. Using the keyboard key **Page down** or **scroll-bars**, move to the bottom on the second page

2) Click on the **File** icon on the standard toolbar

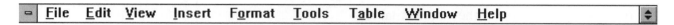

3) From the drop-down menu click on **Page Setup**

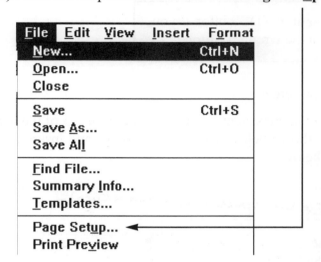

If your screen does not look the same, check that the tab card with the heading "Margins" is on the top. If not, click once on the word "Margins". The measurements on your screen may not be the same as the ones shown here. It does not matter

4) The following screen should appear:

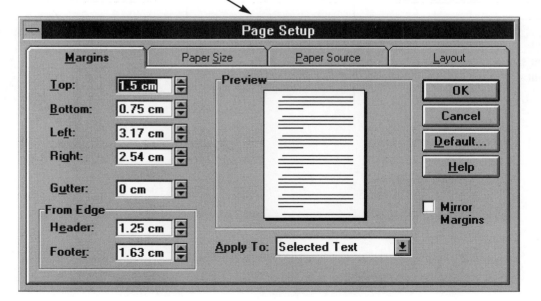

41

8)   Check your display against the copy below

SHORTCUT KEYS (USING WORD)

CHANGING TEXT FORMATTING			
Change the case of letters	Shift + F3	9	B
Make text bold	Ctrl + B	8	A
Underline text	Ctrl + U	10	C
CHANGING FONT AND FONT SIZE	**ACTION REQUIRED**	**PAGE REFERENCE**	
TO	*(Press keys indicated)*	*NUMBER*	*SECTION*
Change the font	Ctrl + shift + F	6	A
Change the font size	Ctrl + shift + P	6	A
Increase the font size to the next available size	Ctrl + shift + >	7	A

> Don't forget the useful UNDO button if you drop the text in the wrong position.

9)   Quick save your document. Leave on screen

10)   The line-spacing of your table is now inconsistent and you need to return 3 of the headings to the top of their columns as shown below. Move the headings and insert a line-space for consistency as indicated below:

SHORTCUT KEYS (USING WORD)

put a line space here (press return)

CHANGING TEXT FORMATTING			
move row to here. Put a line space after			
Change the case of letters	Shift + F3	9	B
Make text bold	Ctrl + B	8	A
Underline text	Ctrl + U	10	C
CHANGING FONT AND FONT SIZE	**ACTION REQUIRED**	**PAGE REFERENCE**	
TO	*(Press keys indicated)*	*NUMBER*	*SECTION*
Change the font	Ctrl + shift + F	6	A
Change the font size	Ctrl + shift + P	6	A
Increase the font size to the next available size	Ctrl + shift + >	7	A

5) Increasing the footer margin will ensure that your page numbers print. The results can be viewed in **Print Preview**

Click alongside the measurement in the footer box ——————————————

6) Either delete the measurement shown and increase the footer measurement by keying in a slightly larger figure, or if you prefer click on the **up arrow** to achieve the same effect

7) As you already are in **Print Preview** you should see the page number appear if you have adjusted the measurement correctly. If you still cannot see (or can only see the top half of the number) increase the footer margin a little more. Repeat as necessary until the page number can be viewed in **Print Preview**

8) Click [**OK**] when you can successfully see the page number 2

9) Print one copy which should contain page number 2. Quick save and clear the screen

> **QUICK METHOD**
>
> **The footer margin can also be dragged up or down in Print Preview where its effect can be seen immediately. See View Rulers, page 35**

MOVING ROWS OF TEXT

It is likely that you will be required to move rows of text in the RSA Stage II Part 2 word processing examination. As the task containing columns will need to be keyed in and not retrieved you could decide to key in the required rows in the correct position at the outset. You may prefer, however, to move the rows using **Word** software after the document has been keyed in – in most instances this can make copying the exercise much easier.

To practise moving rows you are going to move the ''CHANGING TEXT FORMATTING'' block of text above the ''CHANGING FONT AND FONT SIZE'' block of text

4)   Highlight all of the second section of the table (as shown below)

> **QUICK METHOD**
> **To highlight text within a table. Point the cursor into the left margin (so that the arrow head faces towards the right). Click and hold down the left mouse button. Then drag down for the required number of rows.**

SHORTCUT KEYS (USING WORD)			
CHANGING FONT AND FONT SIZE	**ACTION REQUIRED**	**PAGE REFERENCE**	
TO	(Press keys indicated)	NUMBER	SECTION
Change the font	Ctrl + shift + F	6	A
Change the font size	Ctrl + shift + P	6	A
Increase the font size to the next available size	Ctrl + shift + >	7	A
CHANGING TEXT FORMATTING			
Change the case of letters	Shift + F3	9	B
Make text bold	Ctrl + B	8	A
Underline text	Ctrl + U	10	C

5)   Point the mouse arrow into the highlighted text, click and <u>hold down</u> the left mouse button.

As you do this a small rectangle box appears at the bottom of the pointer and a small dotted vertical line is displayed in your text to the right or left of the pointer tip. This indicates the position to which the text will be moved

6)   Keep the mouse button held down while <u>you drag the vertical line</u> to the new position, ie **immediately in front of the heading CHANGING FONT AND FONT SIZE**

CHANGING FONT AND FONT SIZE

7)   Release the mouse button and as you do so the text will move position. The 2 paragraphs should have changed places

PRACTISE PAGE NUMBERING

Exercise 4c

1)	Type in the following text:

A COMMITMENT TO THE FUTURE ← **bold**

Please add page no. top right. Text to be in double line spacing unless indicated.

single spacing

We are one of the world's leading mfrs. of consumer electronic products. We have built this position on total commitment to performance and quality. Research and developement have been a major area of our commit ment and it is this total dedication that means we can fully gntee. all our products for one yr..

we appreciate appreciate our customers and
Our commit ment to complete customer satisfaction has never been greater. In our experiance we find that to acheive this satisfaction we must continue to listen to what our customers have to say, and continue to satisfy their needs. *hit is important*

We fully ack. that modern 'high technology' products need to be easy to use. Our aim is to:
understand

(1)	Provide quick and effective after sales support

(2)	Supply products that are easy to operate with simple to follow instructions *stet*
simple

2)	Satisfy our own stringent standards on product performance and reliability

3)	Continually strive to improve product quality above its already high level

5)	Provide customers with a level of satisfaction and confidence in our products that will far exceed their expectations

now

Our range of products is extensive and we are pleased to now be able to offer you our new home communications products incorporating the latest professional features.

Should you require additional information on any of the products in this leaflet or wish to discuss a particular product in detail, please contact our Customer Care Desk on 2908135. It is helpful if you can refer to the product ref. number).

WE ARE HERE TO HELP YOU ← *change to lowercase with initial caps. & underline*

2)	Save as **PRODUCTS**. Print one copy and carefully check your work against **model answer EX4C** which has been saved on the disk that accompanies this book

MOVING TEXT WITHIN A TABLE (DRAG AND DROP METHOD)

Exercise 17h

1)   Type in the following text and table. The gridlines have been printed here to help you plan your table. Amend as shown

---

INFORMATION TO TRAINERS ← *bold + centre*

The following shortcut keys were ~~inadvertently~~ omitted from the in-house textbook. Please ensure that your trainees are informed *that they can*

~~Use the following~~ *these* shortcut keys to apply character-formatting styles.

SHORTCUT KEYS (USING WORD) ← *bold*			
CHANGING FONT AND FONT SIZE *Change whole row to italics*	ACTION REQUIRED	PAGE REFERENCE	
TO	(Press keys indicated)	NUMBER	SECTION
Change the font	Ctrl + shift + F	6	A
Change the font size	Ctrl + shift + P	6	A
Increase the font size to the next available size	Ctrl + shift + >	7	A
CHANGING TEXT FORMATTING ← *bold*			
Change the case of letters	Shift + F3	9	B
Make text bold	Ctrl + B	8	A
Underline text	Ctrl + U	10	C

---

2)   Carefully check your work. Save your document as **SHORTCUT**. Print preview and print one copy

3)   You will be able to check your work against a model answer later. Leave on screen and continue working with this document on the next page

PRACTISE SUPPRESSING PAGE NUMBERING ON FIRST PAGE

You may wish to commence automatic page numbering with the number 2, from the second page forward. In the Text Processing examination the information on the first page of the examination paper instructs you to "number continuation sheets". In the Word Processing examination you are told to "number second and subsequent pages of a document".

You have just printed a copy of your document **PRODUCTS** (Exercise 4c) with page numbering on both pages. Follow the instructions below to print a second copy with the page numbering on page one suppressed.

Exercise 4d

1)   With the document **PRODUCT** on screen, click on **Insert** on the **Menu Bar**

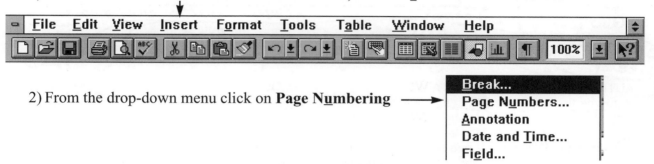

2) From the drop-down menu click on **Page Numbering** ⟶ Break...
Page Numbers...
Annotation
Date and Time...
Field...

3)   The following dialog box will appear on screen:

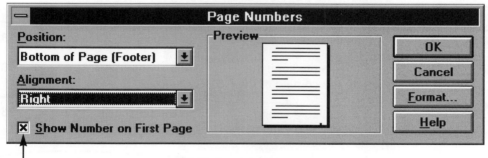

If there is a small **x** in the **Show Number of First Page** box, the number 1 will appear on the first page of your document. You need to remove the **x** from this box – click on the **x** and the box will become empty

4)   Click [**OK**]

5)   Quick save your document and print one copy. Your printouts should now only have a number 2 on the second page. Clear the screen

PRACTISE TABLES – MERGING CELLS AND FORMATTING

Exercise 17g

1)   Retrieve the following document saved as **EX-17G** on the disk that accompanies this book. It was originally saved with a size 10, Arial font – if you wish to change this please do so. (See *Exercise 17f* on the previous page if unsure how to do this.) Amend as shown

> **QUICK METHOD**
> <u>To insert a row.</u>   **Point into the left margin where you want the new row and click once. Click the Table icon – you have a row**

Handwritten annotations: QUOTES (spaced caps). Clear line space. Embolden all main headings. (Please put a clear space between items)

AUTHOR Surname first	QUOTATION First line only	SOURCE	NUMBER / YEAR OF BIRTH
Gay, John	He best can pity, who has felt the woe	unknown	1685
Shakespeare, William	Love sought is good, but giv'n unsought is better	Twelfth Night	1564
Sexon, Anne	In a dream you are never 80	Old	1928
Betjeman, John	Come, friendly bombs, and fall on Slough. It isn't fit for humans now	Slough	1906
Adams, Henry	A friend in power is a friend lost	The Education of Henry Adams	1838
Ward, Julie	Mine eyes have seen the glory of the coming of the Lord	Battle Hymn of the American Republic	1819
Thurber, James	Well, if I called a wrong number, why did you answer it?	The Seal in the Bedroom	1894
Sims, George	It was Christmas Day in the Workhouse	The Dragonet and other poems	1847
Shakespeare, William	Nothing will come of nothing	King Lear	1564
Dryden, John	Beware the fury of a patient man	Absalom and Achitophel	1631

2)   Carefully check your work. Save your document as **QUOTES**. Print one copy

3)   Carefully check your work against **model answer QUOTES** which has been saved on the disk that accompanies this book. Clear the screen

WIDOWS AND ORPHANS

Exercise 4e

1)   Change the *font size* to [12] and the *font* to [Courier] and key in the following text:

WIDOWS AND ORPHANS ← *spaced caps, bold*

Typist. Amend as shown

Widows and orphans is the term used to describe a single line of text that ~~gets~~ *becomes* stranded at the top or bottom of a page. It is not an acceptable display technique to produce work with a single straggling line of text appearing ~~at the top or bottom of a page.~~ *in this way.*

The term 'widow' refers to a single line of text at the top of a printed page. The term 'orphan' refers to the first line of a paragraph left alone at the bottom of a page.

In general you should keep at least 2 lines of a paragraph together on a given page. It there isn't room for 2 lines, you should push the entire paragraph to the beginning of the next page. This is ~~obtained~~ *done* by inserting a 'hard page break', a function which will be covered shortly. ~~in this lesson.~~

It is possible to automatically prevent widows *(embolden)* and orpans *happening* *occurring*. If you choose to use this option, (Word) will adjust your page breaks so that at least 2 lines of a paragrpah always appear on a page. In some cases, this will make your bottom margin slightly larger because fewer lines will be printed to a page. *It is highly recommended that you use the widow and orphan function.*

---

2)   Proof-read and spell-check your work. Save as **WIDOW**

3)   Format the entire document to double line-spacing ←————————————→

4)   Quick save and print one copy. Leave your document on screen. Read and absorb the information contained in this document

5)   Compare your printout with **model answer EX4D** which has been saved on the disk that accompanies this book. Do you have an orphan as in the model answer? (If you do not, it is possible that the 'widow and orphan' option has already been selected or your margin set-up might be slightly different.) Remember an orphan could be more than one word

QUICK METHOD

To highlight the whole document, hold down the Ctrl key and tap the A on the keyboard. Then hold down the Ctrl key once more and tap the number 2 key on the keyboard

CHANGING FONTS AND FONT SIZES WITHIN A TABLE

Exercise 17f

If you have saved a document using a specific font and wish to change the font in order to enhance the appearance of your table it is quite a straightforward procedure. Follow the instructions below to change the font of an existing file

1)   Retrieve your document saved as GRASS (*Exercise 17c*). This file was saved with `Times New Roman` font, sized `10`

PLANT FOOD AND USES ON THE LAWN		EFFECT AND BEST TIME TO APPLY	
Nitrogen	Essential	Lush, green turf	Spring and Summer
Phosphates	Essential	Large root system	Autumn
Potash	Desirable	"Harden" the grass	Spring and Autumn
Lime	Use only in special cases	Only consider using when grass is sparse and overrun by moss	Autumn

2)   Highlight the whole table

QUICK METHOD

**Touch the top of the first column (above "PLANT ....").
The cursor changes to a black downward-pointing arrow.
Click and hold down the mouse button. Drag to the right
until all columns are highlighted**

3)   When everything is highlighted, select a new font and font size. The font chosen below was `Arial Narrow` sized `13`

PLANT FOOD AND USES ON THE LAWN		EFFECT AND BEST TIME TO APPLY	
Nitrogen	Essential	Lush, green turf	Spring and Summer
Phosphates	Essential	Large root system	Autumn
Potash	Desirable	"Harden" the grass	Spring and Autumn
Lime	Use only in special cases	Only consider using when grass is sparse and overrun by moss	Autumn

4)   Quick save your document and clear the screen

6) To check whether the 'widow and orphan' function is on or off, click on the word **For-mat** on the **Menu** bar

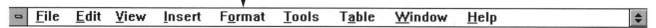

File   Edit   View   Insert   Format   Tools   Table   Window   Help

7) From the drop-down menu click on **Paragraph**. The following dialog box will appear:

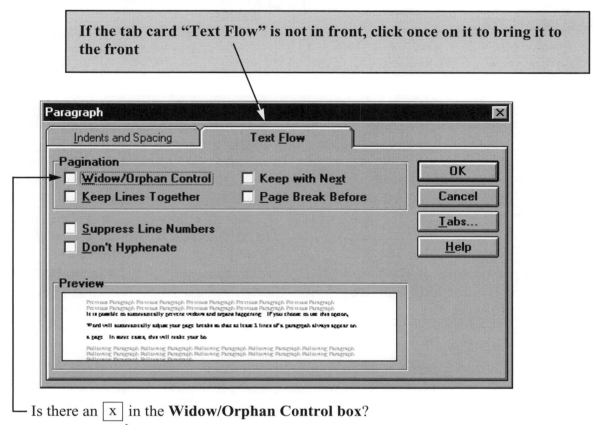

8) Is there an ⟨x⟩ in the **Widow/Orphan Control box**?

☐ Widow/Orphan Control

9) This box must contain an ⟨x⟩ if the **Widow/Orphan** option is to be used

10) Point the cursor into the box and click the left mouse button once to place an ⟨x⟩ in the box(this action repeated also removes an ⟨x⟩)

11) Click [**OK**]

12) Your document on screen should now have 2 lines of text on the second page

13) Quick save your document and print one copy. Clear the screen

4)   Merge cells and amend as shown below:

Put an extra line space clear line between items (marked with a *)

Put an extra line space here so that each row has a clear line space

MUSIC MAKING ← merge 2 heading cells + embolden text	INSTRUMENTS AVAILABLE ← merge 2 heading cells + embolden text	
MUSICIANS AVAILABLE ← merge 2 cells + underline	GUITARS BASES AND SYNTHS ← merge 2 cells and underline. Amend text	
Brilliant drummer [ref 4] Vast experience, all styles, seeks paid gigs.	Status Series 2 matrix bass 4-string £790 [ref 3]	Alesis Q56 with amp-speaker. Paid £1,225 [ref 61]
Experienced engineer available [ref 6] For live work (Swindon based)	Gibson ES335 black 1987 with case £900 [ref 45]	Peavey bass module 200. Still boxed £180 [ref 7]
Lead guitarist, age 22 [ref 55] Looking for band to create new sound influences	Fender Precision bass. Offers [ref 8]	Roland d20 plus speaker. £295 [ref 84]
Black female drummer [ref 44] Seeks band - dance, funk, jazz, rare grooves	Encore coaster electric guitar £85 [ref 9]	Yamaha B50 synth with sequencer. £300 [ref 09]
Bassist keyboard player [ref 70] Loves playing reggae.	Heritage USA 575 acoustic guitar £900 [ref 1]	Classic Pro 1 for sale. Offers [ref 03]
Female guitarist available from May [ref 53] Professional offers only please.	Squire Fender Strat black and white. To swop for bass [ref 5]	Moog Source 16 memory with manual. Offers [ref 7]
Creative male singing drummer [ref 10] Somewhat sloppy but capable of amazing grooves	PR Smith 1993. Excellent condition. Offers [ref 32]	Yamaha Sy35 keyboard. £375 ono [ref 2]
Male singer and songwriter [ref 2] Into pop commercial music	Jackson proff with gig bag. £400 [ref 60]	Kawai K4. £150 [ref 99]

merge these 2 cells and use the delete key so that most text appears on 2 lines where possible

5)   Carefully check your work. Quick save your document and print one copy

6)   Carefully check your work against **model answer EX17E** which has been saved on the disk that accompanies this book. Clear the screen

CONSOLIDATION EXERCISE FOR LESSON 4

TARGET TIME 25 MINUTES

Practise what you have learnt so far by following the instructions below:

1) Key in the following text. Remember to time yourself and fill in your target time sheet

STAIN REMOVAL ← bold

Single line spacing except where indicated. Justify margins.

ADVICE BY ASSOCIATION OF ANTIQUE RESTORERS

Grease, Fats and Oils

Fatty or oily substances, animal, vegetable or mineral in origin, pose annoying *cleaning* problems. Benzoline will cope with them in theory, as will trichlorethylene. However, sometimes stains can be ~~very~~ stubborn and when all else fails, highly refined cigarette-lighter fuel often gives immed. results. *Use a (suficient) amount to remove the stain and (develope) circular rubbing movements as you rub in.* The drawback of solvents is that they attack glue and loosen veneer, but on any *wooden* furniture not venered they work a like a charm. *double line spacing*

Alchohol ← underline

When your guests put glasses down *carelessly* on your furniture it may be that you will be left with a nasty white ring. On polished surfaces alcohol leaves a mark like that of ordinary wetness (for removal see instructions under DAMP STAINS). However, you would be well advised to *recomend* the use of a coaster to your friends and *coleagues.*

DAMP STAINS ← *lower case with initial capitals*

The base of a vase of flowers which has not been wiped dry, leaves a white ring on a polished surface. If the contact has been brief then it is poss. to remove the ring ~~fairly~~ easily. First of all it is necy. to let the ring dry thoroughly, then rub with a little turpentine ↲ letting it soak into the stain. Apply fresh bees wax polish and rub well in. *(no more than a teaspoon)*

2) Save as **STAIN**. Carefully check your work against **model answer CONSOL4 (FIRST PRINTOUT)** which has been saved on the disk that accompanies this book. Print one copy

PRACTISE MERGING CELLS/INSERTING LINE-SPACING AND FORMATTING

Exercise 17e

1)   Type the following table:

MUSIC MAKING		INSTRUMENTS	AVAILABLE
MUSICIANS	AVAILABLE	GUITARS & BASSES	SYNTHS
Brilliant drummer [ref 4]	Vast experience, all styles, seeks paid gigs.	Status Series 2 matrix bass 4-string £790 [ref 3]	Alesis Q56 with amp-speaker. Paid £1,225 [ref 61]
Experienced engineer available [ref 6]	For live work (Swindon based)	Gibson ES335 black 1987 with case £900 [ref 45]	Peavey bass module 200. Still boxed £180 [ref 7]
Lead guitarist, aged 22 [ref 55]	Looking for band to create new sound influences	Fender Precision bass. Offers [ref 8]	Roland d20 plus speaker. £295 [ref 84]
Black female drummer [ref 44]	Seeks band – dance, funk, jazz, rare grooves	Encore coaster electric guitar £85 [ref 9]	Yamaha B50 synth with sequencer £300 [ref 09]
Bassist keyboard player [ref 70]	Loves playing reggae.	Heritage USA 575 acoustic guitar £900 [ref 1]	Classic Pro 1 for sale. Offers [ref 03]
Female guitarist available from May [ref 53]	Professional offers only please.	Squire Fender Strat black and white. To swop for bass [ref 5]	Moog Source 16 memory with manual. Offers [ref 7]
Creative male singing drummer [ref 10]	Somewhat sloppy but capable of amazing grooves	PR Smith 1993. Excellent condition. Offers [ref 32]	Yamaha Sy35 keyboard. £375 ono [ref 2]
Male singer and songwriter [ref 2]	Into pop commercial music	Jackson proff with gig bag. £400 [ref 60]	Kawai K4. £150 [ref 99]

2)   Carefully check your work and save with a name of your choice.

3)   Leave your document on screen

3)   Add the following extra paragraph as a final paragraph to your **STAIN** document on screen:

Wine and Fruit Juice

Providing wine and fruit juice stains have not penetrated too deep they can be treated. The best results are acheived if quick action is taken.

Clean the surface by light sanding, then use muriatic acid diluted with lukewarm water. While the area is still wet with acid, put a few drops of hydrogen peroxide on it. [Burns

It is unfortunate if a cigar or cigarette burns wood. This is not regarded as a stain and nothing can ever remove the discoloration of the wood.

Deep scraping or sanding can mitigate such marks, but it is not a job for an amateur.

---

4)   Add automatic page numbering at the top of all pages. Look back at page 41 if you experience a problem showing the page number

5)   Save as **PRODUCTS** Carefully check your work against **model answer CONSOL4 (SECOND PRINTOUT)** which has been saved on the disk that accompanies this book

PRACTISE MERGING CELLS/INSERTING A LINE-SPACE

Exercise 17d

1) Key in the following text in a table. Use Monotype Corsiva sized 13 or a font of your choice

BOYS	TIME BORN 30 JANUARY	GIRLS	TIME BORN 30 JANUARY
Alann, James R	4.05 am	Barlow, Anne T	3.01 am
Derrick, John P	8.14 am	Lakeman, Charlotte	9.44 am
O'Brien, (baby)	11.55 am	Siri, Petra Z	1.35 pm
Wiltshire, Lomas	3.12 pm	Zabek, Lana R	2.00 pm

2) Carefully check your work and save as **GRASS**. Merge the cells and amend as shown below:

underline headings

BOYS –	TIME BORN 30 JANUARY	GIRLS –	TIME BORN 30 JANUARY
Alann, James R	4.05 am	Barlow, Anne T	3.01 am
Derrick, John P	8.14 am	Lakeman, Charlotte	9.44 am
O'Brien, (baby)	11.55 am	Siri, Petra Z	1.35 pm
Wiltshire, Tomas	3.12 pm	Zabek, Lana R	2.00 pm

add a clear line space

merge these 2 columns   merge these 2 columns

3) Quick save your document and print one copy. It should look identical to the copy below:

<u>BOYS – TIME BORN 30 JANUARY</u>	<u>GIRLS – TIME BORN 30 JANUARY</u>
Alann, James R 4.05 am Derrick, John P 8.14 am O'Brien, (baby) 11.55 am Wiltshire, Tomas 3.12 pm	Barlow, Anne T 3.01 am Lakeman, Charlotte 9.44 am Siri, Petra Z 1.35 pm Zabek, Lana R 2.00 pm

4) Clear the screen.

LESSON 5	OBVIOUS ERRORS OF AGREEMENT PRACTICE
	GRAMMATICAL ERRORS
	CIRCLED ERRORS IN DRAFT WORK
	PRACTISE AMENDING CIRCLED ERRORS IN
	HANDWRITTEN TEXT
	USING APOSTROPHES
	PRACTISE APOSTROPHE WORK
	PRACTISE GRAMMATICAL ERRORS
	AUTOMATIC (SOFT) PAGE BREAK
	HARD PAGE BREAK
	CONSOLIDATION

OBVIOUS ERRORS OF AGREEMENT

Exercise 5a

TARGET TIME 15 MINUTES

1) Type in the following text emphasising the text as indicated. Remember to time your-self and fill in your target time sheet

---

ERRORS TO AVOID

Correct grammar is an essential tool for the production of perfect documents. The examples given below show some of the common errors that people make:

<u>Was or Were</u>

"A list of all the girls, with their pets, <u>were</u> put up on the wall".

The 2 nouns "girls" and "pets" attracted the plural verb "**were**". The subject-word of this sentence is "**list**" which is singular, so the verb should also be singular. The sentence should read:

"A list of all the girls, with their pets, <u>was</u> put up on the wall".

<u>Words wrongly used</u>

Alright – there is no such word. The correct form is **all right**. You would not think of writing **alwrong**, the opposite meaning is written **all wrong**. In other combinations with the word **all**, however, the 2 separate words have become one, with a consequent dropping of the final "l" of "all". For example, almost, already, although. In these the word "all" is less strongly felt; "all ready" has quite a different meaning from "already".

---

2) Save as **GRAMMAR**. Carefully check your work against the above copy and correct any mistakes made. Quick save your work if necessary. Print one copy and clear the screen

PRACTISE MERGING CELLS

Exercise 17c

1)   Key in the following text in a table. Use Times New Roman font, sized 10

PLANT FOOD	USES ON THE LAWN	EFFECT	BEST TIME TO APPLY
Nitrogen	Essential	Lush, green turf	Spring and Summer
Phosphates	Essential	Large root system	Autumn
Potash	Desirable	"Harden" the grass	Spring and Autumn
Lime	Use only in special cases	Only consider using when grass is sparse and overrun by moss	Autumn

2)   Carefully check your work and save as **GRASS**. Merge the cells and amend as shown below:

PLANT FOOD	USES ON THE LAWN	EFFECT	BEST TIME TO APPLY
Nitrogen	Essential	Lush, green turf	Spring and Summer
Phosphates	Essential	Large root system	Autumn
Potash	Desirable	"Harden" the grass	Spring and Autumn
Lime	Use only in special cases	Only consider using when grass is sparse and overrun by moss	Autumn

merge these 2 cells AND

merge these 2 cells

EFFECT AND

Embolden headings

3)   Quick save your document and print one copy. It should look identical to the copy below:

PLANT FOOD AND USES ON THE LAWN		EFFECT AND BEST TIME TO APPLY	
Nitrogen	Essential	Lush, green turf	Spring and Summer
Phosphates	Essential	Large root system	Autumn
Potash	Desirable	"Harden" the grass	Spring and Autumn
Lime	Use only in special cases	Only consider using when grass is sparse and overrun by moss	Autumn

4)   Clear the screen. **You will use this document again later**

PRACTISE GRAMMATICAL ERRORS

Exercise 5b

1) Type a correct copy of the following sentences. Use your printout from the previous page to decide which is the correct word to type

Choose the word you consider to be correct

1) Neither of the students were/was present at the College prize-giving.
2) Have/has either of you ever worked in a pub?
3) Each of the Managers will be allowed to say exactly what she/they think/s.
4) Nobody in the room dared to say what they/he really thought. John thought it was alright.

HELPFUL NOTE. The distributive adjectives and pronouns, eg each, either, nobody, etc, are **singular**, for they imply that each individual person or thing is separately considered. They must be given **singular** verbs and other parts of speech.

2) Carefully check your work and correct any mistakes found. Spell-check and save as **EX5B**

3) Carefully check your work against **model answer EX5B** which has been saved on the disk that accompanies this book. Clear the screen

Exercise 5c

1) The following text contains the type of errors of agreement that you are likely to encounter in the Text Processing examination. Type in the text choosing the correct word/s in each case

1) May I say that we was/were most impressed with the efficiency of your co..
2) I will ask her to contact you when she has/have read the info..
3) Computing arrangements are/is limited.
4) Each new site is/are designed to meet the needs of customers.
5) The warehouse near Bristol have/has the advantage of access to road and rail links.

2) Carefully check your work and correct any mistakes found. Spell-check and save your file as **EX5C**

3) Carefully check your work against **model answer EX5C** which has been saved on the disk that accompanies this book. Clear the screen

INSERTING A BLANK ROW

Exercise 17b

1) You may prefer to insert a blank row using a quicker method. Key in the table below in order to practise this quicker method:

KNEBWORTH CONCERT	READING CONCERT
10 AUGUST	23–25 AUGUST
Oasis	The Stone Roses
The Bootleg Beatles	The Black Grape
The Chemical Brothers	Rage Against the Machine
Ocean Colour Scene	Garbage
The Prodigy	Dodgy
Manic Street Preachers	Sonic Youth

Check your work and save as **ROCKROLL**

2) Place the cursor after the "t" of Concert in the heading – Knebworth Concer**t**

3) Press the **return** (or enter) key on the keyboard

4) Repeat the above technique this time inserting a line space after the dates 10 AUGUST/23–25 AUGUST

KNEBWORTH CONCERT	READING CONCERT
10 August	23–25 AUGUST
Oasis	The Stone Roses
The Bootleg Beatles	The Black Grape
The Chemical Brothers	Rage Against the Machine
Ocean Colour Scene	Garbage
The Prodigy	Dodgy
Manic Street Preachers	Sonic Youth

5) Quick save your document and print one copy. Your printout should look like the copy below. Clear the screen.

KNEBWORTH CONCERT	READING CONCERT
10 AUGUST	23–25 AUGUST
Oasis	The Stone Roses
The Bootleg Beatles	The Black Grape
The Chemical Brothers	Rage Against the Machine
Ocean Colour Scene	Garbage
The Prodigy	Dodgy
Manic Street Preachers	Sonic Youth

CIRCLED ERRORS IN DRAFT WORK

TARGET TIME 7 MINUTES

Exercise 5d

1) Key in the following text. Choose a larger sized font. Remember to time yourself and fill in your target time sheet

---

Justify right margin

It have been decided that an efficient new safety system be introduced into all new cars now coming from Japan. We was most impressed with the system when it were demonstrated for us last week at the motor show.

The result of many years of research are this bonus for the domestic buyer. As ever, the new system now have to be accepted by various countries and it are unlikely that it will be seen in Britain for 3 or 4 years. However, versions is likely to be manufacturered at the company's UK plant.

---

2) Carefully check your work and save as **EX5D.** Carefully check your work against **model answer EX5D** which has been saved on the disk that accompanies this book. Clear the screen

Exercise 5e

TARGET TIME 5 MINUTES

1) Key in the following text in <u>double line-spacing</u>. Remember to time yourself and fill in your target time sheet

---

All kinds of errors will be cir9cled in the RSA Text Processing examination. Errors of agreement (as Task 3) together with spelling, apostrophe and other typo graphical errors could be included. Incorrect punctuation will also be circled, for example a full stop may be missing from the end of a sentence In this case the word ending the sentence, or the word beginning the next sentence may be circled. However, you is not expected to insert additional commas in the text. If you do insert punctuation that significantly alters the meaning of the sentence then you will incur one fault per paper.

---

2) Carefully check your work and save as **EX5E.** Carefully check your work against **model answer EX5E** which has been saved on the disk that accompanies this book. Clear the screen

10) If your heading now occupies 2 lines (as the copy below), place the cursor in the space after the "**L**" of **BRISTOL** and press the **Delete** key on your keyboard. The 2 words should now be on one line (check that you have one space between the 2 words)

BRISTOL SERVICE	COUNTRYWIDE	SERVICE

11) Merge the two main headings **COUNTRYWIDE** and **SERVICE** using the same technique

12) Point the mouse into the left margin and click once to highlight the first row. Embolden the main headings (as shown below) by clicking on the **Bold** icon on the Formatting toolbar

BRISTOL SERVICE		**COUNTRYWIDE SERVICE**	
<u>Colours</u>	<u>7-day</u>	<u>Type A</u>	<u>Type B</u>
Pale lilac	Standard charge	Available immediately	Available immediately
Barely pink	Standard charge	To order	Available immediately
Emerald Green	Standard charge	To order	To order
Gold	Optional extra	To order	To order

13) With the row still highlighted, centre the headings by clicking on the **Centre** icon on the Formatting toolbar

14) Quick save your document

15) Clear the screen

PRACTISE AMENDING CIRCLED ERRORS IN HANDWRITTEN TEXT

Exercise 5f

1) Change your font to [Arial Black] sized [14] or choose a different font yourself.
Type in the following text:

EQUAL OPPS. FOR ALL ← emphasise heading
Telling people not to be prejudiced is about as useful as telling them
to be taller. We (has) produced a short video which uses 5 vignettes
to illustrate the effects and explain the unfortunate personal consequences. ✓ of discrimination
The 5 short scenes each show discrimination by gender, race, sexual
preference, [physical disability] and [nationality]. // Full info. may be found
in our handbook which (alsoo) contains details of (costs) [We also offer
videos on many other subjects related to the workplace, for example
(bussiness) meetings, working with (collaegues) or succeeding with
advertising. Please telephone Stephen 0181 968 0249 for further
info. or fax 0181 964 2163.

2) Spell-check and save as **EQUAL.** Carefully check your work for errors

3) Print one copy and keep it to check later. This document will be retrieved and amended
at the end of this Lesson

Exercise 5g

1) Change your font [CG Omega] sized [14] or choose a different font yourself.
Type in the following text:

approx. 16 small brewing (companys) in the South West (is)
concerned at the threat of cheap lager from abroad. [Rachel
Page from Yate Brewers said that the European ruling could
hit small brewers and (and) force them out of (bussiness). (His)
(colleague), Jessica Bull, said local brewers could not compete
(financialy).

2) Carefully check your work against **model answer EX5G** which has been saved on the
disk that accompanies this book. Clear the screen

INSERTING A BLANK ROW WITHIN A TABLE

4)   You are going to insert a blank row above and below the row beginning ''Colours''

      Place the cursor anywhere in the row beginning **''Colours'' (there is no need to high-light the row)**. Click the right hand mouse button and from the drop-down menu click once on **Insert Rows**. A blank row will be inserted above the row

5)   Place the cursor in the row beginning **''Pale lilac''** and repeat the above action so that there is a clear row (line space) above and below the **''Colours''** row

UNDERLINING TEXT WITHIN A TABLE

6)   Highlight the sub-heading row **''Colours''** and click on the **underline icon** on the For-matting toolbar. Click on a blank cell and your highlight will disappear leaving the text in the row underlined

BRISTOL	SERVICE	COUNTRYWIDE	SERVICE
<u>Colours</u>	<u>7-day</u>	<u>Type A</u>	<u>Type B</u>
Pale lilac	Standard charge	Available immediately	Available immediately
Barely pink	Standard charge	To order	Available immediately
Emerald Green	Standard charge	To order	To order
Gold	Optional extra	To order	To order

MERGING (JOINING) CELLS TOGETHER

7)   Click in the first cell of the table and hold the left mouse down as you drag the mouse to the right to highlight the second cell also (as shown below)

BRISTOL	SERVICE	COUNTRYWIDE	SERVICE

8)   Click on **Table** on the **Menu Bar** ⎯⎯⎯⎯⎯⎯┐

‒	<u>F</u>ile	<u>E</u>dit	<u>V</u>iew	<u>I</u>nsert	F<u>o</u>rmat	<u>T</u>ools	T<u>a</u>ble	<u>W</u>indow	<u>H</u>elp		⬍

9)   From the drop-down menu click on **Merge Cells**

USING APOSTROPHES

Exercise 5h

1)   Type in the following text:

USING THE APOSTROPHE ← emphasise

The apostrophe (have) several functions.

It can be used to indicate the possessive singular case. This is done by adding 's at the end. for example:
[handwritten: typist put extra space either side of 's]

The barber's pole (singular - because it is only one barber)
The boy's head
The typist's chair

It can also be used to indicate the possessive plural case. This is done by adding the apostrophe only, for example:

The babies' rattles (plural - more than one baby and rattle)
~~**Children's games**~~ *childrens' games*
Six months' leave was granted

It can also be used to indicate the omission of a letter or letters from a word:

I'm = I am
I've - I have
I'll = I will
Don't - do not
It's = it is
We'd = we should

✓ Note that in the ~~above~~ *last* example the apostrophe is put where the missing letters would be. *Such ~~abber~~ abbreviations are better avoided in formal composition, except where the writer (are) reproducing conversation.*

---

2)   Carefully check your work on screen against the above copy and correct any mistakes found. If your checking is accurate you should find no errors if you now spell-check.

Spell-check now – were you accurate? If not, then you must check your work more slowly – concentrate on each word. In the examination you will need to be able to check carefully

3)   Print one copy and keep for reference. Save your file **as APOSTRO**. Clear the screen

LESSON 17	TABLE FORMAT
	INSERTING A BLANK ROW WITHIN A TABLE
	UNDERLINING TEXT WITHIN A TABLE
	MERGING (JOINING) CELLS TOGETHER
	PRACTISE MERGING CELLS
	PRACTISE MERGING CELLS/INSERTING A LINE-SPACE
	PRACTISE MERGING CELLS/INSERTING LINE-SPACING AND FORMATTING
	CHANGING FONTS/FONT SIZES WITHIN A TABLE
	MOVING TEXT WITHIN A TABLE (DRAG AND DROP METHOD)
	MOVING ROWS OF TEXT
	PRACTISE MOVING TEXT AND MERGING CELLS
	SPLITTING CELLS WITHIN TABLES
	SORTING WITHIN TABLES
	PRACTISE SORTING WITHIN TABLES
	MOVING COLUMNS WITHIN TABLES
	CONSOLIDATION

TABLE FORMAT

Exercise 17a

In the first book in this series you were taught how to input tables and carry out basic amendment functions. You are now going to build upon that knowledge to produce more complex tables.

1)   Obtain a 4 column, 6 line table using the **Insert Table** icon

2)   Type in the following table. If your work on screen does not show 'gridlines' it is probably because the 'gridlines' option has been turned off. Click on **Table** on the **Menu Bar**, and then click on the word **Gridlines** (at the bottom of the drop-down menu) in order to turn gridlines back on

BRISTOL	SERVICE	COUNTRYWIDE	SERVICE
Colours	7-day	Type A	Type B
Pale lilac	Standard charge	Available immediately	Available immediately
Barely pink	Standard charge	To order	Available immediately
Emerald Green	Standard charge	To order	To order
Gold	Optional extra	To order	To order

3)   Carefully check your work and save with a name of your choice. Leave the table on screen

PRACTISE APOSTROPHE WORK

Exercise 5i

1)   Type a copy of the following sentences, adding the apostrophe to the underlined word. Use your printout from the previous page to help you decide where to add the apostrophe

---

1)   I moved the <u>typists</u> chair to the Personnel Department.
2)   Mrs <u>Greens</u> typewriter needs repairing.
3)   <u>Its</u> much to early to give you an answer.
4)   <u>Joannes</u> desk was moved away from the window.
5)   <u>Dont </u>go to the seaside today, <u>its</u> going to rain.
6)   Only 7 <u>days</u> notice is required.
7)   The <u>ladies</u> hats were in the cupboard.

---

2)   Check your work and correct any mistakes found. If your checking is accurate you should find no errors if you now spell-check. Save your file as **EX5(I)**

3)   Carefully check your work against **model answer EX5(I)** which has been saved on the disk that accompanies this book. Clear the screen

Exercise 5j

1)   Type in the following text. Insert apostrophes as necessary. Choose a different font before commencing this exercise

---

I dont think its any use collecting the childrens toys until Ive had time to mark the prices on these goods. Ill not have time to finish that job today unless I ask for help.

Give the boys shoes to the ladies and the ladies shoes to the boy.

I like reading Dickenss novels and O'Neills poetry.

Im sure that this book is either his or hers, but neither of them claim it. Ill throw it away tomorrow.

---

2)   Check your work and correct any mistakes found. If your checking is accurate you should find no errors if you now spell-check. Save your file as **EX5J**

3)   Carefully check your work against **model answer EX5J** which has been saved on the disk that accompanies this book. Clear the screen

5) Retrieve the following document saved as **COMPUTE**

6) Immediately rename the file **COMPUTE2**. Amend as indicated

KW/CH

Ms. L. Shaneet
"Glenberry"
London Road
BRACKNELL
Berkshire RG12 2UY

Insert phrases as indicated

*Print 2 copies
Please route. One copy
for Technical Support,
one for File*

Dear Madam

recent

Thank you for your letter regarding the purchase of a personal computer. *Insert phrase 3 here* We have set out below the details you require.

Before you decide which computer to buy then you need to ask yourself what you are planning to use a PC for. Most people think of a PC as a machine, like a typewriter, specifically designed to type letters and documents but it is much more than this. The PC is a device for both the businessman and the family. For example spreadsheets can keep track of all household spending and savings accounts, modern PCs can send and receive faxes, and CD-Roms can help educate children with interactive encyclopaedias.

The information you requested about computers is listed below but our advice would be not to worry too much about these details. A good store would ensure that all specifications met your requirements.

*The processor (the "brain" of the machine)
Memory (see below)
Monitor (these vary from 14" to 20")
Software (an operating system such as Windows 95 is essential)
Multimedia (for games, CD-Roms with sound and video)*

// Insert phrase 2

We can offer technical support if you require and can help set-up your computer. (Insert phrase 1)

// Insert phrase 4

Sort into exact alphabetical order + inset 25mm (1") from left margin

Yours faithfully   *Katy Woodbury, Customer Enquiries*

7) Carefully check your work. Spell-check and quick save your document. Print preview and print one copy

8) Carefully check your work against **model answer CONSOL16** which has been saved on the disk that accompanies this book. Clear the screen

PRACTISE GRAMMATICAL ERRORS

Exercise 5k

TARGET TIME 20 MINUTES

1) Retrieve your file saved as **EQUAL**. Check your copy on screen against the copy below. Amend as shown. If you are unsure about shoulder-headings, see the first book in this series

---

Typist. / Please print one copy in double line spacing, amend all circled errors. Add page numbering bottom right. Use "Times New Roman" font sized 12.

EQUAL OPPORTUNITIES FOR ALL ← *centre + embolden*

Videos available ← *Embolden + underline all shoulder headings*

Telling people not to be prejudiced is about as useful as telling them to be taller. We have produced a short video which uses 5 vignettes to illustrate the effects and explain the unfortunate personal consequences of discrimination. The 5 short scenes each show discrimination by gender, race, sexual preference, nationality and physical disability.

Full information may be found in our handbook which also contains details of costs. We also offer videos on many other subjects related to the workplace, for example business meetings, working with colleagues or succeeding with advertising. Please telephone Stephen 0181 968 0249 for further information or fax 0181 964 2163.

Special Educational Needs

This College welcomes (student's) with learning difficulties and disabilities and (offerrs) a wide range of full-time and part-time provision. Full information can be found on page 10 of (are) handbook.

ESOL (English for Speakers of other languages)

We offer a range of courses for people wishing to learn English as a second language. The groups (is) small and will concentrate on speaking, listening, reading and (writting). All ESOL courses are FREE! Please contact the office (typist insert 'phone no. here, it can be found above) and speak to Jane Grant.

---

2) Save your file as **EQUAL2** and then carefully check your work against **model answer EX5K** which has been saved on the disk that accompanies this book. **Look especially where your page breaks occurs** before leaving the work on screen for the next exercise

CONSOLIDATION EXERCISE FOR LESSONS 15 AND 16

Practise what you have learnt in Lessons 15 and 16 by following through the instructions below.

1)   Delete any standard paragraphs saved in the Auto Text box

2)   Create the following standard paragraphs as Auto Text. Save them as indicated

---

If you buy from us you automatically get a 15 months' on site service guarantee. **[save as phrase1]**

There are 2 types of memory, both of which are measured in Megabytes (Mb). Random Access Memory (RAM) measures how much information your computer can store at any instant. These days the most basic machines come with 4 Mb of RAM. **[save as phrase2]**

We are able to offer you a full range of brands, choices and prices as well as having expert staff on hand to explain the technology and cater for all types of enquiry. **[save as phrase3]**

We hope that the above information answers your queries. However if we can be of any further assistance please do not hesitate to contact us. **[save as phrase4]**

---

3)   Carefully check your work and correct any mistakes found

4)   Clear the screen

AUTOMATIC (SOFT) PAGE BREAK

For the Text Processing examination you will find that one task will be so long that it will automatically continue onto a second page. When you print you will have two pages of text.

The computer will automatically advance into a second page when necessary and it will insert a dotted line across the screen when it does so (this is known as a soft page break).

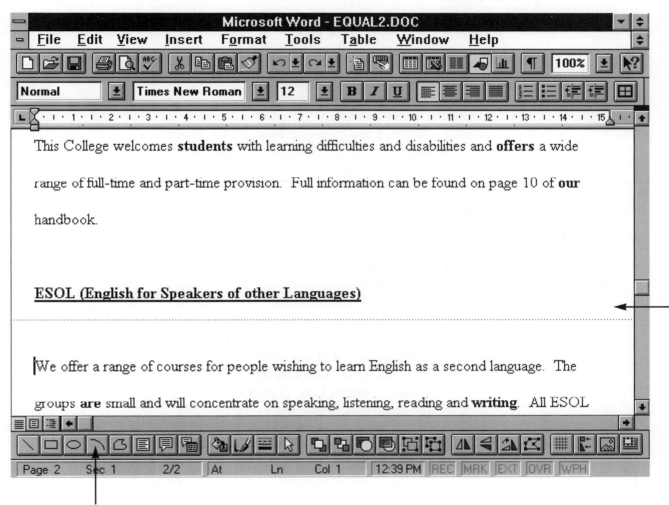

The status bar at the bottom of the screen makes it is easy for you to see exactly where the cursor is situated. Page 1 or 2, as appropriate, will be shown when the cursor is on that page.

1)   With the **EQUAL2** document on screen move the cursor position so that you have the dotted line on screen and then move the cursor above and below the line. At the same time notice the page number change on the status bar at the bottom of the screen

FOOTBALL TERMS

Most football commentators use the everyday soccer terms listed below. Some also sprinkle their commentary with a well worn cliche such as "it's a game of 2 halves".

Centre spot
Corner flag
Foul
Free kick
Goal
Goal line
Header
Penalty spot
Terraces
Touch line

CLASSIC SONGS

Sometimes when a certain piece of music is played it brings back memories. Do any of the following songs bring back good memories for you?

Gerry and the Pacemakers "You'll Never Walk Alone"
Jackson, Michael "Man In The Mirror"
Led Zeppelin "Stairway To Heaven"
Madness "Our House"
Nirvana "Smells Like Teen Spirit"
Presley, Elvis "Love Me Tender"
Queen "Killer Queen"
Rolling Stones "Honky Tonk Women"
The Doors "Light My Fire"

HARD PAGE BREAK

Sometimes you need to instruct the computer to start a new page when you want it to. For example, if you were typing a letter and the computer automatically put the complimentary close on a second page (as below) – this would not be a satisfactory layout. You might wish to transfer a few lines of the last paragraph to the second page also.

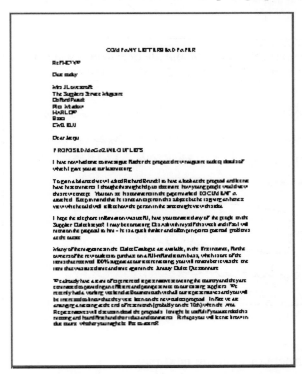
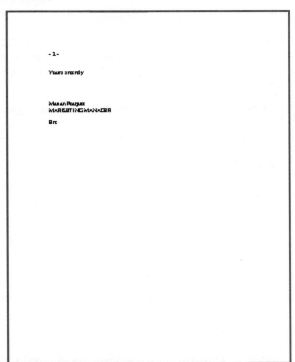

On the other hand the writer of the material might request the typist to leave a larger space at the foot of a page. Perhaps she wants space for adding notes later.

It is also incorrect to leave a heading at the foot of one page and start the text at the beginning of the next.

There are several ways in which you could achieve the desired layout depending upon the situation. Two of these you have already covered – **"Shrink to Fit"** and **"Widows and Orphans"** (Lesson 4). You are now about to add the third method – that of **"Hard Page Break"**.

<u>To instruct the computer to end a page exactly where you want:</u> (Hard Page Break)

1)   With the document **EQUAL2** on screen place the cursor before the third and final subheading

<u>**"ESOL (English for speakers of other Languages)"**</u>

PRACTISE SORTING AND CENTRING LISTS

Exercise 16e

TARGET TIME 10 MINUTES EACH EXERCISE

1)   Type in the following text:

NOTE TO TYPIST - after you have sorted the text into alphabetical order, whilst it is still highlighted click on the centre icon on the formatting toolbar in the normal way

Most football commentators use the everyday soccer terms listed below. Some also sprinkle their commentary with a well worn cliche such as "it's a game of 2 halves".

Free kick
Goal
Touch line
Header
Centre spot
Foul
Corner flag
Terraces
Penalty spot
Goal line

Please sort into alphabetical order

---

2)   Carefully check your work against the correct copy on the next page

3)   Spell-check and save your file with a name of your choosing. Clear the screen

Exercise 16f

1)   Type in the following text:

CLASSIC SONGS

Sometimes when a certain piece of music is played it brings back memories. Do any of the following songs bring back good memories for you?

The Doors "Light My Fire"
Jackson, Michael "Man In The Mirror"
Queen "Killer Queen"
Rolling Stones "Honky Tonk Women"
Led Zeppelin "Stairway To Heaven"
Gerry and the Pacemakers "You'll Never Walk Alone"
Nirvana "Smells Like Teen Spirit"
Madness "Our House"
Presley, Elvis "Love Me Tender"

please sort into alphabetical order + centre

---

2)   Carefully check your work against the correct copy on the next page

3)   Spell-check and save your file with a name of your choosing. Clear the screen

2)   Hold down the **Ctrl** key and press the **return key**

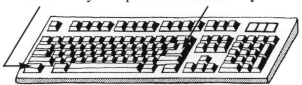

> **If this does not happen check that you are in "Normal View" – see no. 4 below**

3)   A dotted line will appear across the screen with the words **Page Break**** in the centre of the line as below:

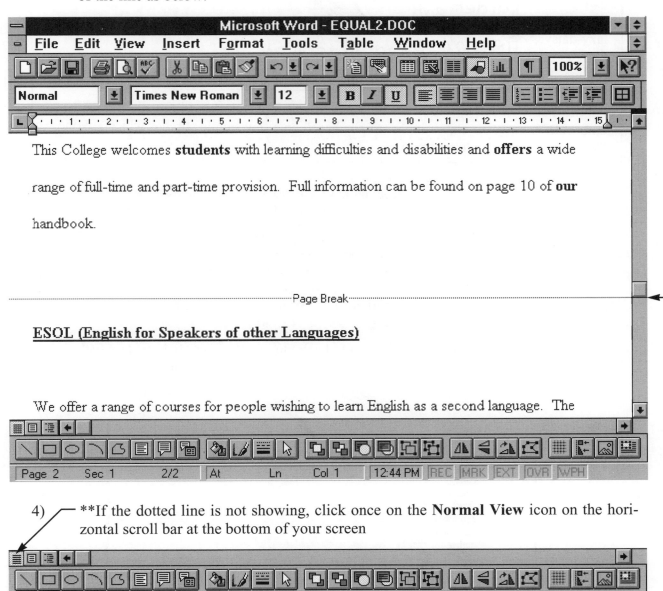

4) ******If the dotted line is not showing, click once on the **Normal View** icon on the horizontal scroll bar at the bottom of your screen

5)   Quick save your document and print one copy before clearing the screen

PRACTISE SORTING AND INDENTING LISTS

Exercise 16d

1) Type in the following text. You are going to sort it and indent it whilst it is still high-lighted

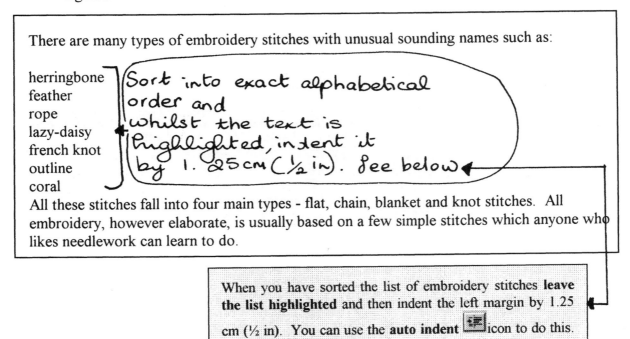

There are many types of embroidery stitches with unusual sounding names such as:

herringbone
feather
rope
lazy-daisy
french knot
outline
coral

Sort into exact alphabetical order and whilst the text is highlighted, indent it by 1.25cm (½ in). See below

All these stitches fall into four main types - flat, chain, blanket and knot stitches. All embroidery, however elaborate, is usually based on a few simple stitches which anyone who likes needlework can learn to do.

When you have sorted the list of embroidery stitches **leave the list highlighted** and then indent the left margin by 1.25 cm (½ in). You can use the **auto indent** icon to do this. (See Lesson 11, page 126, if unsure)

2) Carefully check your work and correct any mistakes found. Spell-check and save your file with a name of your choice

3) Leave the document on screen and check against the copy below. The list of embroi-dery stitches should now be indented as well as in exact alphabetical order

There are many types of embroidery stitches with unusual sounding names such as:

    coral
    feather
    french knot
    herringbone
    lazy-daisy
    outline
    rope

All these stitches fall into four main types - flat, chain, blanket and knot stitches. All embroidery, however elaborate, is usually based on a few simple stitches which anyone who likes needlework can learn to do.

4) Quick save your file. Clear the screen

CONSOLIDATION EXERCISE FOR LESSON 5

> **TARGET TIME 30 MINUTES**

Practise what you have learnt so far by following the instructions below.

1)   Type in the following text. Remember to time yourself and fill in your target time sheet

Double line spacing except where indicated. An extra paragraph will be given to you later. Add page numbering bottom centre.

CERTIFICATES PRESENTED AT THE ANNUAL DINNER ← *emphasize*

leaflet

The photograph on the front cover of this ~~brochure~~ shows a ~~small~~ group of physically disabled young people who gained certificates in Enterprise Communications subjects at the American Foundation in Seattle.

wife of the President

Mrs Hilary Clinton presented the certificates at the Headquarter's last Fri.

Sucessful

The American Foundation has been a charity since 1954 and was set up to encourage ~~young~~ physically disabled young people into corporate industry. The young people has produced many high quality products such as writtting paper, envelopes, letterheaded paper for local companies and misc. other office products.

CERTIFICATE ACCREDITATION

young people

The enthusiasm of the ~~youngsters~~ during their work at the Foundation, and the the overall high quality of the products testify to the value of the programme and the contribution it makes to the student's understanding of the world of work. ✓

Assessment is through an externally marked and set written test and a locally devised and marked project. The results are graded as Merit and Distinction. The Certificates awarded *Pass,* reflect the high quality training given.

emphasize this sentence

RUNNING THE OFFICE

The youngsters run the co.

~~They operate~~ as a small bussines and carry out all the paperwork themselves, iincluding ordering raw materials, stock-taking, visiting potential customers, etc. The Foundation aims ~~at giving~~ students relevant work experience in a number of ways:
to give

An understanding of how businesses work.
Practical ability in a range of skills related to setting up and org. a business.
A knowledge of the basic procedures and techniques of business communications.
An opportunity to apply knowledge and skills in a practical setting and become a responsable member of a working community.

Make this paragraph the last one

PRACTISE SORTING LISTS ALPHABETICALLY

Exercise 16c

1) Retrieve the following document saved as **GEM**. Immediately rename the file **GEM2**. Amend as indicated. <u>**Remember**</u> **if the examination paper instructs you to "right" justify the margin, you are required to "fully" justify it**

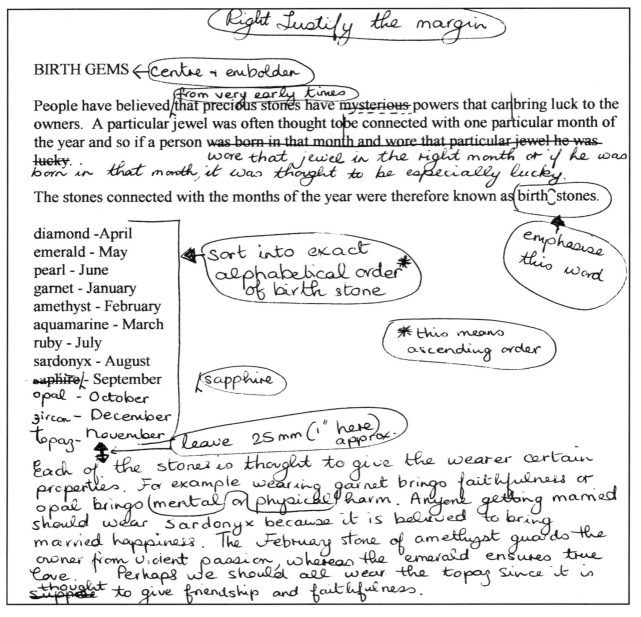

2) Carefully check your work. Quick save your document. Print preview and print one copy

3) Carefully check your work against **model answer EX16C** which has been saved on the disk that accompanies this book. Clear the screen

2) Save your file with a name of your choice. **Remember, you can only use a maximum of 8 alphabetical or numerical letters in a file name. You cannot use a comma, full stop, dash, etc**

3) Add the paragraph below where indicated:

Typist Please insert this paragraph after the 3rd paragraph which ends "..... Local companies and miscellaneous other office products"

After she had presented certificates Mrs Clinton commented:

"These young (peoples)(has) been highly motivated by the opp. to benefit from significant relevant work experience.[I am delighted by (there) progress and congratulate them all today.]
I hope they now go on to ~~get~~ obtain well-paid, worthwhile work within cos. - I know some of them already ~~do~~ have work lined up!"

4) Spell-check your work and correct any mistakes found

5) Carefully check your work against **model answer CONSOL5** which has been saved on the disk that accompanies this book

6) Quick save your file and clear the screen

4)   The following dialog box will appear:

Check that the Sort By box states Paragraphs (if not, click on the downward arrow alongside the box and then click on the word Paragraphs from the drop-down menu)

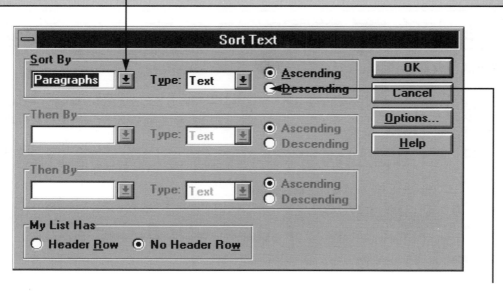

5)   Click in the circle alongside the word **Descending**. You are going to sort the list into descending alphabetical order – any letter of the alphabet beginning with **Z** will therefore come first and any letter of the alphabet beginning with **A** will come last.

6)   Click on | **OK** |. Print one copy and check against model answer **EX16A**

7)   Your list of birds should now be in descending alphabetical order as the one below:

MANY BIRDS MAY BE EASILY SEEN BY THE KEEN BIRD-WATCHER SUCH AS:

Wren
Woodpecker
Swallow
Raven
Pheasant
Linnet
Heron
Hawk
Cormorant

To begin watching birds all that is needed is a sharp eye and a keen ear and a bird book with good coloured pictures.

8)   Highlight the list of birds once more. Click on **Table** on the **Menu Bar.** From the drop-down menu click on **Sort Text**. Check that **Paragraph** has been chosen and this time click on **Ascending**. Click on | **OK** |

9)   Your list should now be in ascending alphabetic order. Quick save and clear the screen

LESSON 6

MEMORANDA AND THE EXAMINATION
SPECIAL MARKS AND ENCLOSURES
INSERTING THE DATE AUTOMATICALLY
BUSINESS LETTERS
USING LETTERHEAD PAPER
HANDWRITTEN BUSINESS LETTERS (copying)
ROUTING COPIES
CONSOLIDATION

MEMORANDA AND THE EXAMINATION

Exercise 6a

TARGET TIME 25 MINUTES

1) Type in the following text. Remember to time yourself and fill in your target time sheet

---

MEMORANDA AND THE RSA STAGE II EXAMS *Double line spacing except where indicated! Page no. bottom left. Justify throughout*

The memorandum task that you will be expected to produce for the above examinations will build upon the knowledge that you gained preparing for the Stage I examination. *s: single spacing*

Once again RSA stationery will not be provided. Memoranda may be produced on pre-printed forms (by keying in entry details) - this of course is much easier if a typewriter is ~~being~~ used. If the examination centre has saved on computer, a template with the main heading details (ie FROM, TO, DATE, REF) then the candidate may retrieve this file and fill in the relevant details. Alternatively the candidate may obtain a new document file and insert the main heading details when he inputs the other memorandum info..

It is very unlikely that the memorandum will be longer than *one* ~~a~~ page, but should it run into 2 pages it is a simple task to type the number 2 at the top of the second page before continuing with text on that page. Automatic page ~~no.~~ could be added if preferred. ✓

numbers

You ~~wwould~~ be wise to keep a small ~~calander~~ by you when you complete this task because it
is very likely *that* ~~you~~ will be asked to fill in a blank space with "next Monday's date" or "the date
of the first Sat. of ~~nezxt~~ month". This instruction reflects normal office practice - a sec. is
often requested to look up ~~approp.~~ *appropriate* dates and insert them ~~when typing~~ *into typed* documents. [As well as
contain *ing* incorrect spellings and misc ~~abbreveations~~ (info. which you should be learning now),
you will be expected to know where to place special marks in the memorandum. Special
marks are informative words such as CONFIDENTIAL, URGENT, PRIVATE and so on.
These inform the recipient and any other members of staff concerned to handle this particular
mail in a certain way. // It is possible that an enclosure may be implied
in the body of the MEMO and, if this is the case you should
automatically add the word/s ENC or ENCS at the foot of the Memo.

MEMORANDUM

---

2) Carefully check your work against **model answer EX6A** which has been saved on the disk that accompanies this book. Save as **MEMOHINT**. Print one copy and **keep for future reference**. Clear the screen

LISTS – SORTING ALPHABETICALLY

Word allows you to sort sentences alphabetically. However if you do not highlight the actual text you wish to be sorted, **Word** will sort the entire document as one unit. In the exercise below you are required to sort only <u>part</u> of the document (ie the list of birds). Follow the instructions to sort the list of birds alphabetically.

Exercise 16b

1)   Highlight the list of birds:

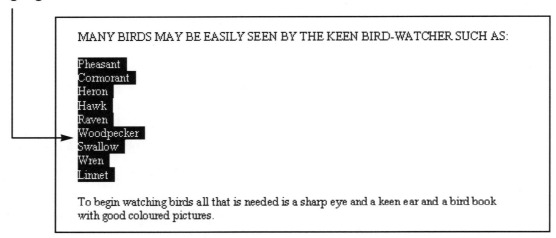

2)   Click on **T<u>a</u>ble** on the **Menu Bar**

3)   From the drop-down menu click on **Sor<u>t</u> Text**

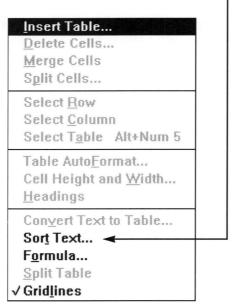

SPECIAL MARKS AND ENCLOSURES

The layout and detailed instructions contained in memoranda were thoroughly covered in the first book of this series. However, the Stage II examinations will also expect you to know where to place special marks, such as CONFIDENTIAL, PERSONAL, URGENT, etc. Look at *Exercise 6b* below for an example of the correct position.

Exercise 6b

1) Type in the following text:

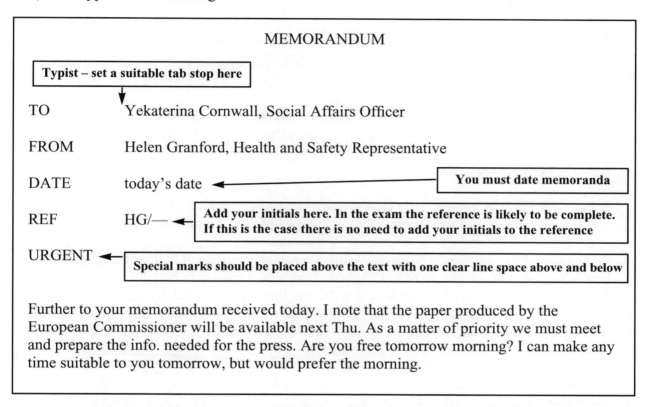

2) Carefully check your work against the above copy and correct any mistakes found. Now spell-check (there should be no more spelling errors if your checking is accurate!).

3) Save your file as **MEMO** and clear the screen

LESSON 16	**LISTS – INSERTING INTO A DOCUMENT AND SORTING ALPHABETICALLY**
	PRACTISE SORTING LISTS ALPHABETICALLY
	PRACTISE SORTING AND INDENTING LISTS
	PRACTISE SORTING AND CENTRING LISTS
	CONSOLIDATION

LISTS – INSERTING INTO A DOCUMENT

Exercise 16a

TARGET TIME 20 MINUTES

1) Retrieve the following document saved as **BIRD.** Immediately rename the file **BIRD2.** Remember to time yourself and fill in your target time sheet. Amend as indicated

BIRDS IN ENGLAND ← *centre*

A bird-watcher who gets up early on a spring morning soon notices that different species of bird begin to sing at different times. This is the start of the famous dawn chorus.

On the whole the length of a bird's day is the same as the number of hours of daylight. So a bird has to work ~~much~~ harder to get food on short winter days than on long summer ones. A few birds spend the winter in the Arctic Circle, and these have to feed during the hours of twilight. As long as a bird is well fed, its warm blood and its feathers help it to keep alive and well in/ *extremely* ~~very~~ cold weather. In Great Britain, birds do not usually die of cold; they become weak because of hunger in the first place. [When food is easy to find a bird may spend hours just flying about, (resting or preening (it's) feathers). However, ~~that~~ this behaviour is more likely to occur in the summer months, In] the winter looking for food will take up much time.

Many birds may be seen by the keen bird-watcher such as:
Pheasant *line space*
Cormor ant
Heron *emphasise this line*
Hawk
Raven
Wood pecker
Swallow
Wren
Linnet // To begin watchingbirds all that is needed is a sharp eye and a keen ear and a bird book with good coloured pictures

2) Carefully check and spell-check your work. Quick save your document and print one copy

3) Carefully check your work against **model answer EX16A** which has been saved on the disk that accompanies this book. Leave the document on screen

Exercise 6c

1) Change the *font size* to `12` and the *font* to `Courier` or `Courier New`

Type in the following text:

> TO Helen Granford, Health + Safety Representative
> FROM Yekaterina Cornwall, Social Affairs Officer
> REF YC/RC
>
> Thank you for your memo. Yes, I agree, we must meet as soon as poss. I have a 9.00 am appointment tomorrow, but I should be free by 9.30 am. I will come to your office at 9.45 am unless you telephone me to re-arrange the time. The papers I have are a little out of date but I will bring them anyway.
>
> (Mark this URGENT)

2) Carefully check your work against the following correct copy

3) Spell-check

4) Save your file as **MEMO2**

5) Clear the screen

MEMORANDUM

TO   Helen Granford, Health and Safety Representative

FROM   Yekaterina Cornwall, Social Affairs Officer

DATE   today's date ← **did you remember to date?**

REF   YC/RC

URGENT

Thank you for your memo. Yes, I agree, we must meet as soon
as possible. I have a 9.00 am appointment tomorrow, but I
should be free by 9.30 am. I will come to your office at
9.45 am unless you telephone me to re-arrange the time.

The papers I have are a little out of date but I will bring
them anyway.

DELETE STANDARD PARAGRAPH

Exercise 15j

1)   Click on **Edit** on the **Menu Bar**

2)   From the drop-down menu click on **Auto Text**

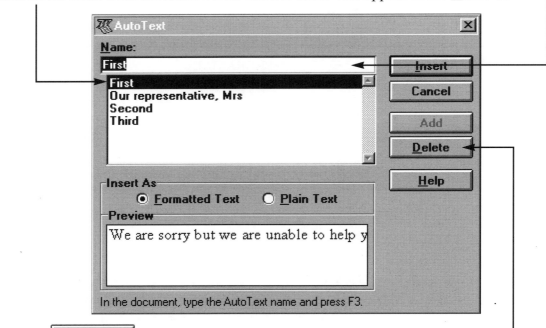

3)   Click on the Auto Text file name **First**. The file name will appear in the **Name** box

4)   Press the ▢ **Delete** key

5)   The file name will disappear and the text will be deleted

6)   Repeat the above instructions to delete the **Second** file

7)   Click on ▢ Close

CONSOLIDATION OF STANDARD PARAGRAPH WORK IS INCLUDED IN THE CONCLUSION EXERCISE AT THE END OF LESSON 16

TARGET TIME 12 MINUTES

1) Type in the following text. Remember to time yourself and fill in your target time sheet. Use a *font* of your choice. The font used here is [Placard SSi] size [14] . Do you remember what to do when an enclosure is implied in the text of a memorandum? If not, look back at the first book in this series because an enclosure is implied in the text below

---

MEMORANDUM *(Please mark PERSONAL)*

TO Jeremy Grant, Wages Clerk,
FROM Hemma Ranratten, Personnel Officer
REF HR/DD

It has come to our notice *(my)* that one or *(many)* 2 discrepancies have occurred in your computer accounts. I We would like to discuss this matter with you as soon as poss. [You will understand that these errors is a serious matter for the staff concerned and the Comapny. I am enclosing a printout of the errors made during the last calendar month - you will notice that there are 24 errors in total on the list. [Can you please attend a meeting in my office at 10.00 am on [typist please give next Monday's date] in order to discuss these matters. Miss Blackburn, your Supervisor will be invited to this meeting and you may invite your Union Representative if you wish. [Please confirm that you will attend.

---

2) Carefully check your work on screen against **model answer EX6D** which has been saved on the disk that accompanies this book

3) Save your file as **JGRANT**. Print one copy and clear the screen

4) Now compare your printed copy with the model answer. If your checking skills are good you should have no mistakes. If you do have errors, you need to pay more attention to your checking. Check slowly, perhaps keep a finger on each copy as you proceed. In order to pass the examination you must be able to spot your errors!

PRACTISE MERGING STANDARD PARAGRAPHS INTO VARIOUS DOCUMENTS

Exercise 15i

TARGET TIME 25 MINUTES

1) Type in the following text. Remember to time yourself and fill in your target time sheet

---

(Insert phrases as indicated)

Our ref RP/WR/30

Mr C J Wong
65 Stotbury Road
ANDOVER
Hampshire
SP4 5AG

Dear Mr Wong

Thank you for your recent *telephone* enquiry. We are pleased to let you know that we do supply the Atlantic II Woods that you require. *As you probably know* Atlantic has now become one of the UK's biggest selling jumbo woods. The cost depends upon whether you require steel or graphite. Steel costs £45.00 and graphite £55.00 *inclusive of VAT and postage.*

We are delighted to inform you that ~~You may be unaware that~~ we are offering a 10% discount on all golfing accessories *at the moment* and I am enclosing our catalogue which you might find of interest. All details of costs together with an order form can be found within the catalogue.

(Insert Phrase stored as Second)

(Insert Phrase stored as Third)

Yours sincerely

Roland Pullinger
MANAGER

---

2) Carefully check and spell-check your work. Quick save your document and print one copy

3) Carefully check your work against **model answer EX15(I)** which has been saved on the disk that accompanies this book. Clear the screen

INSERTING THE DATE AUTOMATICALLY

When using open punctuation (ie omitting unnecessary commas, etc) you should not use a comma within or after the actual date. The date should be typed in figures and it should be in the order of day, month, year, eg 12 March 1998.

It is possible and can be fun to instruct **Word** to insert the date for you. To do this:

1) Position the cursor at the point where you want to insert the date (in this case at the top of the screen)

2) Click on the word **Insert** on the **Menu Bar**

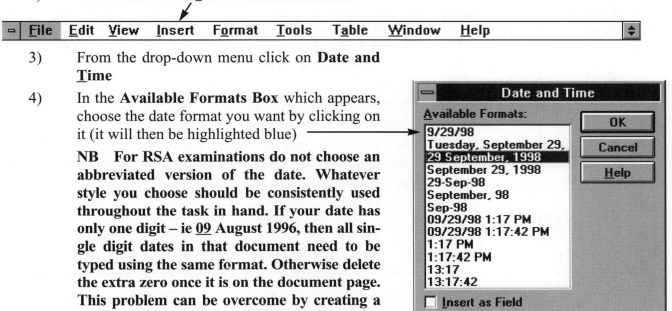

| File | Edit | View | Insert | Format | Tools | Table | Window | Help |

3) From the drop-down menu click on **Date and Time**

4) In the **Available Formats Box** which appears, choose the date format you want by clicking on it (it will then be highlighted blue)

   NB   For RSA examinations do not choose an abbreviated version of the date. Whatever style you choose should be consistently used throughout the task in hand. If your date has only one digit – ie <u>09</u> August 1996, then all single digit dates in that document need to be typed using the same format. Otherwise delete the extra zero once it is on the document page. This problem can be overcome by creating a Macro which, as it is advanced work, is covered in the third book in this series.

5) Click on | **OK** |

Exercise 6e

1) With the date on your screen, copy the above instructions (leaving out the screen graphics) and save your work as **DATE**. Add the text below as a final paragraph:

> SHORT CUT‸ (line space)
> It is possible to insert the date by following the above instructions. However, it is even quicker if the keyboard is used to insert the current date. Once the format of the date has been chosen you can quickly insert the date by holding <u>down</u> the **Alt** (alternative) and **Shift** key on the keyboard and pressing **D**. Let all keys go and the date will appear. You can add the current time in a similar manner with the **Alt**, **Shift**, and **T**. [Highlight the date or time and press the **delete** key on your keyboard if you wish to subsequently remove them.

2) Check your work and correct any mistakes before saving with a name of your choice. Quick save and print one copy for future reference and then clear the screen

PRACTISE MERGING STANDARD PARAGRAPHS INTO VARIOUS DOCUMENTS

Exercise 15g

1)   Type in the following text:

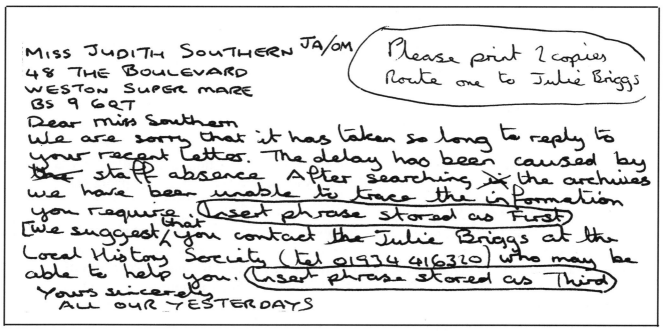

David Ward   LS/--

280 Peache Road

Teddington Middlesex, TW11 8AR

Dear Sir

Thank you for your letter received today (Insert phrase stored as First)

[We do not sell handmade willow baskets but I have passed your letter to a colleague who may be able to help you. My colleague who runs "Craftsmen Incorporated" in Totnes Devon, will contact you direct.

Yours faithfully

Lyn Saltcombe, 123 DESIGNS

(Insert phrase as indicated)

2)   Carefully check your work. Quick save your document and print one copy. Carefully check your work against **model answer EX15G** which has been saved on the disk that accompanies this book. Clear the screen

Exercise 15h

1)   Type in the following text:

MISS JUDITH SOUTHERN JA/OM

48 THE BOULEVARD

WESTON SUPER MARE

BS 9 6QT

Dear miss Southern

We are sorry that it has taken so long to reply to your recent letter. The delay has been caused by staff absence. After searching the archives we have been unable to trace the information you require. (Insert phrase stored as First)

[We suggest that you contact the Julie Briggs at the Local History Society (tel 01934 416320) who may be able to help you. (Insert phrase stored as Third)

Yours sincerely

ALL OUR YESTERDAYS

(Please print 2 copies. Route one to Julie Briggs)

2)   Carefully check your work. Quick save your document and print one copy. Carefully check your work against **model answer EX15H** which has been saved on the disk that accompanies this book. Clear the screen

Exercise 6f

1) Type in the following text:

Mark this Confidential

MEMORANDUM

To David Nesbitt, Financial Director

From Jidadeep Singh, Human Resources Officer

Ref   AA/ORB/it.

I recently read in the newspaper (photocopy enclosed) of the decision of the English Schools Football Association not to pay their team coaches out-of-pocket expenses for carrying out their duties. As you know Allan Alexander has been an ESFA coach (for many years) and until now we have granted him leave of absence without pay when he has been on coaching duty. Allan discussed this matter with me last Friday [give date] He has decided that because of the financial situation he really cannot afford to carry on with his England duties and will, (regretably) have to turn the honour down.

Allan, a former professional footballer, (and it seems such in the sport today) has discovered some of the best young players a pity that his talent will be lost to the game. He has appealed to the ESFA but they are in financial difficulties at present — although longterm they hope to provide financial help to ✓ their coaches once more.

I am contacting you with the request that either an ex gratia payment be made to Allan or we permit him to take paid leave. This would help him continue this worthwhile work until the ESFA sort their finances out, and I think it could perhaps provide us with some good publicity. I can let you have more details in due course if you wish.

---

2) Carefully check your work and correct any mistakes found

3) Spell-check and save your file as **FOOTBALL**. Print one copy

4) Carefully check your work against **model answer EX6F** which has been saved on the disk that accompanies this book. Clear the screen

PRACTISE CREATING AND SAVING STANDARD PARAGRAPHS

Exercise 15f

1) Type the following sentences which are going to be stored as standard paragraphs for later retrieval:

> We are sorry but we are unable to help you.
>
> We hope that this information will be helpful.
>
> Please do not hesitate to contact us if we can be of further assistance.

2) Click on the **Show/Hide** icon on the standard toolbar and highlight the <u>first</u> sentence. Do not highlight the ¶ icon. If you highlight ¶ then your retrieved Auto Text will also insert a return. (See *Exercise 15b* for more information)

3) Click on the **Insert Auto Text** icon on the **Standard Toolbar** –

4) Delete any name that appears in the **Name** box. Key in the file name – First

5) Click on Add

6) Highlight the other 2 sentences <u>one at a time</u>. Repeat the above instructions and Save these files with the Auto Text file names given below. When you have finished clear the screen

> We hope that this information will be helpful. **save as** Second
>
> Please do not hesitate to contact us if we can be of further assistance. **save as** Third

INSERTING A FILE INTO A DOCUMENT ON SCREEN

In the RSA examination you will **not** be expected to key in and save your own standard paragraphs. The examination paper itself will request that you insert text from a different file in a certain position within a document. To do this:

With the relevant document on screen and the cursor placed where you wish to insert the text, click on **Insert** on the **Menu Bar**. From the drop-down menu click on **File**. Click on the file name you need from the appropriate directory (your examination centre will advise you where it has been saved). The file will merge into your document on screen but you may need to edit out unwanted text.

BUSINESS LETTERS

Exercise 6g

1)   The layout and detailed instructions contained in business letters were thoroughly covered in the first book of this series. Refresh your memory by copying the letter below. Notice especially the positioning of the special instructions 'URGENT' – this was covered in the first book but special marks are more likely to be required in the Stage II examinations

---

INTERCONTINENTAL TRAVEL COMPANY
11 The Ridge
Stratford Place
LONDON   W1N OER

Tel 01675 466 501
Fax 01675 466 504

DW/SO

Date today

URGENT
Wayside Inn Holidays
1093 East Main Street
STAUNTON
West Virginia
USA

Dr Sirs

PROPOSED HOLIDAY PACKAGES

We are a well-reputed, experianced holiday company with 4 shops in London and branches throughout England. We have decided that we would like to offer package holidays to the States and this is my reason for contacting you. Could you let us have various several draft itineraries of different holiday packages together with price details? We propose offering various "interest" holidays (eg golf, tennis) alongside the more usual choices. We look forward to hearing from you.

Yours ffly
INTERCONTINENTAL TRAVEL COMPANY

Ms Debbie Wilson
Office Manager

---

2)   Carefully check your work and correct any mistakes found. Spell-check and save your file as **HOLIDAY**. Print one copy on letterhead paper (see overleaf for details of letterhead paper). Carefully check your work against **model answer EX6G** which has been saved on the disk that accompanies this book. Clear the screen

Carefully check your work against the following correct copy:

Letter Head Paper

Your ref GM/SF
Our ref RL/PC

Today's date

Mr Graham McGill
"Presents Galore"
67 High Street
KINVER
ST4 7TL

Dear Mr McGill

Many thanks for your recent letter regarding our products. I think you will find that quite a lot of our goods would appeal to your customers.

Our representative, Mrs Patricia Oaten, will be in the Staffordshire area next week and could call upon you if you wish. I will ask Patricia to telephone you to arrange a convenient time.

Yours sincerely

Roger Linklater
SALES

MEMORANDUM

TO   Mrs R Allan, Furniture Sales
FROM   Rosamund Ducal, Customer Services
DATE   Today's
REF   RD/– – ◄— | **your initials** |

Thank you for your memo. I am sorry to learn of the problems that you are experiencing with Mr George Reading who purchased one of our pine dining room tables. My advice would be to send Mr Reading a letter asking him if he would like Patricia to call upon him to discuss this problem. A standard phrase I often use is – Our representative, Mrs Patricia Oaten, will be in the Staffordshire area next week and could call upon you if you wish.

If you give Patricia his name and address together with his telephone number she will contact him to arrange a suitable date and time.

USING LETTERHEAD PAPER

When printing letters do not forget to make allowances at the top margin of the page for the letterhead – either press the return key at the top of your document page before you type the reference, or change the top margin by clicking on **File** and then **Page Setup.** The amount of space needed will depend upon the depth of the letterhead

The RSA will not supply letterhead paper for the examination but your examination centre will provide you with appropriate paper. <u>Do not use plain paper for printing the letter</u>.

Exercise 6h

TARGET TIME 25 MINUTES

1)   Key in the following text. Remember to time yourself and fill in your target time sheet

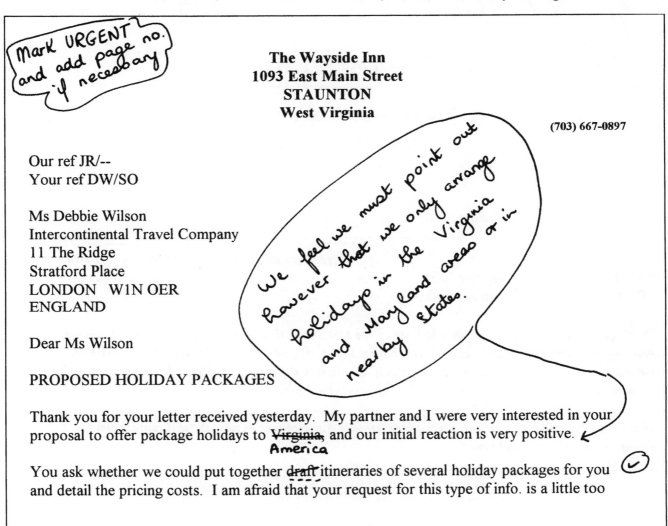

Mark URGENT and add page no. if necessary

The Wayside Inn
1093 East Main Street
STAUNTON
West Virginia

(703) 667-0897

Our ref JR/--
Your ref DW/SO

Ms Debbie Wilson
Intercontinental Travel Company
11 The Ridge
Stratford Place
LONDON   W1N OER
ENGLAND

Dear Ms Wilson

PROPOSED HOLIDAY PACKAGES

We feel we must point out however that we only arrange holidays in the Virginia and Maryland areas or in nearby states.

Thank you for your letter received yesterday. My partner and I were very interested in your proposal to offer package holidays to ~~Virginia,~~ and our initial reaction is very positive.
America

You ask whether we could put together ~~draft~~ itineraries of several holiday packages for you and detail the pricing costs. I am afraid that your request for this type of info. is a little too

68

PRACTISE MERGING STANDARD PARAGRAPHS INTO A DOCUMENT

Exercise 15d

1)   Type in the following text:

Your ref GM/SF
Our ref RL/PC

Please type this letter with a justified margin

Mr. Graham McGill "Presents Galore" 67 High Street
KINVER   ST4 7TL
Dear Mr. McGill
Many thanks for your recent letter regarding our products.
I think you will find that quite a lot of our goods
would appeal to your customers.
Insert the standard paragraph phrase stored as "Our representative" here. I will ask Patricia to telephone you to arrange a convenient time.
Yours Sincerely, Roger Linklater, SALES

2)   Carefully check your work against the correct copy on the next page

3)   Spell-check and save your file as **ENQUIRY**. Clear the screen

Exercise 15e

1)   Type in the following text:

Please use an appropriate reference in this memo

**MEMO TO Mrs R Allan, Furniture Sales
FROM Rosamund Ducal, Customer Services**

Thank you for your memo. I am sorry to learn of the problems that you are experiencing with Mr George Reading who purchased one of our pine dining room tables. My advice would be to send Mr Reading a letter asking him if he would like Patricia to call upon him to discuss this problem. A standard phrase I often use is - *insert phrase stored as "Our representative" here*

If you give Patricia his name and address together with his telephone number she will contact him to arrange a suitable date and time.

2)   Carefully check your work against the correct copy on the next page

3)   Spell-check and save your file as **COMPLAINT**. Clear the screen

vague for us to give you a detailed response immed. and it would be necy. for you to provide us with ~~some~~ idea of proposed price range/s, length of stay and type of holiday/s you require.
a firm

We have listed below several general options for your consideration:

it would be

Option 1   One week in Washington DC (poss. *to* include exercursions) followed by one week in the Shenandoah Valley. This would combine the busy life of our capital City with the beautiful Shenandoah Valley area.

Option 2   The Blue Ridge Mountains area. This would include countryside/hiking/horse riding followed by one week at the Shenvalee golf resort.

Option 3   One week at historic Williamsburg (once one of England's American colonies) plus one week *at* the beautiful Virginia Beach. This holiday would allow the travellor to relax at the seaside after enjoying a week of sight seeing.

Option 4   New York, Washington and Virginia Beach. Perhaps a holiday for the energetic or young at heart travvelor.

Own transport or coach would be poss. on all the above options. If you can let me have more in depth detail of your requirements, I will contact local transport providers and hoteliers and put together detailed itineraries and prices on the above options. If you would care to list holiday destinations in Virginia that you think would be popular I will be pleased to work out detailed itineries for them.

Yours ffly
WAYSIDE INN HOLIDAYS

Change paragraph headings into shoulder headings

James Rosenthal
TRAVEL CONSULTANT

2)   Spell-check and save your file as **USA**. Print one copy

3)   Carefully check your work against **model answer EX6H** which has been saved on the disk that accompanies this book. Clear the screen

4) You are going to insert into the document the standard paragraph that you have saved. **Normally you would insert Auto Text <u>as you type a document</u>, but on this first practise occasion we will insert it into an existing letter**. Position the cursor immediately before the word "**We**" in the last line of the letter on screen

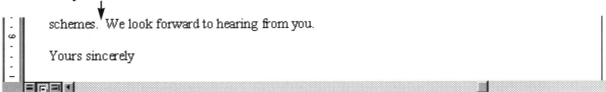

5) Type the word **Our** (this is the first word of the saved Auto Text file name). Press the space bar once. **It is important always to put one space after the Auto Text file name**

6) Click on the **Insert Auto Text** icon on the **Standard Toolbar**

7) Your standard paragraph should be inserted as below. Had you left the "hidden" non-printing return character then after the inserted sentence a return would also have been inserted

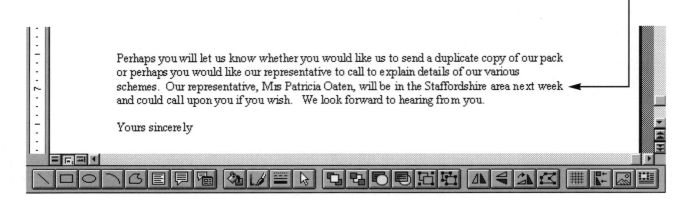

8) Quick save your file

9) Clear the screen

PRACTISE HANDWRITTEN BUSINESS LETTERS

Exercise 6i

TARGET TIME 25 MINUTES

1) Key in the following text. Remember to time yourself and fill in your target time sheet

Our ref MS/DG   (Use a font of your choice for this letter)

Mr and Mrs D Heape, 11 The Lawns, Clevedon, BRISTOL, BS19 6MG

Dr Mr and Mrs Heape

FRIENDS OF QUEEN ELIZABETH HOSPITAL SCHOOL

I am pleased to report that the past year has been a very successful one
for the friends and would like to thank all who have supported our efforts.
With your help we have been able to provide the school with over £3,000.
It has been decided to use this money to buy much needed computer
equipment for the boys together with a rowing ergometer.

Sports day was enjoyed by everyone despite the cold weather, apparently we
seem to choose the coldest and wettest day in June every year! Lyn
Blakes organised everyone very efficiently with help from her catering
team. Thank you everyone. Events for next year include a joint
3rd and 4th year social evening on 20th Oct. plus our 5th Nov. celebrations.
An important date for your diary is the Christmas Party - this year it
will be held Dec 8th. If your son is leaving school this summer I
would recommend that you keep in contact with the school. If you
would like to receive all the School Diaries, Newsletters and AGM
details for the next 5 yrs. please send to the "accounts friends" a
cheque for £10.00 made payable to QEH, Mark your envelope "A/cs
-friends".

please emphasize last sentence

Yours sncly.

June Woodword
Sec. to the friends of QEH   with best wishes for a happy
                                         summer break.

2) Save as **QEH**. Carefully check your work on screen against **model answer EX6(I)**
    which has been saved on the disk that accompanies this book. Now spell-check (there
    should not be any errors because you have already checked). Print one copy and clear
    the screen

MERGING STANDARD PARAGRAPHS INTO A DOCUMENT

Exercise 15c

1)   Type in the following text:

LETTER HEAD PAPER

HH/UF

Miss A Hobbs
376a Challicroft Road
LEEK
Staffordshire
ST13 5HH

Dear Miss Hobbs

EXTRA BENEFIT INSURANCE

Some time ago you contacted our company requesting information on household insurance.
We sent you our "Household pack" by return of post. As this is some weeks ago now and
we have not heard from you, we wonder whether you have in fact received these details.

Perhaps you will let us know whether you would like us to send a duplicate copy of our
pack or perhaps you would like our representative to call to explain details of our various
schemes. We look forward to hearing from you.

Yours sincerely

Hannah Hahn
INSURANCE DEPARTMENT

---

2)   Carefully check your work. Spell-check and correct any mistakes found

3)   Save your file as **STANDARD** and leave on screen

ROUTING COPIES

In the office, extra copies of letters and memoranda are sometimes printed and the names of all the recipients of any extra copies are added at the bottom of the document.

This practice is reflected by the RSA examination board. For example on a letter the typist may be requested to take "a top, plus 2 copies – one for the file and one for Mr Daniel Brown". In this case the bottom of the letter should be set out as the example below:

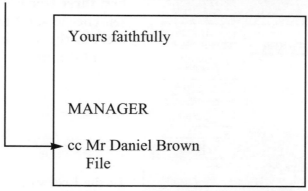

Yours faithfully

MANAGER

cc Mr Daniel Brown
    File

The "cc" stands for "carbon copy" which is rather an old fashioned term nowadays. It refers to the days when typewriters were normally used to produce correspondence. The typist would insert carbon paper between sheets of paper in order to make copies of the work ... be thankful you are working on a word processor because correcting a carbon copy was not easy.

The details should be printed on all copies, unless you are explicitly told otherwise. The actual copies should be printed on plain paper if you are typing a letter and you should neatly tick against the name of the recipients or file as the case may be. For example:

TOP COPY	*2nd COPY*	*3rd COPY*
Yours faithfully	Yours faithfully	Yours faithfully
MANAGER	MANAGER	MANAGER

cc Daniel Brown
      File
	cc Daniel Brown ✔
	      File
		cc Daniel Brown
		      File ✔

Practise routing carbon copies in the next exercise.

5) Click on the **Insert Auto Text** icon on the **Standard Toolbar**

6) The following dialog box will appear:

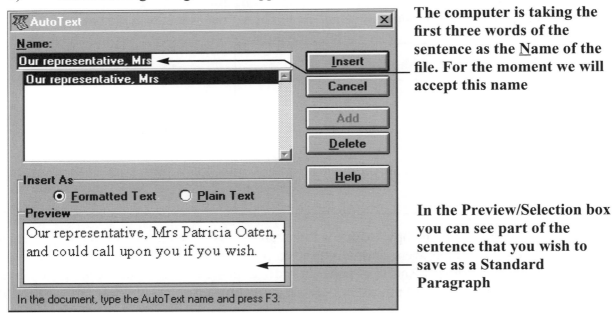

The computer is taking the first three words of the sentence as the <u>N</u>ame of the file. For the moment we will accept this name

In the Preview/Selection box you can see part of the sentence that you wish to save as a Standard Paragraph

7) Click on [**Add**] and your standard paragraph is now saved

8) Click on the **Show/Hide** ¶ icon once again to remove non-printing characters from the screen

9) Delete the sentence so that we can use the document page to prepare our letter, into which we will place the Auto Text which we have just stored

PRACTISE ROUTING COPIES

Exercise 6j

TARGET TIME 15 MINUTES

1) Type in the following text in a font of your choice. The one used below is ARIAL font, size 12 point

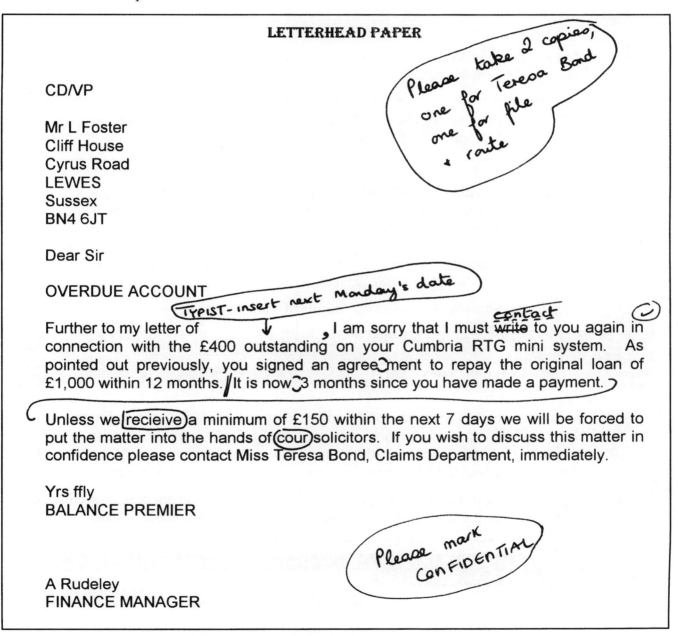

2) Save as **DEBT**. Print one copy and carefully check your work against **model answer EX6J** which has been saved on the disk that accompanies this book. Clear the screen

CREATING AND SAVING A STANDARD PARAGRAPH

Using The "Auto Text" And The "Show/Hide" Icons

Auto Text allows you to store frequently used text and graphics and insert them over and over again in various documents. The stored text can be as short as a single character or as long as several pages. Auto Text can be very useful for inserting frequently used words and paragraphs. For example an estate agent may frequently use the expressions "in excellent condition" or "with a double garage". These expressions can be easily and accurately inserted with a simple keystroke; thus saving time.

Exercise 15b

1)   You are going to save as Auto Text a standard paragraph for eventual re-use. To do this type the sentence below:

> Our representative, Mrs Patricia Oaten, will be in the Staffordshire area next week and could call upon you if you wish.

When you save Auto Text, **Word** will automatically save any returns, tab indentations, etc that you may have used when creating the Auto Text paragraph. When you eventually recall the saved text, the saved returns etc will also be recalled. This may not be what you require, so it is better to check <u>before</u> you save any Auto Text that any saved returns etc are actually required. To do this you use the **Show/Hide** icon (see Lesson 10, page 115, for full **Show/Hide** details).

2)   Click on the **Show/Hide** icon on the **Standard Toolbar**

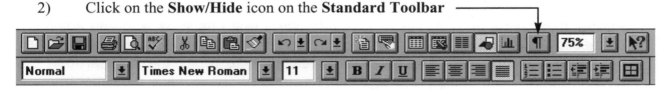

3)   When this icon has been pressed the screen shows all the "hidden" non-printing characters, including paragraph marks and space marks. For example a space bar is shown by a raised full stop, and the mark to start a new paragraph looks like ¶. **You must be careful not to highlight this mark when carrying out the next instruction**

4)   Highlight the text but <u>not the return mark</u>. Of course, if you did not press the return key when keying in the above paragraph you will not have a return mark on screen

> Our·representative,·Mrs·Patricia·Oaten,·will·be·in·the·Staffordshire·area·next·week·and·
> could·call·upon·you·if·you·wish¶

CONSOLIDATION EXERCISE FOR LESSON 6

Practise what you have learnt so far by following the instructions below.

Exercise 6k

1)   Key in the following text. Remember to time yourself and fill in your target time sheet

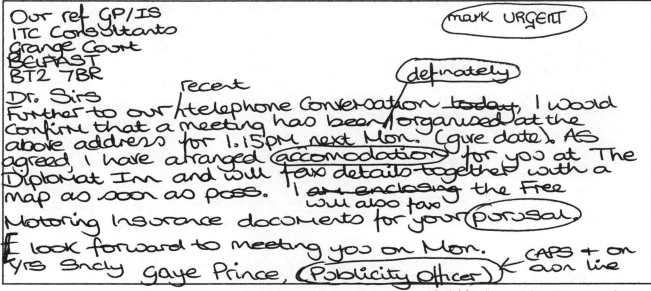

2)   Carefully check your work and correct any mistakes found. Save your file as **MOTOR**

3)   Print one copy and clear the screen

Exercise 6l

1)   Key in the following text. Remember to time yourself and fill in your target time sheet

2   Spell-check and save this file with a name of your choice. Print one copy and clear the screen. Carefully check both pieces of work against model answer **CONSOL6** which has been saved on the disk that accompanies this book. Clear the screen

LESSON 15	STANDARD PARAGRAPHS
	CREATING AND SAVING A STANDARD PARAGRAPH USING THE "AUTO TEXT" AND THE "SHOW/HIDE" ICONS
	MERGING STANDARD PARAGRAPHS INTO A DOCUMENT
	PRACTISE CREATING AND SAVING STANDARD PARAGRAPHS
	PRACTISE MERGING STANDARD PARAGRAPHS INTO VARIOUS DOCUMENTS
	DELETE STANDARD PARAGRAPH

Exercise 15a

TARGET TIME 12 MINUTES

STANDARD PARAGRAPHS

1) Type in the following text. Remember to time yourself and fill in your target time sheet. Adjust the line length to 14 cm (5½")

> THE ADVANTAGES OF STANDARD PARAGRAPHS *(Single spacing + justified)*
>
> Many companies often use the same wording + paragraphs on many of their ~~documents~~ letters. For example, insurance policies, solicitors' letters or overdue a/c warnings will often ~~have~~ use common "standard" paragraphs.
>
> It is poss. to type ~~in~~ and store ~~on disk~~ all of these (paraphs). Each paragraph must be given (it's) own number or reference name. Later when staff wish to write a different document using the same text, it is a simple matter to (retrieve) the "standard" paragraph once more.
>
> Using pre-saved paragraphs has many advantages in the office, not least of which is the (saved time).
>
> The ability to build up a document using pre-saved paragraphs is known by several names. Some people call it "boilerplating," other "blockbuilding or "standard paragraphs" Word software books refer to it as "auto text." Whatever name is used the principles are the same.
>
> (Recalling accurate pre-saved text also reduces keying-in errors)

2) Carefully check your work and correct any mistakes found. Spell-check. Save your file as **PARAS.** Print one copy if you wish and clear the screen

176

LESSON 7	WORKING WITH MORE THAN ONE DOCUMENT
	LOCATING INFORMATION
	AUTO NUMBERING (PARAGRAPHS)
	PUTTING A LINE SPACE BETWEEN AUTO
	NUMBERED ITEMS
	WORKING WITH MORE THAN ONE
	HANDWRITTEN DOCUMENT
	LOCATING SPECIFIC INFORMATION WITHIN A
	DOCUMENT AND WITHIN HANDWRITTEN
	DOCUMENTS
	CONSOLIDATION

WORKING WITH MORE THAN ONE DOCUMENT

In the examination you will be required to use information contained in one document in order to complete a second document. The following exercises will give you an opportunity to practise this

Exercise 7a

TARGET TIME 8 MINUTES

1) Type in the following text. Remember to time yourself and fill in your target time sheet

FOREST FIRE BREAKS UP SCOUT CAMP

Some 1,000 Scouts and Cubs, attending an international camp, were evacuated from the camp on the edge of Sherwood Forest after 2 tents caught fire.

It is thought that the cause of the fire were burning debris. It is also thought that the local village community centres are being asked if they can help.

Army units were this weekend helping 120 Nottinghamshire firefighters called out to 2 severe fires within Sherwood Forest. It is thought that if the heatwave in Britain continues the threat of forest fires will stay with us well into the autumn.

2) Carefully check your work and correct any mistakes found. Spell-check

3) Save your file as **SCOUTS** and print one copy. Clear the screen

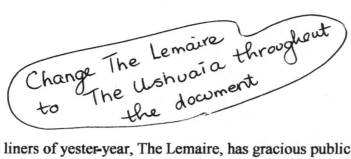

Change The Lemaire to The Ushuaia throughout the document

Like the grand liners of yester-year, The Lemaire, has gracious public rooms and intimate corners for quiet moments of relaxation. Her sweeping decks afford ~~plent~~ *plenty* of room for whale-watching, photography, or just admiring the spectacular scenery.

Single line spacing

Prices range from £4,100 for a standard inside (grade C) cabin to £5,400 (grade A) for a deluxe outside suite. Price is per person and based on double occupancy. Bonus savings are available on ~~bookins~~ *all bookings* made before 29 April - details available from your travel agent.

C

Treat yourself to a special Christmas this year, join us for spectacular celebrations and experience the dramatic beauty of the Antartic.

A

For immediate reservations see your travel agent or telephone our reservations consultations on 0800 436936

insert C

Included in your cruise is the round-trip airfare from the UK, plus free regional air connections from major UK airports.

The New Cruising Lines Plc (centre + bold) Southampton

The quality of service is second to none

2) Carefully check your work. Spell-check and quick save your document

3) Print preview and print one copy

4) Carefully check your work against **model answer CONSOL14** which has been saved on the disk that accompanies this book. Clear the screen

LOCATING INFORMATION

Exercise 7b

TARGET TIME 10 MINUTES

1) Change the ***font*** and *font size* to one of your choice. Type in the following text. Fill in the missing gaps from SCOUT document you have just printed. The font used below is

   `Footlight MT Light` sized `15`

MEMO *(Can you please mark this URGENT - BY HAND and deliver as soon as typed. I have lost the fax containing the details - can you please find + fill in the gaps please.)*

To   Clive, News Editor   From Jeremy, Sports Desk   Ref JP/WE

One of my sporting contacts in ~~Nottingham~~ *Newcastle* has sent me a fax which I think could prove to be a big news story for your department. It seems that approx. .... Scouts and Cubs have been evacuated from an .... camp on the edge of Sherwood Forest. .... is thought to be the likely cause of the fire. Army units have been called out to help the .... local firefighters. *(please say number involved here)*

Is this of interest to you? Your telephone line has been permanently busy lately so I will have my sec. deliver this memo immed. My contact's name is Jim Hurley and you can telephone him on 0912-861344

---

2) Save your work with a name of your choice.

3) Carefully check your work against **model answer EX7B** which has been saved on the disk that accompanies this book.

4) Clear the screen

CONSOLIDATION EXERCISE FOR LESSON 14

Practise what you have learnt so far by following through the instructions below.

> **TARGET TIME 20 MINUTES**

1) Retrieve the following document saved as **CRUISE**. Immediately rename the file **CRUISE2**. Remember to time yourself and fill in your target time sheet. Amend as indicated

Change to double line spacing (except where indicated) and use a justified right margin. Adjust line length to either (A) 12.5cm (5") or (B) 50 characters. If proportional spacing is used please adjust to (A)

Please insert CHRISTMAS CRUISE as a header on every page

SOUTH AMERICA - ANTARCTICA - THE FALKLAND ISLANDS

The White Continent is the most spectacular travel destination on earth and you could experience it! *emphasise*

single line spacing

Experience the dramatic beauty
Experience the glacial wilderness
Experience a different Christmas

Copy this section to [A] Leave in single line spacing

You'll ~~view~~ *see* colonies of frolicking penguins, whales and ice shimmering icebergs - all from the comfort of your luxury cruise ship. *on the ice*

move this section to [B]

You'll spend 5 nights in vivacious Buenos Aires where you will be able to shop, dine and dance and enjoy ~~the sophisticated haunts of this swinging~~ *this sophisticated* city. You'll see the famous Avenida 9 de Julio (one of the widest streets in the world), The Palace of Argentine Congress, the President's Headquarters (The Pink House) and did you know that apart from New York and ~~and~~ London no other capital in the world has *as* ~~so~~ many theatres as Buenos Aires.

A one-night stopover in the charming Falklands will give you a taste of Victorian England. *The charm of these special islanders will make you wish you could stay longer.*

[B]

Your cruise ship will be THE LEMAIRE ~~build~~ *built 2 years ago* especially for Arctic cruising. Her ice-~~strengthend~~ *strengthened* hull, 23,050 tons, huge fin stabilisers and rapid cruising speed work together to assure a smooth ride. A state of the art waste disposal system ensures environmentally friendly cruising. The Lemaire also carries/twin-engined, fibreglass helicopter to scout ice conditions. *Alongside ~~the~~ her technical capabilities are distinctive on-board features.*

AUTO NUMBERING (PARAGRAPHS)

It is possible to add numbering automatically to your paragraphs which will save you so much time. It is also fun to use

Exercise 7c

1)   Key in the following text:

THEATRE PRODUCTIONS (centre + bold)

If you join Stage Savers you will save 25% on all your ticket prices for the following productions. Plan ahead - don't miss out on the play you really meant to see!

The Tempest
The Last Yankee
Cinderella (Christmas production)
Old Wicked Songs
When The Kissing Stopped
A Streetcar Named Desire

2)   Save your file as **PLAYS**. You are going to enumerate the above list of plays using the automatic numbering icon

3)   Highlight the plays **(be careful not to highlight the line space above or below)**

4)   Click on the **Numbering** icon on the **Formatting toolbar**

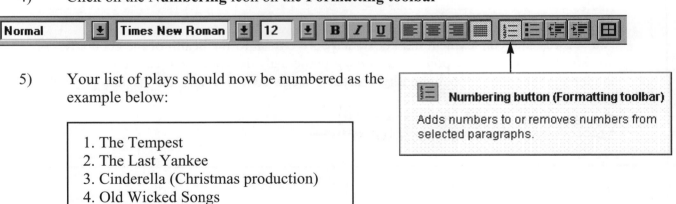

5)   Your list of plays should now be numbered as the example below:

> 1. The Tempest
> 2. The Last Yankee
> 3. Cinderella (Christmas production)
> 4. Old Wicked Songs
> 5. When The Kissing Stopped
> 6. A Streetcar Named Desire

Numbering button (Formatting toolbar)

Adds numbers to or removes numbers from selected paragraphs.

PRACTISE COPYING TEXT

Exercise 14l

1)   Retrieve the following document saved as **MANAGE2.** Immediately rename the file **MANAGE3.** Remember to time yourself and fill in your target time sheet. Amend as indicated

TARGET TIME 1 MINUTE

MANAGEMENT OR MIS-MANAGEMENT?

Copy this emboldened section to [A]

I ask the question **"does the dismantling of departments and the erosion of job security have damaging repercussion for the economy?"**

There is no doubt that those gold watches awarded for long and faithful corporate service are fast becoming antiques. These days, faithful servants of companies are more likely to be offered a redundancy package. Anyone who has reached the age of forty-something begins to wonder how safe they are in their job.

The pressures for change, it would seem, are impossible to resist. The old-style departments are vanishing, they are either fragmenting into small units scattered around the business, or their work is being contracted out. The implications of this change is enormous - staff left behind find themselves working longer hours and giving up their own time just to complete the work. Contractors may not understand the intricacies of the business in the same depth as full-time permanent staff, and needless mistakes may be made.

Job security and employment market stability are crucial to the health of the economy. A workforce flexible to the point of becoming perpetually de-skilled and casual can have no confidence in itself. Job insecurity creates a siege economy and that is not good for business.

I ask the question again [A]

~~MANAGEMENT OR MIS-MANAGEMENT?~~

---

2)   Carefully check your work

3)   Quick save your file and print one copy if you wish. Clear the screen

PUTTING A LINE SPACE BETWEEN AUTO NUMBERED ITEMS

You may need to put a clear line space between auto numbered items as **Example A** below:

Example A

1. The Tempest
2. The Last Yankee
3. Cinderella (Christmas production)
4. Old Wicked Songs
5. When The Kissing Stopped
6. A Streetcar Named Desire

Pressing the return key does not insert a clear line space (it will insert another number) when auto numbering has been used. You have a choice of 2 methods. Try them both now:

Method 1 (useful when <u>all</u> paragraphs need to be in double line-spacing)

1.   Highlight the text (be careful not to highlight the line space above and below the text)

2.   Hold down the Ctrl key on the keyboard and press the number 2

3.   Your list should now be in double line-spacing

4.   Use the Undo button to enable you to try the second method below.

Method 2 (you can select where you wish an extra line space to be inserted)

1.   Position the cursor at the end of the line <u>above</u> where you wish to insert a line space. In this case position the cursor in the space after the **e** of **The Last Yankee**
1.   The Tempest
2.   The Last Yankee ⟵
3.   Cinderella (Christmas production)

2.   Hold down the **Shift** key on the keyboard and press the **Return** key

1.   The Tempest
2.   The Last Yankee

3.   Cinderella (Christmas production)

3.   You should now have an extra line space below The Last Yankee

4.   When you have finished practising with this document clear the screen. Do not save the file when prompted by the computer to do so

There is more advanced information on auto numbering in the third book of this series.

PRACTISE COPYING SENTENCES

Exercise 14 j(2)

1)   Retrieve the following document saved as **JOB.** Immediately rename the file **JOB2**. Amend as indicated

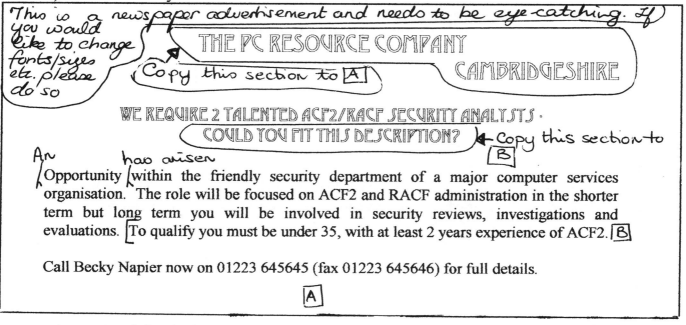

2)   Carefully check your work. Quick save your document and print one copy

3)   Carefully check your work against **model answer EX14J** which has been saved on the disk that accompanies this book. Clear the screen

Exercise 14k

1)   Retrieve the following document saved as **CLUB.** Immediately rename the file **CLUB2**. Amend as indicated

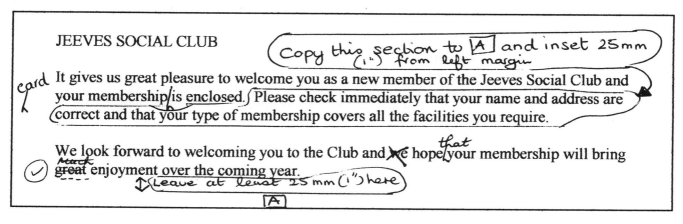

2)   Carefully check your work. Quick save your document and print one copy

3)   Carefully check your work against **model answer EX14K** which has been saved on the disk that accompanies this book. Clear the screen

Exercise 7d

1)   Type in the following text in single line-spacing. Remember to use auto numbering

---

FIVE WAYS TO HELP YOURSELF IN EXAMINATIONS

1)   Always read ~~very~~ *extremely* carefully all the instructions for each task before you start.

2)   Use common-sense both in deciphering manuscripts and also in arranging matter.

3)   If you are not sure how to set out any piece of typing, follow the ~~setting~~ *layout* of the test paper which is usually a good guide as to what is ~~needed~~ *wanted*.

4)   Be consistent with spelling, particularly with words ~~which~~ *that* can be spelt in 2 ways, such as 'realise or realize'.

5)   Prepare well in advance. Make sure that you learn all the abbreviations, corrections, signs, amendments etc. It will help you if you know the performance criteria and the assessment faults that your work will be judged against. If you know that continuation sheets must be numbered, or that you will be expected to fill in missing gaps in one document with info. contained in another, then you will not panic or wonder what to do in the actual exam.

---

2)   Carefully check your work and correct any mistakes found

3)   Spell-check and save your file with a name of your choice

4)   Print one copy and clear the screen

Exercise 7e

1)   Type in the following text in double line-spacing. Fill in the missing gaps from the **Exercise 7d** that you have just printed

---

fill in appropriate number

I have recently read a document aimed at preparing candidate's for RSA examinations. It contained ...✗... seperate points which I found interesting. It pointed out the need for consistency with spelling, particularly with words which have different American and English spellings such as '............ or realize' which is something I had not thought about before. If you is taking an examination shortly I would advise you to read this document - it's title is ....   *(Please use double-line spacing)*

---

2)   Spell-check and save this file with a name of your choice

3)   Print one copy and clear the screen

4)   Carefully check your work against **model answers EX7D and EX7E** which has been saved on the disk that accompanies this book

3)   Amend as shown:

(Please amend as shown)

THE FOLLOWING ARE SOME COMMON ABBREVIATIONS IN USE TODAY

ABBREVIATIONS

Typist — Copy each numbered item (one at a time) to the bottom of the page. Embolden it and then add the unemboldened text as shown below

1)   A/C   account current~~current~~
2)   Alt   alternate ~~or altitude~~
3)   BC   before Christ
4)   cfi   cost of freight and insurance
5)   Enc   enclosure
6)   HMSO Her (His) Majesty's Stationery Office   ← **amend this entry**
7)   HRH   Her (His) Royal Highness
8)   NB   (Latin - nota bene) = note well
9)   PS   (Latin - post scriptum) written after (a postscript)
10) VIP   very important person

SOME EXAMPLES OF THE ABOVE USED IN SENTENCES (note there is not an example for each number above)

(Typist. please do not number the sentences below)

~~1)~~ **A/C   account current.** Jack asked his bank for overdraft facilities on his a/c.

~~2)~~ **Alt   alternate.** When the Alt key is held down on the computer keyboard, other keys may pressed at the same time in order to carry out certain functions.

~~4)~~ **cfi   cost of freight and insurance.** The total cost of the invoice did not include cfi.

~~5)~~ **Enc   enclosure.** At the foot of a business letter the abbreviation 'Enc' is typed. This highlights to all concerned that another document has been enclosed with the letter.

~~8)~~ **NB   (Latin - nota bene) = note well.** When writers wish to convey an important message to their readers, the abbreviation NB will be placed before the relevant sentence.

~~10)~~ **PS   (Latin - post scriptum) written after (a postscript).**   If you see the abbreviation PS with text written after it at the end of a letter, you know at once that the author of the letter wrote the PS after the main bulk of the letter had been finished.

---

4)   Carefully check your work. Quick save your document and print one copy

5)   Carefully check your work against **model answer EX14J** which has been saved on the disk that accompanies this book. Clear the screen

WORKING WITH MORE THAN ONE HANDWRITTEN DOCUMENT

Exercise 7f

TARGET TIME 20 MINUTES

1) Type in the following text. Remember to time yourself and fill in your target time sheet

THE MARTOCK ESTATE (bold & centred)
NEW HOUSES by Critchen Developers

This new estate consists of 15 cottage-type dwellings built with a large courtyard shape. Each cottage is built on traditional lines but incorporates all modern ~~the latest~~ amenities. The fitted kitchens are fully equipped with a dish-washer, cooker and fridge/freezer and all are spacious enough to contain a dining area if ~~it is~~ ✓ needed ~~required~~.

All the windows (is) double-glazed and every room is heated by a gas central heating system. Each cottage has at least one garage plus a parking area, and the spacious gardens at the rear have already been landscaped. The front of each property has a small enclosed gardens ~~looking~~ which looks out onto the village green complete with maypole! There are 3 different types of property but we have described THE EXECUTIVE HOUSE for you below:

THE EXECUTIVE HOUSE comprising - [ground floor - entrance porch, large living room, kitchen, sitting room, study and music room, plus downstairs WC.

first floor - landing with access to 4 bedrooms, 2 double, 2 single). The master bedroom is en-suite and the single bedrooms have shower/WC. Double garage and parking area. Highly recomended.

DOUBLE LINE SPACING

Prices vary from £150,00 - £280,000 depending upon plot size. For further details contact Messrs Dewbury and Son, Castleton House, The Quads, Barnstaple, Devon, EX31 3DE

QUAD

2) Carefully check and spell-check your work. Save your file with a name of your choice

3) Print one copy and carefully check your work against **model answer EX7F** which has been saved on the disk that accompanies this book. Clear the screen

2)   Carefully check your work and correct any mistakes found

3)   Quick save and leave on screen

4)   Highlight the heading MANAGEMENT OR MIS-MANAGEMENT?

5)   Click on the **Copy** icon on the **Standard Toolbar**

6)   You are going to copy this heading to the end of your document. Move the cursor to the end of the document and press the return key twice

7)   Click on the **Paste** icon on the **Standard Toolbar.** Wait ......

8)   The heading should now be at the top and bottom of your document

9)   Carefully check your work. Quick save your document and print one copy

10)   Carefully check your work against **model answer EX14(I)** which has been saved on the disk that accompanies this book. Clear the screen

PRACTISE COPYING SENTENCES

Exercise 14j

1)   Retrieve the following document saved as **MIXED**

2)   Immediately rename the file **MIXED2**. The sentences need to be copied so that the document looks like the one overleaf. Use the above instructions to copy them to the specified locations

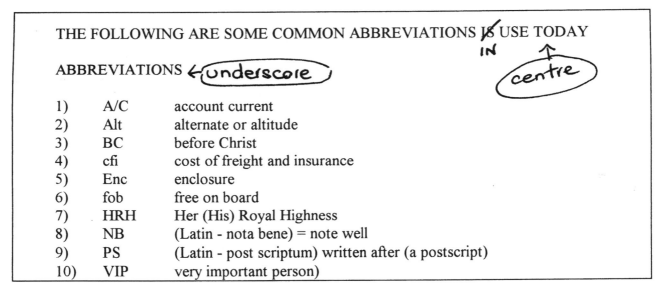

Exercise 7g

1) Type in the following text. Find the missing information from your previous document. Remember to time yourself and fill in your target time sheet

---

COMPANY LETTERHEAD PAPER

TYPIST
Please send this letter to mr J Stephens and miss D Woodward, Flat 4a, Henge House, Wakefield West Yorkshire. Our ref JJ/-- Check it carefully because John drafted it in a hurry + I think you will find numerous errors.

Dear John and Debbie

I (beleive) I (has) at last found the ~~house~~ Cottage for which you have been searching. It is in the countryside yet near enough to the Motor-way for your travelling requirements. It is new but built along traditional lines. It has 4 bedrooms (2 --- /2 ---) plus ample shower-rooms. It has a large rear garden. In fact it seems to have everything you requested.

There are 15 ~~houses~~ Cottages on this new estate built by C------ D------ but only 4 of these ~~houses~~ Cottages would ~~suit~~ meet your needs, in fact one of the EXECUTIVE HOUSES even has a tiny stream running past the foot of the garden (another of your requests!)

I am enclosing full details. It is (defanetly) worth taking a look - if you get in touch quickly I will arrange immed. viewing.

Yrs Sncly.
Jacqueline Johnson
Enc

Best wishes

---

2) Carefully check and spell-check your work. Save your file with a name of your choice

3) Print one copy and carefully check your work against **model answer EX7G** which has been saved on the disk that accompanies this book. Clear the screen

PRACTISE COPYING SENTENCES

Exercise 14i

1) Retrieve the following document saved as **MANAGE.** Immediately rename the file **MANAGE2**. Remember to time yourself and fill in your target time sheet. Amend as indicated

Hint to typist. The exam board will say right justify when they wish you to fully justify

Right justify text change to single line spacing

MANAGEMENT OR MIS-MANAGEMENT? ←Centre

embolden

I ask the question "does the dismantling of departments and the erosion of job security have damaging reper cussion for the economy?"

There is no doubt that those gold watches awarded for long and faithful corporate service are fast becoming antiques. These days, faithful servants of large companies are more likely to be offered a redundancy package. Anyone who has reached the age of forty-something begins to wonder how safe they are in their job. The pressures for change, it would seem, are impossible to resist. The old-style departments are vanishing, they are either fragmenting into small units scattered around the business, or their work is being contracted out. The implications of this change range is enormous - staff left in the job ✓ find themselves working longer hours and giving up their own time just to get the work.

huge

behind

completed If they don't complete the work, who knows - they may be next to say a forced goodbye. Contracters may not understand the intricies of the business the same as full-time permanent staff, and needless mistakes may be made.

Contractors

intricacies   in   depth

Job security and employment market stability are crucial to the health of the economy. A workforce flexible to the point of becoming perpetually de-skilled and casual can have no confidence in itself. Job insecurity creates a siege economy, and that is not good for business.

LOCATING SPECIFIC INFORMATION WITHIN A DOCUMENT

Exercise 7h

1) Type in the following text. Expand any gaps from the information given within the task

---

Double line spacing

HOTEL BUSINESS BOOMS ← *emphasize*

Bristols' new found status as a tourist destination is giving the hotel industry a huge bo0st. Virtually every hotel is showing a growth in business over last year, according to the Bristol Hotels Association.

The Associations' spokesperson said today that there were a new spirit of co-operation between hotels, the attractions and the City Council. He felt that in general all 3 worked closely together through the Tourism Forum.

He reported that another initiative "Conference Bristol" was beginning to flourish and generate business that would in the past have gone to other cities. The rise in the American market through its Aer Lingus connection had also played a part in the acomodation factor. In fact one member of the T............. F.............whose hotel was near Pensford reported that she was thinking of marketing her estableshment as being "near Bristol" because *she felt* it would fhave greater appeal.

---

2) Carefully check and spell-check your work. Save your file as **BRISTOL**

3) Print one copy and clear the screen

4) Carefully check your work against **model answer EX7H** which has been saved on the disk that accompanies this book

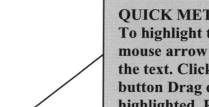

QUICK METHOD
To highlight the paragraph – point the mouse arrow in the left margin towards the text. Click and hold down the mouse button Drag down until the 4 lines are highlighted. Release the mouse button

3) Highlight the following paragraph:

> **Attention Corporate and Society Golf organisers!**
>
> Telephone Duncan MacRae NOW to find out how to make your company day complete.

4) Click on the **Copy** icon on the **Standard Toolbar**

5) You are going to copy this heading to the end of your document. Move the cursor to the end of the document and press the return key twice

6) Click on the **Paste** icon on the **Standard Toolbar.** Wait ......

7) The paragraph should now be in its original position and at the bottom of your document

8) Quick save and clear the screen

LOCATING SPECIFIC INFORMATION WITHIN HANDWRITTEN DOCUMENTS

1)   Type the 2 tasks on this page. Expand any gaps from the information given within the text. Spell-check and save each file with a name of your choice

2)   Print one copy of each and clear the screen. Carefully check your work against **model answer EX7I&7J** which has been saved on the disk that accompanies this book

Exercise 7i

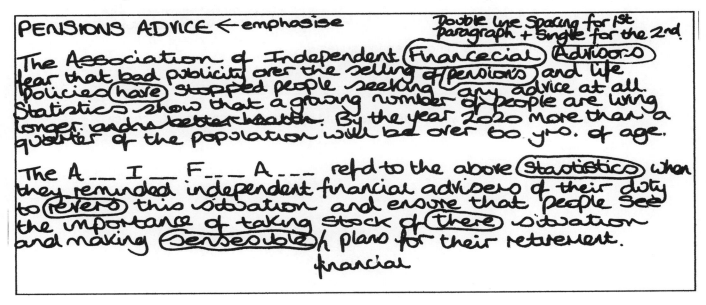

The Statistics of Education, volume 2, School Leavers; Social Trends, reported that fewer girl's than boys take GCE 'A' levels, especially in maths, chemistry and physics and fewer males than females pursue second chance routes, such as an Open University course - although this gap is closing.// At 11 yrs. of age girls perform as well if not better than boys in the sciences, but by the age of 16 when CSE's are encountered not ✓ girls are performing not as well less well. Experts in the education field have put forward many theories as to why girls do not perform as well as boys in the sciences. Many beleive that false labelling has a self-fulfilling prophecy - if girls are labelled "unmathematical" they begin to beleeve they cannot "do maths". The S___ of E___ also highlighted that fewer boys than girls prepare for teacher education.

Exercise 7j

PENSIONS ADVICE ← emphasise   Double line spacing for 1st paragraph + single for the 2nd.

The Association of Independent Financecial Advisors fear that bad publicity over the selling of pensions and life policies have stopped people seeking any advice at all. Statistics show that a growing number of people are living longer and in better health. By the year 2020 more than a quarter of the population will be over 60 yrs. of age.

The A__ I__ F___ A___ refd to the above Statistics when they reminded independent financial advisers of their duty to reverse this situation and ensure that people see the importance of taking stock of there situation and making sensesouble plans for their retirement.
         financial

COPYING TEXT TO A SPECIFIC LOCATION WITHIN THE SAME DOCUMENT

The Stage II word processing examination will request you to <u>copy</u> a certain section of text to another location within the same document. When your document is subsequently printed you will have 2 identical sections of text within the one document. Complete the following exercise in order to practise this.

Exercise 14h

1) Key in the following text using a font of your choice. The font used here is
   Arial sized 11

Expand '&' to 'and' on each occasion

Single line spacing

THE DOWNS GOLF AND COUNTRY CLUB ← *bold*

Membership notice: ← *bold and underlined*

The Downs G___ and _____ Club are pleased to announce that a limited number of 3 and 5 day Memberships are still available. Contact PGA Professional, Duncan MacRae, for more information.

Attention Corporate & Society Golf organisers! ← *bold and underlined*

Telephone Duncan MacRae NOW to find out how to make your company day complete.

Facilities include:

27 holes of championship golf
practise facilities
squash courts and snooker tables
3 restaurants & 4 bars
pro-shop
Corporate/conference/wedding reception suites

Typist Please number these items (remember the quick method – see Lesson 7, page 76)

---

2) Carefully check your work. Spell-check and save with a name of your choice

CONSOLIDATION EXERCISE FOR LESSON 7

Practise what you have learnt so far by following the instructions below.

TARGET TIME 20 MINUTES FOR EACH TASK

1) Type in the following text. Remember to time yourself and fill in your target time sheet

TROPICAL DEFORESTATION ← *embolden* (*single spacing unless indicated*)

Britain is one of the largest consumers of hardwood in the (devtelloped) world and if this hardwood is imported from ~~badly managed or~~ unsustainable sources such as the rain forests, then the tropical forests of the world will only have a limited life span. Clearly we are all (responssible) in helping to perserve tropical forests. They play an important role in maintaining the regional and global climate of the world and as many as half of the (Earths') species live in these forests, which cover less than 2% of the globe.// As the forests disappear, the pace of soil erosion accelerates. In Guatemala, an average of around 1,200 tonnes of soil are lost/from each square kilometre of land. As a result it becomes harder to/feed the *↳every year* population and in (coutnries) like India and Bangledesh, the silt shortens the life of dams and *this* can cause wide spread flooding in low land areas.

Uses of tropical timber for ~~items such as~~ furniture, doors, window frames, construction, boat-making and even coffins is not necy. - there are environmentally (acceptbale) alternatives to every item. The Timber Trade Federation have agreed in principle a Code of Conduct which ensures that only tropical timber from sustainably managed sources be allowed into Britain. ✓ *forests*

When choosing wood products consumers are advised to look out for the "Good Wood Guide Seal of Approval". The Seal is awarded on a yearly basis and DIY outlets, timber yards, product mfrs., department and furniture stores are all eligible to apply for the Seal of Approval. The aim of the Seal is to assist the consumer and give them the opp. of choice and encourage the timber industry to switch to tropical hardwoods that have been grown sustainably, for example in plantations established on already degraded land.

The National Association of Retail ~~Farnd~~ Furnishers have endorsed the Code and helped Friends of the Earth produce a guide for consumers.

If you contact F___ of the E___ they can give you more details of the C__ of C___ together with a publications list that will ensure you can make an informed choice when choosing (products') made of wood.

last paragraph emboldend in double line spacing →

2) Carefully check your work and save as **FOREST**. Print one copy and carefully check your work against **model answer CONSOL7** which has been saved on the disk that accompanies this book

83

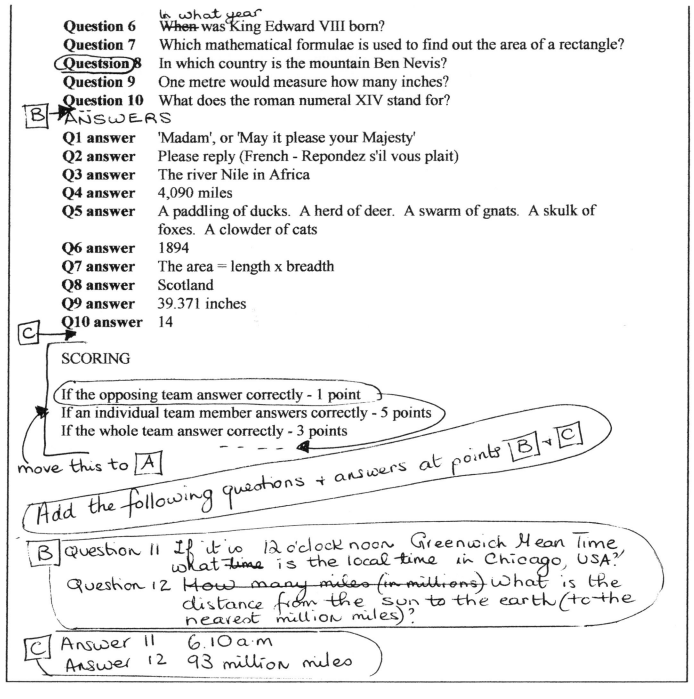

Question 6 ~~When~~ *In what year* was King Edward VIII born?

Question 7 Which mathematical formulae is used to find out the area of a rectangle?

Questsion 8 In which country is the mountain Ben Nevis?

Question 9 One metre would measure how many inches?

Question 10 What does the roman numeral XIV stand for?

[B] ANSWERS

Q1 answer 'Madam', or 'May it please your Majesty'

Q2 answer Please reply (French - Repondez s'il vous plait)

Q3 answer The river Nile in Africa

Q4 answer 4,090 miles

Q5 answer A paddling of ducks. A herd of deer. A swarm of gnats. A skulk of foxes. A clowder of cats

Q6 answer 1894

Q7 answer The area = length x breadth

Q8 answer Scotland

Q9 answer 39.371 inches

Q10 answer 14

[C]

SCORING

If the opposing team answer correctly - 1 point

If an individual team member answers correctly - 5 points

If the whole team answer correctly - 3 points

move this to [A]

Add the following questions + answers at points [B] + [C]

[B] Question 11 If it is 12 o'clock noon Greenwich Mean Time, what ~~time~~ is the local time in Chicago, USA?

Question 12 ~~How many miles (in millions)~~ What is the distance from the sun to the earth (to the nearest million miles)?

[C] Answer 11   6.10 a.m

Answer 12   93 million miles

2) Carefully check your work. Quick save your document and print one copy

3) Carefully check your work against **model answer EX14G** which has been saved on the disk that accompanies this book. Clear the screen

166

SECOND TASK FOR CONSOLIDATION LESSON 7

1) Type in the following text. Remember to time yourself and fill in your target time sheet

---

Please mark URGENT

MEMO
To Rachel Webber, Marketing
FROM Simon McCarthy, Sales
REF SM/--

I have recently read an article about a new Code of Conduct that the T..... T..... F...... have *agreed* with regard to tropical timber imports and have enclosed a photocopy for your info. As (responsible) mfrs. I (definately) think we must seek to obtain the Seal of Approval. (Foriegn) imports of wood play a large part in our org. and although we already only buy tropical hardwoods grown on sustainable plantations, I believe we should ensure that consumers know this fact. // I have asked my sec. to contact the above federation and the N..... A..... of R..... F...... for further written details - (altho) from telephone enquiries she has discovered that the closing date for registration this year is the end of next month. In view of this deadline I think we should meet to (discus) preliminary matters. [Can you let me know several dates next week when you would be free and I will ask my sec. to arrange a / meeting?

/ mutually
convenient

---

2) Carefully check your work and save with a name of your choice. Print one copy and carefully check your work against **model answer CONSOL7B** which has been saved on the disk that accompanies this book. Clear the screen

PRACTISE MOVING TEXT WITH THE "CUT AND PASTE" METHOD

TARGET TIME 25 MINUTES

Exercise 14g

1) Retrieve the following document saved as **QUIZ.** Immediately rename the file **QUIZ2.** Remember to time yourself and fill in your target time sheet. AMEND as indicated

Change to double line spacing (unless indicated). Change QUIZZ to Quiz throughout document. Insert the words MIND TEASERS as a header on every page

GENERAL KNOWLEDGE QUIZZ ← *(centre + embolden)*

of adults

It is intended that the quizz be used with 2 teams/ The questions are not suitable for young children who will find them difficult. Answers are provided at the end.

An impartial judge needs to be appointed to rule on disputes. Before the quizz starts ~~all~~ *both* teams must agree that the decision of the judge is final.

of one minute

It is recommended that a time limit/be set for questions to be answered

These 3 paragraphs in single spacing

✓

RULES

Each member of the team must answer a question individually in turn. If the answer given is incorrect then the question is open to all/members ~~of the team.~~ *team* If the whole team does not answer correctly then the question is offered to the opposing team.

[A]

QUESTIONS ← *embolden all Questions + numbers*

Question 1 How would you begin a letter to the Queen?
Question 2 What do the initials RSVP stand for?
Question 3 What is the name of the longest river in the world?
Question 4 How long is the longest river in the world?
Question 5 *When* sheep are gathered together we call them a <u>flock</u> of sheep. What is the name to describe the following animals when they are gathered together as a group? (One mark for each correct answer)

single line spacing 1.25cm (½")

Ducks
Deer
Gnats
Foxes
Cats

These 5 in single spacing

LESSON 8   EXAMINATION HINTS
CONSISTENCY IN TEXT
CONSISTENCY IN DISPLAY – PARAGRAPH
HEADINGS
COPING WITH EXAMINATION STRESS
MOCK RSA TEXT PROCESSING II Part 1 EXAM

EXAMINATION HINTS

Exercise 8a

1)   Type in the following text. The font used here is Times New Roman sized 11

DISCUSS ANY QUERIES   **EXAMINATION HINTS**   *Embolden all shoulder headings*

Dont leave all the work until the last minute. Make sure you know and can expand correctly all abbreviations and that you can spell the listed spellings and there derivations.

GENERAL

Stress builds up if you become anxious. Discuss any queries you may have regarding the *yr. work* examination paper with your teacher. Get thing's into perspective; there are thousands of other examination candidates who are just as nervous! *people*

THE NIGHT BEFORE THE EXAMINATION   *emphasize*

Look through work that have already been marked. Remind yourself of errors that you have *frequently make;* made, errors that you are not going to make on THE DAY! Do you always remember to date memos and letters? Do you set out business letters correctly? What about enclosures - do you alway's remember to add ENC? If you think it necy. set the alarm clock. You do'not want too be late.

THE DAY OF THE EXAMINATION

Start the day absolutely normally. Have your usual break fast, and pick comfortable, loose- *choose* fitting clothes (it may be hot in the examination room). Collect together anything you wish to take - you are allowed use of an English and mother-tongue dictionery a ruler and *to use* something with which to right might be useful and if you are using a typewriter it is very important you rememeber correcting materials// Allow yourself plenty of time to travel to the examination centre, You do not want to arrive stressed because of traffic delays.

---

2)   Carefully check your work and save your file as **EXAM**. Print one copy and clear the screen

3)   Carefully check your work against **model answer EX8A** which has been saved on the disk that accompanies this book

3)   Amend as below:

Add a header to each page - You AND YOUR EYES

↑ *Leave at least 25—(1") here between header + heading on each page*

CONTACT LENSES ← *centre*

Does the thought of inserting contact lenses into your eyes make you squirm?

Three
~~8~~ million people in this country wear contact lenses. [Before they tried ~~A~~lmost all of them felt that they would never be able to **insert** them. From a survey carried out by ~~the~~ Conutab who produce contact lens care products around the world, it seems that **removing** contact lenses proved more difficult to new users of the product. // [A]

← *page break*
Cleaning

It will be necessary to clean your lenses daily to remove dust and naturally **occurring** eye mucus which accumulates on the lens surface. Daily cleaning is a quick and simple operation and takes no more than ~~two~~ or ~~three~~ minutes. Overnight you will need to disinfect your lenses to destroy micro-organisms such as **fungi and bacteria that** can grow on them.

Your optician will take care to explain how to insert and remove the lenses when you first use them. The optician will also explain how to take care of your lenses because it is especially important to keep them clean.

← *page break*
Protein removal

↑ *move to* [A]

Protein is produced **naturally** in **everyone's** tears and deposits tend to collect on contact lenses causing discomfort. If allowed to build up, protein films can become extremely difficult to remove. Regular weekly use of protein removers will help prevent unwanted protein build up.

4)   Carefully check your work. Quick save your document and print one copy

5)   Carefully check your work against **model answer EX14F** which has been saved on the disk that accompanies this book. Clear the screen

CONSISTENCY IN TEXT

Exercise 8b

1)   Type in the following text:

Richard Jarvis lives in an enormous house by the seaside. The accomodation has large rooms and very big gardens at the front and back, although Richard is not keen on gardening.

Dick has 2 brothers. The oldest one works in a Foriegn Bank and his younger brother has applied for a bussines course at the local College. Ricky attends the local College. He is studying a course in accountancy; he was always good at maths. *[very]*

Rich has a temp. job in a garage. The pay is not very good but at least it covers spending money.

---

2)   Read through what you have just typed. Do you think that this passage is about one person or 4 different people? Using nicknames for the name Richard has caused ambiguity. In business communications, of course, you are not likely to find this type of confusion but it is important that you remember to be consistent in the style and format of presentation used and consistent in the use of abbreviations, spellings, etc. otherwise your work will not be well presented and could be confusing to the reader

3)   Clear the screen without saving the above document

Exercise 8c

1)   Type in the following text

CONSISTENCY IN PRESENTATION

7 six and 12 – should be 7 6 and 12 or seven, six and twelve.
7% and 6 per cent should be 7% and 6% or 7 per cent and 6 per cent.
1200 and 2.30 pm should be 1200 and 1430 or 12.00 pm and 2.30 pm.
£24 and £6.00 should be £24 and £6 or £24.00 and £6.00.

---

2)   Carefully check your work against the above copy and then save with a name of your choice

3)   Print one copy and keep for future reference. Clear the screen

MOVING TEXT WITH THE "CUT AND PASTE" METHOD

The second method of moving text is to use the "cut and paste" method. You will find it easier to use "cut and paste" with longer documents when the text has to be moved some distance. For full details see the first book in this series. Alternatively to refresh your memory, look at the Quick Reference Section which can be printed out from the disk which accompanies this book.

TARGET TIME 15 MINUTES

Exercise 14f

1) Key in the following text with a font of your choice. The font used here is Arial sized 11. Remember to time yourself and fill in your target time sheet

CONTACT LENSES *Justify right margin (remember if the exam paper instructs this it means fully justify)*

Does the thought of inserting contact lenses into your eyes make you squirm?

3 million people in this country wear contact lenses. Before they tried almost all of them felt that they would never be able to insert them. From a survey carried out by the Conutab who produce contact lens care products around the world, it seems that removing contact lenses proved more difficult to new users of the product.
bold + underline

Cleaning

It will be necessary to clean your lenses daily to remove dust and naturally occuring eye mucus which accumulates on the lens surface. Daily cleaning is a quick and simple operation and takes no more than two or three minutes. Overnight you will need to disinfect your lenses to destroy micro-organisms such as bacteria and fungi than can *that* grow on them.

Your optician will take care to explain how to insert and remove the lenses when you first use them. The optician will also explain how to take care of your lenses because it is especially important to keep them clean.

Protein removal

Protein is produced natually in everyones tears and deposits tend to collect on contact lenses causing discomfort. If allowed to build up, protein films can become extremely difficult to remove. *Regular weekly use of protein removers will help prevent unwanted protein build up.*

2) Carefully check your work. Spell-check and save with a name of your choice

Exercise 8d

1)   Keeping in mind consistency of style, type in the following text which has several errors of consistency that are not highlighted in any way

---

At 1700 they ordered a taxi to take them to the airport, but they became worried when it had *[had been]* not arrived by 5.30 pm. They telephoned the taxi company and was told that it was 'on it's way'. At that minute it arrived. The taxi was expensive - it cost them £14.00 although when ordered they had been given an approx. price of £11. A 7% tip was also automatically added to this price. Again they had been told it would be five per cent. They paid because they were in a hurry, but decided that on return from holiday they would write and complain. At the airport they met the rest of they're party, and the party leader checked the confirmation details. She became worried when she counted 12 people present because the confirmation invoice stated reservation had been made for three single rooms and four double rooms.

---

2)   Save your file as **AIRPORT.** Print one copy and clear the screen

3)   Carefully check your work against **model answer EX8D** which has been saved on the disk that accompanies this book

Exercise 8e

1)   Type in the following text:

Reminder to examination candidates ← bold

CONSISTENCY IN PRESENTATION ← bold + centre

WORDS OR FIGURES ← underline

There are no hard and fast rules about weather to type numbers in words or figures, but it will be confusing if you start a sentence with a number, eg "1 of us will be late". If the number "one" begins a sentence, type it as a word - "One of us will be late". Complex numbers are clearer if written in words, eg "She counted one thousand, one hundred and sixty two birds" is a long-winded way of typing "She counted 1,162 birds". Some schools of thought say that the number "one" should be typed as a word and all other numbers typed as figures. tHIS is an easy way to remember to display numbers correctly, and perhaps it is a display method you might like to adopt.

---

2)   Check your work against the above copy. Save your file as **WORDS** and print one copy before clearing the screen. Keep for future reference

3)   Amend as below:

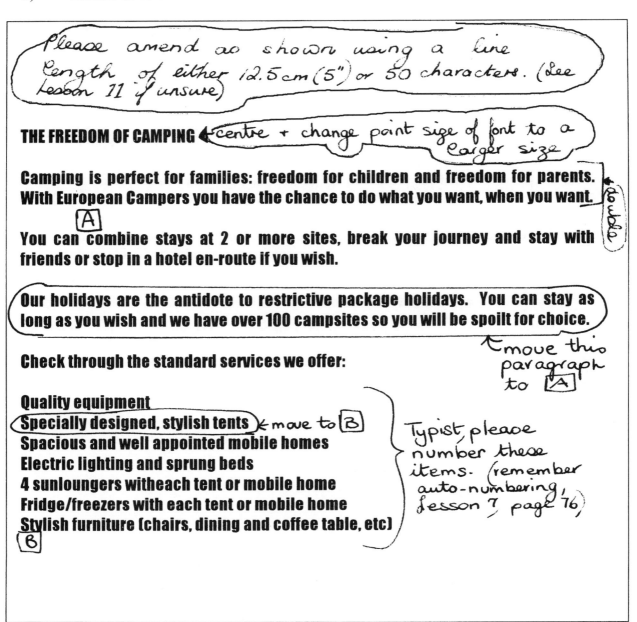

Please amend as shown using a line length of either 12.5 cm (5") or 50 characters. (See Lesson 11 if unsure)

THE FREEDOM OF CAMPING ← *centre + change point size of font to a larger size*

Camping is perfect for families: freedom for children and freedom for parents. With European Campers you have the chance to do what you want, when you want. *double*

A

You can combine stays at 2 or more sites, break your journey and stay with friends or stop in a hotel en-route if you wish.

Our holidays are the antidote to restrictive package holidays. You can stay as long as you wish and we have over 100 campsites so you will be spoilt for choice.

← *move this paragraph to A*

Check through the standard services we offer:

Quality equipment
Specially designed, stylish tents ← *move to B*
Spacious and well appointed mobile homes
Electric lighting and sprung beds
4 sunloungers witheach tent or mobile home
Fridge/freezers with each tent or mobile home
Stylish furniture (chairs, dining and coffee table, etc)
B

Typist, please number these items. (remember auto-numbering, lesson 7 page 76)

4)   Carefully check your work. Quick save your document and print one copy

5)   Carefully check your work against **model answer EX14E** which has been saved on the disk that accompanies this book. Clear the screen

CONSISTENCY IN DISPLAY – PARAGRAPH HEADINGS

Exercise 8f

1)   Look carefully at the following text. Can you see the inconsistency in presentation of the paragraph sub-headings? In the exam it is probable that any shoulder-headings used will be uniform in appearance, although it is likely that you will be requested to transpose the actual shoulder-headings. However, at work ensure that you present shoulder-headings in a uniform manner, and should the examination paper request you to do the same you will already have adopted good working habits. **Exam tip** – remember there should always be at least one clear line space before and after separate items within a document

2)   Type in the text below:

Amend as shown   COPING WITH EXAMINATION STRESS ← *bold*

BENEFICIAL EFFFECT

If examination revision is "getting to you", leave it, go for a walk, and then come back to it. Dont be to strict with yourself if you know you has worked steadily. Simple muscle-relaxing or breathing exercises for 10 min$utes might help.

Relaxation Techniques
It is recognized that a little stress can have a beneficial effect. Actors (and examination *exam* ✓) candidates) often give there best performance after suffering from pre-performance nerves. ~~The negative aspects are related to anxiety and strain.~~ There are ways of dealing with them.

Watch what you eat

Eat plenty of fresh fruit and vegetables, and avoid too much coffee. You need a "well body" at this stage - dont survive on snacks. A carefully balanced diet is what is needed.

SMOKING AND DRINKING ← *change all shoulder headings to this format*

Cigarrettes and alchohol are **not** going to help you overcome nerves, even if you think they might, and they could well have the effect of making you more nervous.

DISCUSSIONS WITH FRIENDS
Meeting friends and ~~discuss~~ *discussing* problems can ~~assist~~ *help* you ~~to clarify things in your mind~~. However, do not panic if you're friends seem more confident than you - they might be bluffing! Some people need to bolster up they're own confidence just before an exam, ~~just~~ Make sure that this does not have the opposite effect on your confidence.

---

3)   Carefully check your work and correct any mistakes found

PRACTISE MOVING TEXT TO A SPECIFIC LOCATION (USING DRAG AND DROP METHOD)

TARGET TIME 15 MINUTES

Exercise 14e

1) Key in the following text with a font of your choice. The font used here is `Impact` sized `13`. Remember to time yourself and fill in your target time sheet

---

THE FREEDOM OF CAMPING   *(Use single spacing as shown)*

Camping is perfect for families: freedom for children and freedom for parents. With European Campers you have the chance to do what you want, when you want.

You can combine stays at 2 or more sites, break your journey and stay with friends or stop in a hotel en-route if you wish.

Our holidays are the antidote to restrictive package holidays. You can stay as long as you wish and we have over 100 campsites so you will be spoilt for choice.

Check through the standard services we offer:

Quality equipment
Specially designed, stylish tents
Spacious and well appointed mobile homes
Electric lighting and sprung beds
4 sunloungers witheach tent or mobile home
Fridge/freezers with each tent or mobile home
Stylish furniture (chairs, dining and coffee table, etc)

(Fully justify margins)

---

2) Carefully check your work. Spell-check and save with a name of your choice

4)   Spell-check and save your file with a name of your choice

5)   Leave the document on screen and amend as below:

Be prepared

COPING WITH EXAMINATION STRESS   *Double line spacing unless indicated*

RELAXATION TECHNIQUES   *Insert this paragraph in single line spacing*

If examination revision is "getting to you", leave it, go for a walk, and then come back to it. **Don't** be **too** strict with yourself if you know you **have** worked steadily. Simple muscle-relaxing or breathing exercises for 10 **minutes** might help.

throughout your course

BENEFICIAL EFFECT

It is recognized that a little stress can have a beneficial effect. Actors (and **exam** candidates) often give **their** best performance after suffering from pre-performance nerves. *The negative aspects are related to anxiety. There are ways of overcoming this — being prepared will help in this case.*

WATCH WHAT YOU EAT

Eat plenty of fresh fruit and vegetables, and avoid too much coffee. You need a "well body" at this stage - **don't** survive on snacks. A carefully balanced diet is what is needed, *so take time off for proper meals.*

SMOKING AND DRINKING

Alcohol and cigarettes are **not** going to help you **overcome** nerves, even if you think they might, and they could well have the effect of making you more nervous.

DISCUSSIONS WITH FRIENDS

Meeting friends and **discussing** problems can **help** you. However, do not panic if **your** friends seem more confident than you - they might be bluffing! Some people need to bolster up **their** own confidence just before an exam. Make sure that this does not have the opposite effect on your confidence.

DO YOUR BEST
Remember, you can but do your best. Nobody has the right to expect more of you.

Each exam candidate is an individual whose approach will be different. However, all candidates who work steadily throughout their course have a far better chance of success than those who leave their efforts to the last minute.

---

6)   Add page numbering. Check and print preview your document before printing one copy

7)   Carefully check your work against **model answer EX8F** which has been saved on the disk that accompanies this book

PRACTISE LOCATING AND CORRECTING INFORMATION

There are 2 methods that can be used when text needs to be moved. The "cut and paste" and "dragging with mouse" methods were both fully covered in the first book in this series. Either consult the first book for detailed instructions or see the Quick Reference Section which can be printed out from the disk that accompanies this book.

It is better to use "cut and paste" with longer documents when the text has to be moved some distance. It is easier to manipulate the mouse to "drag text" to its new position if the text is only being moved a short distance. **In the Stage II word processing examination, text to be moved will be circled in the document with an instruction where it has to be moved to. For example "move to A ". The position it has to be moved to will also be marked A**

Moving text with the mouse (drag and drop)

Exercise 14d

1)   Retrieve the following document saved as **NAMES.** Immediately rename the file **NAMES2**. Amend as indicated

The meaning of first names

move to A → Anthony	(Latin) worthy of praise
Agatha	(Greek) good, kind
Adam	(Hebrew) red man, earth man
Adela	(German) of noble birth
Alan B	(Celtic) harmony
Alexander	(Greek) a defender of helper of men
Alice	(Greek) truth, nobility
Alison	Scots alternative for Alice
Anita	(Spanish) gracious
Ann/Anna/Anne	(Hebrew) grace
A	
Arthur	(Celtic) high, noble
Auberey	(German) ruler, spirit
Avril	(French) April in French

use the drag + drop method to move to the end of the typed list (the place marked with an A)

2)   Carefully check your work and correct any mistakes found. Spell-check

3)   Quick save your file and clear the screen

MOCK RSA TEXT PROCESSING II Part 1 EXAMINATION

Time how long it takes you to complete the following 3 documents. In the examination you will be allowed $1\frac{1}{4}$ hours to complete all tasks. Remember to use letterhead paper as appropriate. If you are using a word processor you are allowed to print out after the $1\frac{1}{4}$ hours if you prefer, however, no amendments can be made to text if you choose to print after time.

Document 1

mark this CONFIDENTIAL

Our ref KS/GH
Mr W B Akram
Flat 6b
Hollyquest Rise
LIVERPOOL L68 2AF

Dr Mr Akram

You will no doubt have read of the proposal for this society and the Social Union Society to merge and subsequently convert to a public limited co.

I wanted to write to you personally to clarify a number of important points and to reassure you of our intention to keep your best interests in mind. The exact timing of the merger has not been finalised yet but once it takes place you will have access to the branches of both society's. After flotation members of the present societies will receive some form of benefit. Full details are unknown at present, but I would like to confirm that you could be eligible for benefit in view of the fact that your a/c. was opened before 14 August 19--. I think I should alert you to the fact, however that your benefit allocation might be reduced if the a/c. balance is reduced at any time during the flotation period. At present I am unable to give you any other details. However I will write to you as soon as more info. becomes available. Should you have any queries please contact me or telephone the head office information line direct - (Freefone 0800 44 44 84).

Yrs. sncly.
Ken Shooter
BRANCH MANAGER

I am enclosing a brief financail information sheet detailing your a/c.

90

Exercise 14c

TARGET TIME 10 MINUTES

1) Retrieve the following document saved as **WARNING.** Immediately rename the file **WARNING2.** Remember to time yourself and fill in your target time sheet. Amend as indicated. **You will need information from the previous document in this task**

MEMO

TO Ruby Sanger, Human Resources Officer
From Rory Coleman, Personnel Officer
RC/BS

(line space clear)

UNSOLICITED ADVERTISEMENTS *(emphasise heading)*

I noticed in the staff magazine for this ~~quarter~~ *season* that several advertisements were slipped inside. On glancing through these leaflets I was very concerned to read the leaflet from Zurich Central Banking House – did you ~~actually~~ read this leaflet before giving permission for it to be issued to all staff? I disagree strongly with the idea that we should be seen to endorse such advertisements by issuing them to staff (albeit through the staff magazine). The last sentence was ~~particularly~~ offensive to me. ~~but~~ Overall there are 3 ~~main~~ reasons I feel this kind of advertisement should not be encouraged:

(Check this information and amend if necessary)

a) young people should not be encouraged to 'get into debt'

b) all our staff will believe that we think Zurich Central is a sound finance house

c) personal loans are a personal matter - if staff require them then it is up to them to seek details. We should not be putting ideas into their heads.

I would like your comments as soon as possible

(in this particular advertisement)

I would like to know whether any of your staff were involved in inserting leaflets in magazines, and if so the number of hours taken and a break down of costs to the company. I would also like to know whether Zurich Central paid the company for the free advertising?

---

2) Carefully check your work and correct any mistakes found. Quick save your file and print one copy

3) Check the printouts for **LOAN** and **WARNING2** against **model answers EX14B and EX14C** which have been saved on the disk that accompanies this book. Clear the screen

Document 2

Memo

To: All Staff.

From: Ken Shooter, Branch Manager.

Ref: KS/GH.

You will be aware of the proposed merger between our building society and the S___ U __ S___. I have received info. from the Chairman which I believe will be of interest to all staff, he especially points out emphasises that there are no proposals for staff redundancies. A booklet "The proposed merger" have been prepared for staff use and I have requested a copy for each member of staff.

I think it very important that we meet as a team to enable me to outline the Chairman's message and to give us all the opp. to voice our opinions and worries. I would therefore be pleased if you could remain on the premises after the books have been balanced next Tuesday afternoon, (give date).

I hope to be able to give out the booklets at our meeting together with a telephone information line to head office.

I hope that you will be able to be present.

PRACTISE LOCATING AND CORRECTING INFORMATION

Exercise 14b

TARGET TIME 10 MINUTES

1) Type in the following text. Remember to time yourself and fill in your target time sheet. **You will need information from this document in the next task**

Single line spacing

UNSECURED PERSONAL LOAN *centre*

As a Confederation member, you can now take advantage of an attractive loan rate offered by ZURICH Central Finance House. There is / no need to put off that long awaited holiday or / now that new car - ~~it's yours right now!~~ you can have it now! [We offer an (attractive guaranteed) rate of interest which is only 21.3% and is fixed so you will know exactly how much you are paying throughout ~~the period of the personal~~ the loan period. You can borrow up to £15,000 and choose a repayment period up to 7 years. ~~It could not be simpler~~ Remember our loans are unsecured so you will not be putting your ~~house~~ home at risk. Let Zurich Central help you - we can issue funds on the same day. // Apply direct to Zurich Central Finance House (Tel 01-497-302170) - young applicants particularly welcome.

---

2) Carefully check your work and correct any mistakes found. Spell-check and save your file as **LOAN.** Print one copy and clear the screen

---

Did you find all the incorrect statements? Check your printout against the one below. All errors have been changed and the correct answer has been underlined

NOTES ON POSITIVE <u>THINKING (OR ACTION)</u> COURSES
1) Patricia <u>Wright</u> felt her life was "stuck in a rut".
2) Patricia was <u>22</u> years of age and was single.
3) She worked in a supermarket in the local <u>city</u> and she <u>loathed</u> her work.
4) She <u>saw</u> an advertisement for a positive <u>thinking</u> course and decided to <u>telephone</u>.
5) She retrained by returning to College and taking secretarial examinations at evening class. – [this is correct information]
6) She has now moved to London and works <u>as a secretary</u>.
7) You can take control of your life by telephoning <u>0116 2143777</u>

Document 3

MASON BUILDING SOCIETY *← emphasize*

Single line spacing except where indicated

Progress Report

The proposal for our Society and the Social Union Society to merge and subsequently be converted to a public limited company is proceeding as expected.   The shares of the new society will be listed on the London Stock Exchange in due course. The purpose of this short newsbrief is to clarify a number of points for all senior staff.

Staff employment

~~I think~~ *It* it is important at the outset to say that ~~we have~~ *there are* no proposals for redundancy. It is envisaged that the branches of both existing societies will remain open under the new society. In fact we see this merger as a positive step forward for our staff, (experiance) shows that it ~~will~~ *is likely* increase career *(too)* prospects.

Future growth

Employees and customers ~~alike~~ will have an opportunity to become the owners of a large, competitive and successful quoted co.. It is intended to structure the conversion and flotation so that the main beneficiaries will be investing and borrowing members of the present societies. Benefits will mainly take the form of a distribution of shares. It *is intended this bonus will be paid to members of both (society's) at the time of the merger.*

Implementation *on conversion to a public limited company*

Proposals *,on conversion* /will be put to (memebrs) of the combined society following the merger, ~~on the conversation to a public limited company~~. Exact timing will depend on a number of factors, including the satisfaction of refd. legal and regulatory processes.

emphasise last sentence and justify to the left

Patricia Wright felt her life was "stuck in a rut" 2 years ago and when she broke her arm in a car accident it seemed the final straw. ~~Whilst she was home recovering from the accident she took time to reflect upon her life~~. She was 22 years of age, single and working in a supermarket in the local ~~town.~~ city She loathed her work. It was boring, repetitive and not particularly well-paid. However, the people she worked with were friendly, and what else could she do anyway. It wasn't far to travel. She saw our advertisement for positive thinking courses and decided to ~~join us. Now she has a well-paid job in London and is much happier with her life.~~ telephone. She enrolled on a 4 week positive action course, where under the guidance of our tutor she learnt to take control of her life. She decided to re-train and returned to college to take secretarial exams at evening class. Now she has moved to London and works as a secretary and life is exciting once more.

Why not take control of your life - telephone us now. We can help.

Tel 0116 2143777

2) Carefully check your work. Spell-check and quick save your file. Print one copy

3) Carefully check your work against **model answer EX14A** which has been saved on the disk that accompanies this book

4) Type in the following text. Use your printed **DREAMS2** document to check that the information is correct. If found to be incorrect please insert correct information

NOTES ON POSITIVE DREAMS COURSES

1) Patricia Right felt her life was "stuck in a rut".
2) Patricia was 23 years of age and was single.
3) She worked in a supermarket in the local town and she liked her work.
4) She heard a radio advertisement for a positive dreams course and decided to write for information.
5) She retrained by returning to College and taking secretarial examinations at evening class.
6) She has now moved to London and works as a secretary.
7) You can take control of your life by telephoning 0117 92143777.

5) Carefully check your work and correct any mistakes found. Spell-check and save your file as **ANSWERS**

6) Print preview and print one copy. Clear the screen

7) In the RSA examination one task will contain information that will be incorrect in some way, just as some of the information above was not correct. You will be able to check this information from another task as you did here with the **DREAM2** document. I know you will be glad to learn that in the actual examination it is likely that only one statement will be false and your attention will be drawn to it in some way by the examiner. Probably it will be ringed

8) To check that you found all the above errors see the bottom of the next page

<u>Share accounts</u> / *emphasize these 2 words*

It has been decided that with effect from five pm /today all new share accounts opened will not be eligible for bonus shares in the combined new society. <u>It is necy. for this info. to be conveyed to new customers when they join.</u>

<u>Eligibility</u>

To be eligible to take part in any vote that may occur an investing member must have a balance of at least £150 at 5.00 pm today.

<u>Bonuses</u>

One of the conditions of eligiblity to receive bonus shares after flotation is that customer's remain members continuously throughout the flotation process. Customers must be alerted to the fact that any reduction in the balance of their a/c(s) might gntee. a reduc7tion in the bonus benefits which they could receive on flotation.

Summary

The accompanying booket should help branch managers clarify a number of important personal and financal points that staff and customers might raise. A temp. telephone info. line has been set up for all staff and customers. (See page 12 of the booklet).

Your board is /in no doubt that the proposal to merge the 2 societies will be in the best interests of all concerned.

typist/operator insert final paragraph here

J J Kinder

Chairman ← *at least one line space here*

14 August 19__

it can be found on the next page. In the actual exam it will be handed to you separately

93

LESSON 14	LOCATING AND CHECKING DOCUMENT INFORMATION
	PRACTISE LOCATING AND CORRECTING INFORMATION
	MOVING TEXT TO A SPECIFIC LOCATION WITHIN THE SAME DOCUMENT
	MOVING TEXT WITH THE MOUSE ("drag and drop" and "cut and paste" methods)
	PRACTISE MOVING TEXT using both methods
	COPYING TEXT TO A SPECIFIC LOCATION WITHIN THE SAME DOCUMENT
	PRACTISE COPYING TEXT
	CONSOLIDATION

LOCATING AND CHECKING DOCUMENT INFORMATION

Exercise 14a

1) Retrieve the following document saved as **DREAMS.** Immediately rename the file **DREAMS2**. Amend as indicated

Double line spacing unless indicated. Justified right Margin. Adjust line length to either (a) 15.3cm (6") or (b) 60 characters. If Proportional spacing is used please adjust line length to (a)

DO YOU HAVE DREAMS? ← Centre

[margin note: Indent this Section 38mm (1½") from left Margin and put into single spacing]

Achieving your dreams begins right now .... ~~We all know that life is not a dress rehearsal but we tend to put that thought to the back of our mind and just get on with life as it comes~~. The attitude of your mind plays a crucial part in what you achieve in life. If you think to yourself "I can't do that!" then you won't be able to do it. If you can't be bothered to put the effort into examinations, then you won't pass them. If you don't make the time to sit down and sort our [out] the priorities in your life, then you will continue to muddle through and take what comes - whether you like it or not.

typist/operator: this is the extra paragrah for document 3

↓

Advice to Branch Managers

Please insert in double line spacing

We beleive that in the interest of goodwill you should as soon as poss. hold a meeting with

your staff and explain the currant situation. Further copies of the accompanying booklet

"The proposed merger" can be obtained from Head Office for staff use. Please ensure that all

staff know of the temp. info. telephone line that has been set up for their use. We also

recomend that you write a personal note to current account holders giving them brief details

of the current situation - they also should be informed of the info. ~~telephone~~ line.

When you have printed all documents, carefully check them against the model answers saved as **TEXTEXAM** on the disk that accompanies this book.

Well done! you have covered all the necessary criteria to enable you to take the RSA Text Processing Stage II part 1 examination. You should now practise several past papers.

Good luck in the examination!

CONSOLIDATION EXERCISE FOR LESSONS 12 AND 13

TARGET TIME 30 MINUTES

Practise what you have learnt so far by following through the instructions below.

1)   Retrieve the following document saved as **FERRIES**. Immediately rename as **FERRIES2**. Remember to time yourself and fill in your target time sheet. Amend as indicated

Change to double line spacing (except where indicated) + use a justified right margin. Adjust the line length to either (a) 14cm (5½") or (b) 55 characters. If proportional spacing is used, please adjust line length to (a). Insert THE FRENCH SHOPPERS as a header on every page

British store-owners are delighted that there is a pounding of bargain-hunting French feet alighting from the cross-Channel ferries at present. The financial position of the French franc and the British pound makes the time ripe for a French invasion of ~~shoppers~~ **shops.** *single spacing for this paragraph*

TAKING THE FERRY TO THE SHOPS ← *centre all headings*

Ferry companies have been heaving under the weights of shoppers set on a short break in the UK. "Le great British bargain" is much sought after in Oxford Street. *French* The ferry companies are anxious to encourage this softening of the French attitude towards previously untouchable British fashion, and are tempting customers with bargain/*price* crossings.

POPULAR BUYS

garments are Winter ~~clothing is one of~~ the most popular buys. The quality of British woollens with the price tag they carry is a temptation, and bedding can be a third of the price of similar quality **goods** found in France. Classic clothes are also selling well and the simple black jacket is one of the most popular suitcase items on the return journey.

Change ferry (or ferries) to boat (or boats) throughout

UNUSUAL ITEMS

recent According to research made by the ferry companies it is not only clothes that the French are buying. They also cram their suitcases with items such as dark British beers, English marmalade and bacon, *and surprisingly tins of pet food are another best seller - but nobody is quite sure why this should be!*

TWO-WAY TRAFFIC

✓ In a questionnaire ~~completed~~ *fitted in* by 83% of ferry passengers in the ~~first~~ *last* 2 weeks of ~~June,~~ *July* the majority of passengers ~~are~~ *were* taking their car across the Channel to fill the car boot with *in order* foreign food and drink. *This is excellent news for the ferry companies and for the retail trade on both sides of the channel.*

2)   Quick save your file and carefully check your work. Print preview and print one copy

3)   Carefully check your work against **model answer CONSOL13** which has been saved on the disk that accompanies this book. Clear the screen

LESSON 9   COPYING A DISK
MAKING A DIRECTORY
COPYING A DISK TO A NETWORKED DRIVE

1)   Switch on and load Word for Windows 6 software

2)   Check that you are working on the correct disk drive. Your work should save onto your personal disk, usually in Drive A

3)   Documents have already been prepared for your subsequent retrieval for this section of the book. **A disk containing these documents has been provided and it is strongly advised that you copy this disk before use**. You may also prefer to copy the disk direct to Drive C as it will make retrieval quicker. Instructions on how to do this are set out below.

COPYING A DISK

Note: *You will need the disk to be copied and a blank disk.*

1)   Open the 'Main' group in **Program Manager**

Main

2)   Double-click on '**File Manager**'

PRACTISE MANUAL SEARCH AND REPLACE

Exercise 13d

> **TARGET TIME 25 MINUTES**

1) Retrieve the following document saved as **GERMS.** Immediately rename the file **GERMS2**. Remember to time yourself and fill in your target time sheet. Amend as indicated

Change to double line spacing (except where indicated) and use a justified right margin. Adjust line length to either (a) 14 cm (5½") or (b) 55 characters. Change germs to bacteria throughout.

BEWARE, BEWARE: GERMS ARE EVERYWHERE! *← centre + bold*

reported cases of / *↕ ← please leave at least 50 mm (2") here.*

It is a very uncomfortable fact that food poisoning in this country have increased five-fold over the past 10 years. 37,010 were reported in the last 6 months alone, and it is estimated that for everyone reported case there are 10 that go unreported. [Horror stories of environmental health officers finding rat droppings in restaurants may make headlines but germs multiply in much less dramatic circumstances. Ignorance of basic food hygiene rules encourage germs to multiply. Even the humble salad may be contaminated with germs if it isn't washed properly or a cream cake may be contaminated with staphylacoccus if it has been lying around in warm conditions. ✓

Typist Number 2nd page only

THE BARBECUE
The barbecue can be a source of germs if the same utensils are used to put raw meat on the grill and to remove it when ~~cooked~~ *it is finished. Barbecue cooking also tends to burn* ~~Burning~~ foods on the outside leaving the inside raw *and this* is another hotbed for germ infestation.

THE KITCHEN
Short of running the kitchen like an operating *theatre* there are a number of things that can be done at home to avoid food poisoning caused by germs:

Indent these items by 25 mm (1") from left margin

1) Store and prepare raw and cooked food separately
2) Check food is ~~throughly~~ cooked *thoroughly* | *single line spacing*
3) Follow use-by dates rigidly
4) ~~Store and prepare raw and cooked food separately~~

THE GERMS
There are many different bugs but the most common is salmonella, which is found in meat and poultry left in warm, moist conditions. Raw eggs can also be a source of salmonella poisoning. Listeria is another common bug found especially in soft cheese.

2) Spell-check and quick save your file. Print preview and print one copy.

3) Carefully check your work against **model answer EX13D** which has been saved on the disk that accompanies this book. Clear the screen

File Manager will then load and it will look similar to this. You will not have the same file names but it is not important

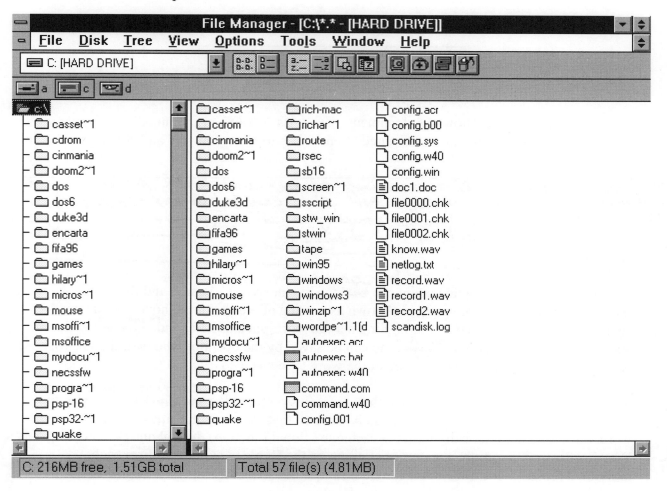

3) Click once on the 'Disk' menu (top left of screen)

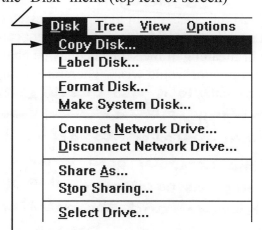

4) Click once on '**Copy Disk**'

SEARCH AND REPLACE IN MULTI-PAGE DOCUMENT

Exercise 13c

TARGET TIME 30 MINUTES

1) Retrieve the following document saved as **GLOBAL.** Immediately rename as **GLOBAL2.** Amend as indicated. Remember to time yourself and fill in your target time sheet

Change to double line spacing. Please number all pages. Use a justified right margin. Adjust the line length to (a) 15.3cm (6") or (b) 60 characters. If proportional spacing is used please adjust line length to a). Change document to file throughout.

GLOBAL FUNCTION

Editing a word processing document can ~~be done~~ *be carried out* in many ways. Search and Replace is a term used to edit a word or sentence (known as a string of words) throughout a document. By instructing the computer to search for a certain word, such as RED and ~~replace~~ *replacing* it with another word, such as BLUE, ~~much~~ *a lot of* time can be saved by the operator who would other wise have to carefully find each occurrence of the word to be changed.

Search and replace can be used so that the operator is prompted to ~~say whether~~ *confirm that* they wish the word changed (manual function) or it can be used so that the computer finds the target word/words and automatically replaces each one (global function) throughout *the document* When using **Word** software it is simply a matter of clicking on the **Replace** icon to confirm each individual replacement when manual mode is required. When the operator wishes to use the global replacement he simply clicks on the **Replace All** icon.

leave at least 76mm (3") here

The global function can be very useful especially in long, complicated documents, when it would be onerous to search out specific words. Global replacement can cause problems *However,* ~~however,~~ because the grammar or meaning of the sentence may be changed by the computer when it is not what the computer operator would wish. Therefore the operator needs to be *very* careful when using global replacement. It is also possible to use the global function when paginating ~~a document.~~ ~~with some software.~~ Global pagination allows the operator to define how many lines are *required* ~~wanted~~ /on each page and then the computer goes through the document inserting page breaks as necessary. This *x*function is not without problems, however, and the operator needs to check page by page and change the page breaks if required. Sometimes S..... and R....... is known as Edit and Find but the principles are the same.

2) Quick save your file. Print Preview and print your file. Carefully check your work against **model answer EX13C** which has been saved on the disk that accompanies this book. Clear the screen

5)   The following window will appear:

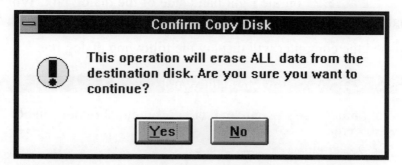

6)   Click on '**Yes**'

The following window will appear:

7)   Insert the disk you wish to copy and then click on [**OK**]

8) Click on 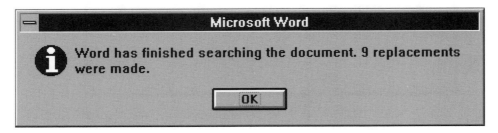 on the right hand side of the dialog box. **Word** begins searching through your document finding the letters '**red**' and replacing with '**blue**'

9) When finished the computer will display the following dialog box:

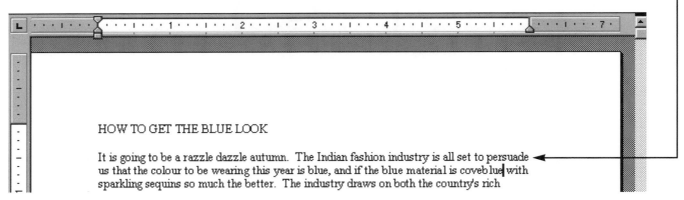

10) Check that your dialog box states **9 replacements**

11) If your box stated that **10 replacements** had been made it is because you overlooked placing an **x** in the [☐ Find **W**hole Words Only] box

As previously mentioned the letters "red" can be found in the word "cove<u>red</u>" in the second line of the text. If you forgot to place an **x** in this box your text will read as follows:

HOW TO GET THE BLUE LOOK

It is going to be a razzle dazzle autumn. The Indian fashion industry is all set to persuade ← us that the colour to be wearing this year is blue, and if the blue material is coveblue| with sparkling sequins so much the better. The industry draws on both the country's rich

12) Amend your text if necessary

13) Check through your document. All the words "red" should now read "blue"

14) Quick save your document

15) Clear the screen

The copying process will begin. Half way through the copying process the following window will be displayed:

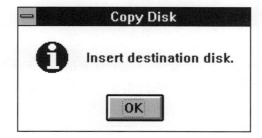

8)   Insert the disk you wish to copy the disk onto

IMPORTANT – The disk you are copying onto should not contain any documents you want to keep because they will all be deleted!

    Make sure the disk is not 'write protected'. To do this turn the disk on its back (label downwards), and move the tab on the bottom right-hand side so that it covers the hole.

    If your disk is 'write protected' you cannot change any of the information on it

---

9)   After checking the important points above click on [**OK**   ]

The computer will now copy the contents of the other disk onto your other disk

10)   After the disk has finished copying the computer will return to File Manager. From there you can either copy another disk or exit.

To quit hold down [**ALT**] key on your keyboard and then tap [**F4**] or click on the file menu and select exit

SEARCH AND REPLACE – GLOBAL AMENDMENT (INSTRUCTING WORD TO AUTOMATICALLY CHANGE SPECIFIC TEXT WITHOUT STOPPING)

Exercise 13b

1) Retrieve the following document saved as **RED.** Immediately rename the file **RED2.** Read through this document and you will notice the number of times the word RED has been used

---

HOW TO GET THE RED LOOK

It is going to be a razzle dazzle autumn. The Indian fashion industry is all set to persuade us that the colour to be wearing this year is red, and if the red material is covered with sparkling sequins so much the better. The industry draws on both the country's rich cultural tradition and an available skilled workforce in order to produce this profusion of red delights.

Sequinned red skirts in chiffon with cropped red shirt-jackets are already hitting the High Street shops, and red floral slip dresses with beadwork are selling like hot cakes in exclusive fashion boutiques. Even shoe manufacturers have caught the red bug – a glance in the window of any of the chain shoe shops will confirm that the colour for the season is red.

---

2) You are going to instruct the computer to automatically change RED to BLUE throughout the entire document without you confirming the replacement on each occasion. Check that your cursor is at the beginning of the document

3) Click on **Edit on the Menu Bar**

4) Click on **Replace**

5) Type the word red in the **Find What** box

6) Type the word blue in the **Replace With** box

7) Check the rest of the dialog box is correct. Look especially at the ☐ **Find Whole Words Only** box. The letters 'red' can also be found in the word cov<u>ered</u> (this word can also be found in *Exercise 13b*).

   If you do not place an **x** in this box you will find the word 'covered' will be changed to 'coveblue'. (See page 149 if unsure)

CREATING A DIRECTORY (ON DRIVE C)

1) Open the 'Main' group in **Program Manager**

Main

2) Double-click on '**File Manager**'

3) Make sure the 'root of drive C' is highlighted, as below. If it is not highlighted click on
icon

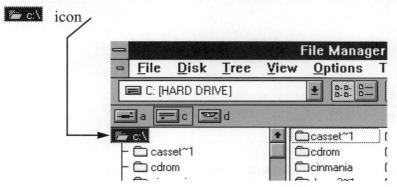

4) Click once on **File** to bring down the 'File' menu

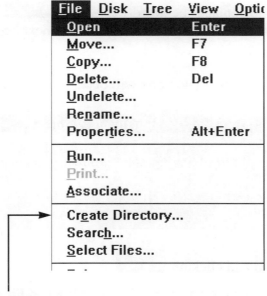

5) Click on '**Create Directory**'

11) The computer will stop on the title – EXERCISE which will appear in reverse high-light

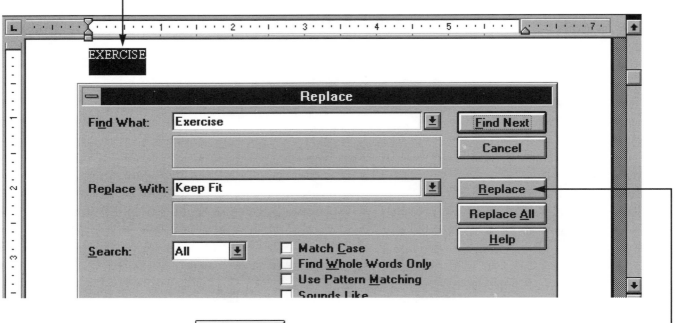

12) Click on the word **Replace**

The computer will highlight the next occurrence of the word **exercise**. Check that you wish to change each word the computer highlights and press **Replace** to confirm your decision on each occasion.

If you <u>do not</u> wish to replace the word click on **Find Next** and **Word** will not replace the highlighted word, but will move on to the next occurrence

13) When finished the following dialog box will occur:

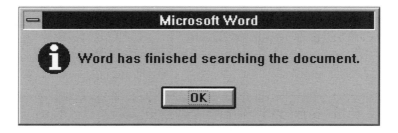

14) Click on **OK** and click on **Close**

15) Check through the document on screen. The words Keep Fit should now have replaced exercise. Quick save the document and clear the screen

The following window will appear:

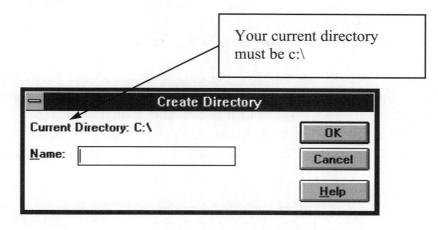

Your current directory must be c:\

6) Type in the name of your directory then click on [OK]

Example

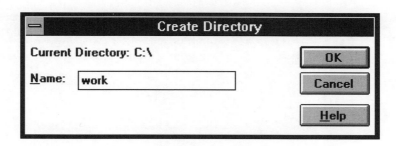

TIP: The name of your directory cannot be over 8 characters in length and cannot contain any of the following characters:. " / \ [ ] : * | < > + = ; , ?

---

7) After the directory has been made you will be returned to File Manager. From there you can either create another directory or quit

To quit hold down [**ALT**] and then tap [**F4**] or select exit from the file menu

The word ALL needs to be shown here. If it shows 'down' or 'up' click on the downward arrow alongside the box and choose ALL (because you wish to search ALL the document, not down or up from the cursor position).

If you started using the Search and Replace command with your cursor half way down the page, this is quite all right, because when Word has searched to the end of the document it will ask if you wish to continue checking from the beginning. Just click on 'yes' and Word will continue searching the text you had missed.

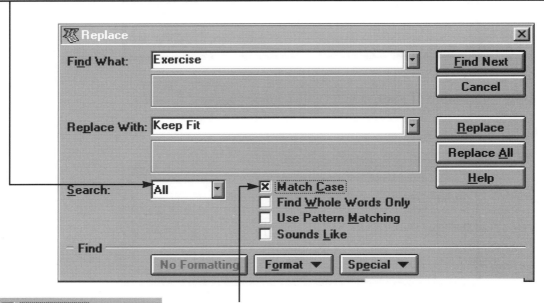

Match Case If an **x** shows in this box only words that exactly match the word typed in the **Find What** box will be found. If you typed **Exercise** with a capital **E** then **exercise** or **EXERCISE** (all capitals) will not be found. **TO REMOVE AN x – CLICK ON IT**.

Find Whole Words Only This is useful if you are searching for a word such as **"action"** which could be found in other words, such as **"reaction"**. If an **x** is in the box only the word itself will be found.

Use Pattern Matching This is a more advanced feature. If the **x** is in this box you can type a query in the **Find What** box such as **Ta?e**. All the words with this pattern, such as "tape", "tale", "tame", etc will then be found.

Sounds Like An **x** in this box will instruct the computer to stop on words which sound similar to the one typed. For example if the word **to** had been inserted in the **Find What** box, words such as "too" or "two" etc will also be found.

9) You do not need an **x** in any of the boxes for this particular search and replace. **TO REMOVE AN x – CLICK ON IT**

10) Click on **Find Next**

COPYING A DISK TO DRIVE C

1)   Open the 'Main' group in **Program Manager**

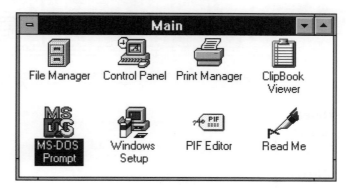

2)   Double-click on '**File Manager**'

File Manager will load. It will look similar to this:

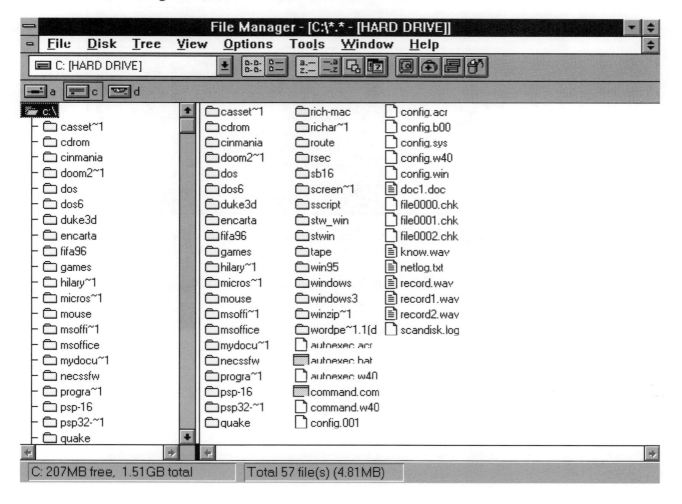

4)   Click on **Edit** on the **Menu Bar**

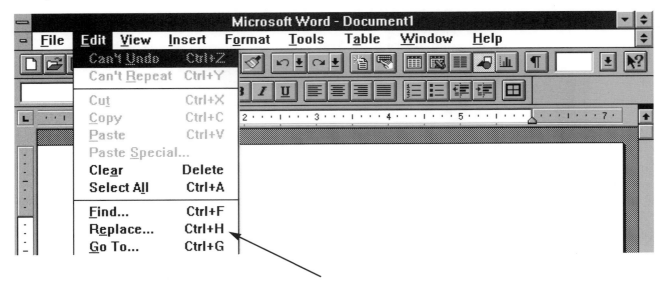

5)   From the drop-down menu click on **Replace**

6)   The cursor should be flashing in the **Find What** box. If there is any text in this box delete it. Key in the word – exercise

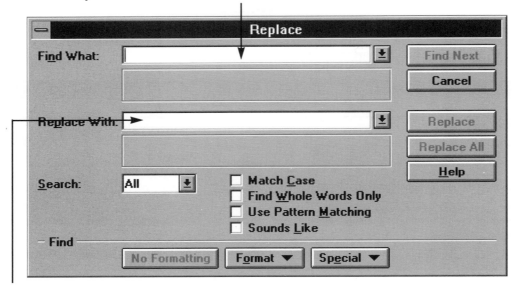

7)   Click in the **Replace With** box. If there is any text in this box delete it. Key in the words – Keep Fit

8)   You need to check the other items in this dialog box. See next page

3)   Insert the disk to be copied

4)   Click on the A drive icon

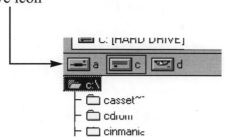

5)   You are going to highlight the files you wish to copy to the C drive.

QUICK METHOD

Click on the first file in the list, for example: (Note – your file names will be different)

6)   Hold down the [**SHIFT**] key on the keyboard and then click on the last file in the list. This selects ('highlights') all the files listed on the disk

The above example would now look like the illustration overleaf.

LESSON 13	SEARCH AND REPLACE
	SEARCH AND REPLACE – MANUAL AMENDMENT
	SEARCH AND REPLACE – GLOBAL AMENDMENT
	SEARCH AND REPLACE IN MULTI-PAGE DOCUMENT
	PRACTISE MANUAL SEARCH AND REPLACE
	CONSOLIDATION (for Lessons 12 and 13)

SEARCH AND REPLACE

It is possible to instruct **Word** to search a document for a certain word (or words) and replace them with another word (or words). You can either instruct **Word** to go through the document automatically changing specific text or you can instruct **Word** to stop at every instance of the word you wish to change and decide whether you wish to change it in every instance.

SEARCH AND REPLACE – MANUAL AMENDMENT (REQUESTING WORD TO STOP EACH TIME IT FINDS THE REQUIRED WORD)

Exercise 13a

1) Retrieve the following document saved as **KEEPFIT**

2) Immediately rename the file **KEEPFIT2**

EXERCISE

Exercise is often a solitary endeavour. You may jog on an empty road, swim laps in

watery isolation or pump iron without a training partner. Sometimes exercise is peaceful,

even invigorating; sometimes exercise is just plain lonely. That's when it's fun to be part of

an organised exercise group.

3) Read the passage through and notice the number of times the word "Exercise" is used. You are going to instruct the computer to change the word "Exercise" to "Keep Fit" using the MANUAL facility

7) Tap [**F8**]on the keyboard. The following window will appear:

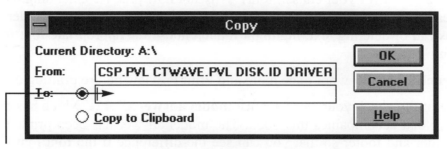

8) Type **C:** or the letter of the network drive you wish to copy to (ex. **G:**) in the window box, and then the name of your directory

For example if you have a directory on the C drive called SAMPLE, you would type the following in the window:

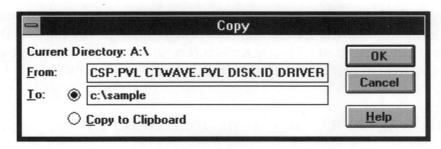

16) Click on the **Page Numbers icon** 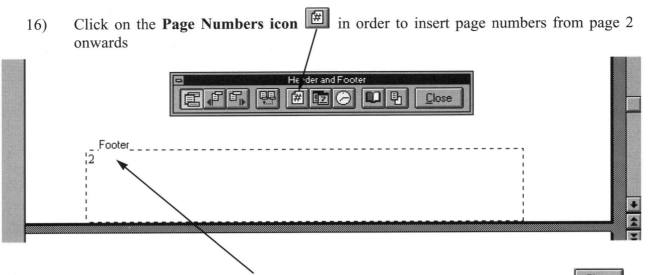 in order to insert page numbers from page 2 onwards

17) Notice that the number "**2**" has appeared in the Footer box before clicking on Close

18) Quick save your work and then Print Preview. You should be able to see the same header at the top of each page, but only the page number 2 will have printed

19) It is likely that the font used for the header is the default font and not **Book Antiqua** sized **12** (or your chosen font). Why not now practise amending the font used in the header and footer? Re-read page 141 "Amending existing Header or Footer" and instead of deleting text, highlight it and choose the appropriate font from the **Formatting Toolbar**

20) Quick save your work once more and Print Preview before printing one copy

21) Carefully check your work against **model answer EX12F** which has been saved on the disk that accompanies this book. The model answer has been printed with the default header and footer so that you can see the difference if the font/font size has not been changed

22) Clear the screen

REMINDER .... IMPORTANT NOTE TO TYPIST

Always remember to number the second page. In the exam you will be expected to automatically number the second and subsequent pages of any document. This instruction will be printed within general information on the front page of the examination paper. THE INSTRUCTIONS WILL NOT BE PRINTED ON EACH EXAM DOCUMENT.

IT IS IMPORTANT THAT YOU REMEMBER TO DO THIS!

For extra practice retrieve *Exercise 12a*, *Exercise 12b* and *Exercise 12c* and insert page numbers <u>on the second and subsequent</u> pages only.

9)   Click on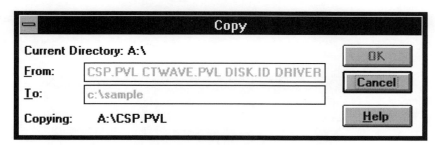

The files will then start copying from your disk to the directory on the destination drive. In my example the dialog box would look like this:

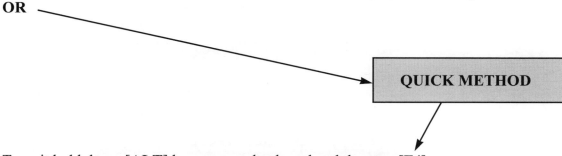

10) After the disk has finished copying the computer will return to File Manager. From there you can exit – click on the word **File** and then on **Exit** from the drop-down menu, **OR**

QUICK METHOD

To quit hold down [**ALT**] key on your keyboard and then tap [**F4**]

13) Click on the **Show Next icon** 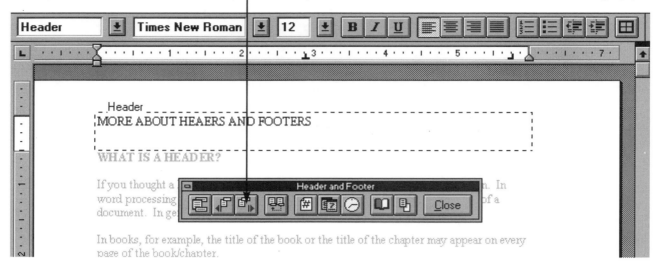 (this will move the document on to the second page)

14) You will now be given a second **Header** box. Whatever you type in this box will appear on the second and subsequent pages of your document. In this case you require the same header as on the first page so once more type – MORE ABOUT HEADERS AND FOOTERS

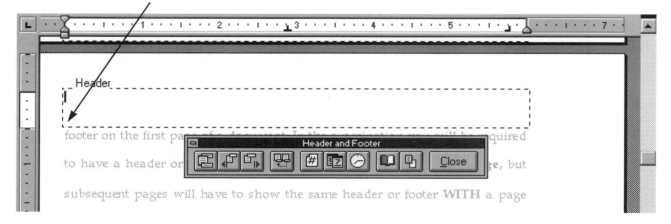

15) Click on the **Switch between Header and Footer icon**  in order to insert a footer (which in this case is going to be the page number)

LESSON 10   **OPENING/RENAMING AN EXISTING DOCUMENT**

PRACTISE OPENING/RENAMING AN EXISTING FILE

PRACTISE ROUTING COPIES

ALLOCATION OF VERTICAL SPACE

INSERTING SPACE WITHIN NEW TEXT – using `Courier` **font and** `Times New Roman` **font**

SHOW/HIDE ICON

NORMAL VIEW AND PAGE LAYOUT VIEW

PRACTISE OPENING AND RENAMING AN EXISTING DOCUMENT AND INSERTING SPACE WITHIN RETRIEVED TEXT

INSERTING SPACE WITHIN RETRIEVED TEXT

CONSOLIDATION

If you are unsure how to carry out any of the word processing functions in this book refer to the **QUICK REFERENCE** section. The basic functions are covered in more detail in the first book in this series.

A disk containing documents for you to retrieve has been provided with this book. The second half of the book concentrates on the RSA Word Processing II examination in which documents will be retrieved and amended. You will need access to the documents contained on the disk from this point forward. Please read the previous Lesson (Lesson 9) for further details.

OPENING AND RENAMING AN EXISTING DOCUMENT

It is often necessary at work to update an existing document file. When an existing document has to be amended and reprinted it is often wise to keep the original file intact because you may wish to retrieve the original version at some later date. In the RSA word processing examination you will be required to retrieve (open) a document and amend it. You would be sensible to leave the original file intact and work on a copy of it. If you should then make irreversible errors with your copy, you can refer back to the original and copy once more in order to start again. Follow the instructions below in order to do this.

Exercise 10a

1)   Open a new document file in the usual way

       Follow the instructions to insert the file **RETRIEVE** into this new document. You will then keep the original file intact and be able to retrieve it again in its original form if required. The **RETRIEVE** document has been saved on the disk that accompanies this book.

8) When the **Page** Setup dialog box is shown, click on the tab heading **Layout** (in order to bring it to the top)

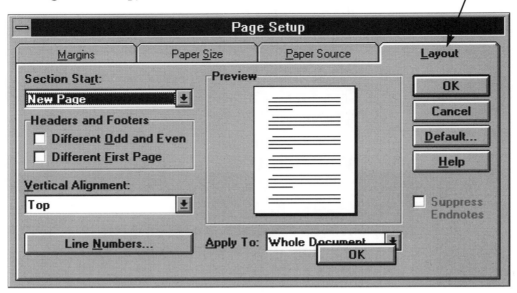

9) Under the Headers and Footers section click in the box beside "**Different First Page**". An "**x**" will appear in the box

10) Click on OK

11) The following "First Page Header" box will appear:

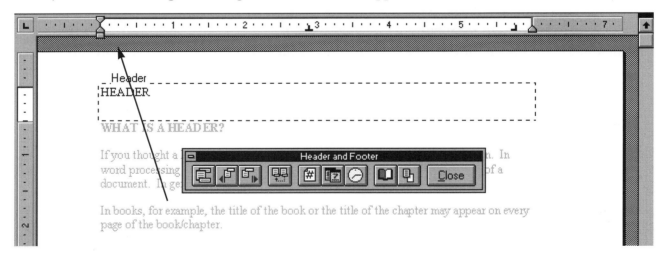

12) Type in the header (left aligned) – MORE ABOUT HEADERS AND FOOTERS

2)   Click on **Insert** on the **Standard Toolbar**

3)   From the drop-down menu that appears click on **File**

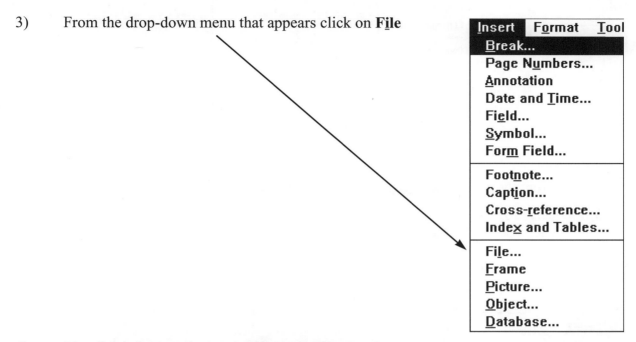

4)   The dialog box on the opposite page will appear on screen

You need to find the file named **retrieve.doc**. It is not possible to tell you in exactly which directory or sub-directory the file **retrieve.doc** has been placed. It depends upon where the information on the disk which accompanies this book has been filed.

Look back at Lesson 9 if you are unsure about this or about using the disk that accompanies this book.

4) **It is important that the cursor is in the first page of your document**. Check that it is and then click on <u>V</u>**iew** on the **Menu Bar**

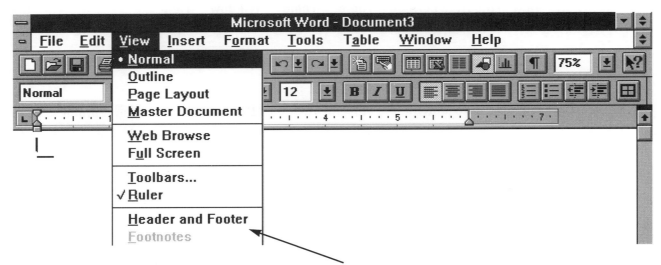

5) From the drop-down menu click on **Header and Footer**

6) The program will switch temporarily to **Page Layout view** if you are in **Normal View**. (See page 116 if unsure about Page Layout and Normal View.) The Header toolbar will now be placed on the top of your document

7) Click on the **Page Setup icon**

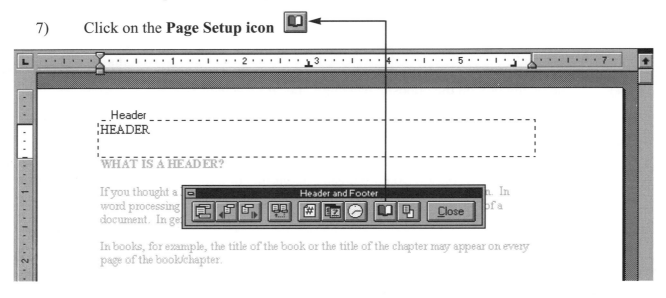

Once you can see the name **retrieve.doc** in the list underneath the **File Name:** box

click on the name once and press [OK]

Alternatively you will save time if you double-click the left hand mouse button quickly on the **retrieve.doc** name in the actual list (this retrieves the file immediately without the

need to press [OK])

QUICK METHOD

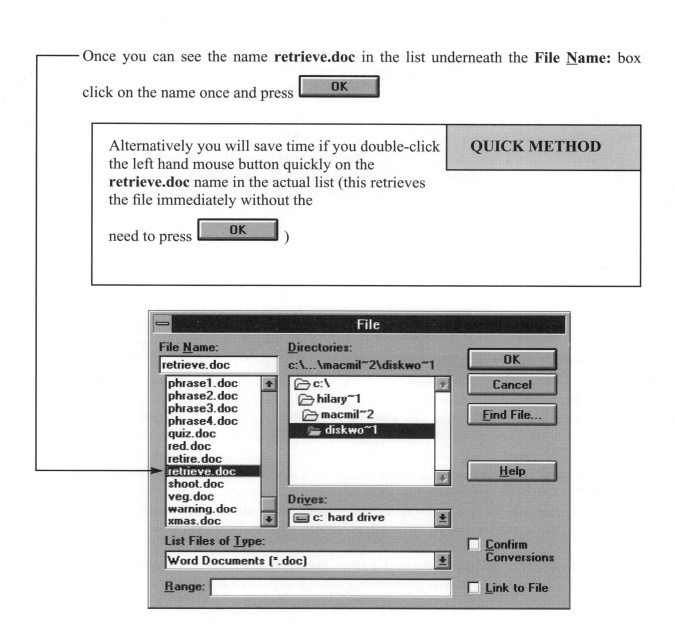

---

5) Once the text is on screen you need to save it in the usual way before you commence work. Save your file as **RETRIEV2**. Remember – the name you use to save your file <u>must</u> always be 8 or less <u>alphabetic</u> or <u>numeric</u> characters in length. You cannot use a comma, space, full stop etc

---

When retrieving and renaming an original file it will help you remember which file it is if you use the same name and add the number 2 to the renamed copy of the file. If your existing file name is 8 characters then you might have to shorten it slightly for the renamed version, as in the example above.

---

6) Check that you are saving in the correct directory and drive (see the first book in this series if you are unsure). Click on [OK] The document on screen will now be renamed **RETRIEV2** and this name will appear at the very top of the screen

INSERTING HEADERS/FOOTERS, AND PAGE NUMBERING THE SECOND AND SUBSEQUENT DOCUMENT PAGES

In the RSA Word Processing Stage II Part 2 examination you will be expected to number the second and subsequent pages of any document. This will involve you in suppressing page numbering on the first page, which is quite straightforward if headers and footers are not involved. (You have already covered this in Lesson 4, page 44.) However, in the word processing exam it is possible that you will have headers and footers in a multi-page document. Follow the instructions below in order to carry this out.

Exercise 12f

1) Key in the text below in a font of your choice. The font used here is `Book Antiqua` sized `12`

USES OF HEADERS AND FOOTERS *(bold)* *(Double line spacing & justified throughout please)*

As the names imply A header normally sits at the top of each page in your document and footer sits at the bottom. In general, both footers and headers serve as pointers for the reader. For example in magazines they give info. such as the issue, date of publication, name and perhaps volume number. In books, they often include a chapter or section area. You can create headers and footers that range from one word to multiple paragraphs. You can format them using many of the same features you use for body text. For example you can change the font or font size within a header or footer, or embolden certain words if you ~~require~~ prefer.

You can also add graphics, such as a logo and define different headers or footers for odd and even pages. It also possible to have a different header or footer on the first page of a document ~~only~~. You can even control the position of headers and footers to place them anywhere on the printed page - this rather makes a nonesense of the description HEADers and FOOTers, because they are no longer at the head or foot of a page. Many of these features are too advanced for this intermediate book but you do need to know how to put a different header or footer on the first page of a document. In the examination you will be required to have a header or footer **WITHOUT** a page number on the first page, but subsequent pages will have to show the same header or footer **WITH A PAGE NUMBER.** *(please type in lower case)*

Except when spell checking you can only see the header or footer that you have inserted when working in Page Layout view. If you are working in Normal or Outline view they will be hidden from the screen - they are still there however! You can also see the layout of headers and footers with the Print Preview command. All these features have been covered elsewhere in this book - do look them up in the index if you are in any way unsure. *and read about them*

---

2) Carefully check your work and correct any mistakes found. Spell-check

3) Save your file with a name of your choice and leave on screen

7) Amend the **RETRIEV2** file on screen as indicated

Justify right margin.

Typist-please ensure that consistent layout used for all numbers.

RETRIEVING A DOCUMENT ← bold

One of the joys of using a word processor is that it is so easy to amend ~~mistakes~~ errors. Years ago when only typewriters were used it was a mammoth job to correct ~~errors~~ mistakes, especially if several carbon copies were involved. In those days the typist would have spent ~~1~~ one or 2 minutes rubbing out the error, or 'painting' it out with correcting fluid and waiting for the fluid to dry, before being able to insert the character/s.

Re-typing amended work was another long process in those days. In the first place the typist would copy type the work. The author of the work would then amend it and return it to the typist for re-~~typing~~ typing again - this re-~~typing~~ typing process could be repeated ~~three~~ or ~~4~~ times. On each re-type the typist would have to start from scratch ~~again~~ once more.

It could be very irksome to re-type the same text over and over just because the author wished to add a word here or a paragraph there. The long suffering typist often felt like screaming at the author ~~to "make up his or her mind!"~~.

Nowadays with work stored on computer, changing text is much easier. In fact bosses now sometimes make unnecessary changes because they see it as such a simple matter. The Word Processing II Part 1 examination reflects this ~~changing~~ ability to recall text and amend it; in fact ~~3~~ of the ~~four~~ tasks will involve the candidate ~~to~~ recalling previously stored text (the words "stored" and "saved" have the same meaning in this context).

The second part of this book reflects office and examination practice in that much of the work you will use ~~have~~ has already been saved on disk. You will be told the document name in each case and you are very strongly advised to rename the file immediately you have retrieved it.

By renaming you will protect the original copy. This is a useful habit to adopt at work and in exams, because should you make lots of errors or lose chunks of text when amending you always have the original to retrieve once more for a fresh start.

8) Carefully check your work. Spell-check

9) Quick save your work and print one copy

10) Carefully check your work against **model answer EX10A** which has been saved on the disk that accompanies this book

108

DELETE OR AMEND EXISTING HEADER OR FOOTER

Exercise 12e

1)   Retrieve the document saved as **XMAS2**

2)   Immediately rename the file **XMAS3**

3)   Click on **View** on the **Menu Bar**

4)   From the drop-down menu click on **Header and Footer**

5)   The following toolbar and rectangular **Header** box will appear (the header you typed will be shown)

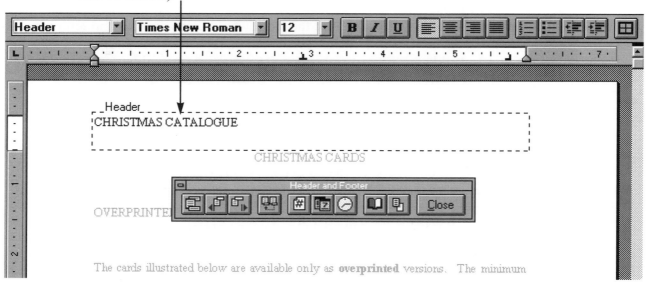

6)   Delete the words CHRISTMAS CATALOGUE.

If you experience a problem deleting existing text with just the keyboard delete keys, try highlighting the text first and then press the **Delete** key.

Usually the only text which causes problems when deleting is text inserted using a 'Field' command (as with the page numbering)

7)   Type the new header – GIFT IDEAS

8)   Click on the **Switch between Header and Footer** icon

9)   Delete the existing footer – SECTION 3 – CARDS

10)   Type the new footer – CHRISTMAS CARDS

11)   Click on ▢ **Close**   **Print Preview** and quick save your document. If you wish print one copy before clearing the screen. Carefully check your work (on screen or in print) against **model answer EX12E** which has been saved on the disk that accompanies this book

PRACTISE RETRIEVING AND RENAMING AN EXISTING FILE

Exercise 10b

1)   Retrieve the file saved as **MOBILE** which has been saved on the disk which accompanies this book. Rename your file as **MOBILE2** before amending as shown below:

SHOPMOBILITY ←centre ← bold   *Double line spacing throughout*

The first time I heard of Shopmobility was in the City of Bath. I was shopping with my
very
daughter when we passed one of their shops. The window was full of wheelchairs and four
wheel scooters and the sign invited people with physical disabilities to use them in order to see
there was a
Bath. [It was because of this chance encounter that I found myself one weeks later taking my
80 year old father on a trip around Bath. Actually the truth was that he was taking me - hiring
an electric scooter gave him once again the freedom to an active life. He rushed around at top
speed, maneuvering along the pedestrianised shopping streets and in and out of the stores. *At
one point I lost him in Marks & Spencers, but as I saw
him maneuvering backwards amongst the mens' trousers with
an enormous grin all over his face, I knew he was not lost -
in fact it was the opposite because he had found freedom once more!*

2)   Carefully check your amendments against the above copy. Quick save your file and clear the screen

Exercise 10c

1)   Retrieve the file saved as **VEG** which has been saved on the disk which accompanies this book. Rename your file as **VEG2** before amending as shown below:

Troubles with the Veg*etables* ←CAPS

✓ There is perhaps nothing more distressing for the gardener than to see a whole crop wiped
upsetting   *amateur*
out. There are many reasons for problems, but on the whole they fall into three main
categories// Pests which attack plants make up the first category. Some pests are so small
that they cannot be easily seen - mites, eelworms, etc. Others, such as birds and cats, are much
larger.//Disease caused by fungi make up the second category. Fungi can be prevented by
spraying, but the other diseases caused by viruses and bacteria can rarely be controlled in this
Manner way.//The last category produces disease-like symptoms but is not caused by a living   *it*
organism. Perhaps we should call this category disorders. Disorders show that something is
or has been wrong with the growing environment. *General disorders could be
caused by wind or frost, too little or too much water,
too little organic matter, etc.*

2)   Carefully check your amendments against the above copy. Quick save your file and clear the screen

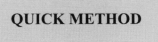

INSERT PAGE NUMBERS WITHIN A FOOTER

1) With the **LABELS** document on screen click on **V**iew and then click on **Header and Footer**

2) From the toolbar shown click on the **Switch Between Header and Footer** icon

3) Tap the **Tab** key on the keyboard. The **I** beam will move to the middle of the **Footer** box.

The **Tab** key is used to separate elements in a header or footer. By default Word defines tab stops for the centre and flush-right positions. If the margins or tabs are not as default then the position of your header (or footer) will vary. The advanced formatting of headers and footers can be found in the third book in this series

4) Type in the words   SUMMER EDITION

5) Tap the **Tab** key on the keyboard once more. (The **I** beam will now move to the right side of the **Footer** box.) From the toolbar shown click on the **Page Number** icon. The page number "1" will appear justified to the right

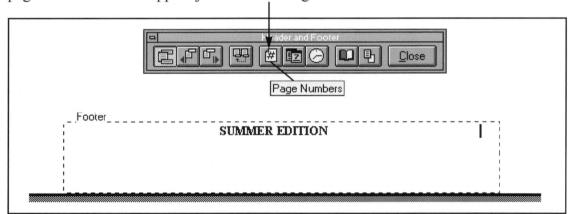

NB Whichever page you happen to be on at the time this command is given will display the correct page number.

6) Click on [Close] **Print Preview** your document to check that your footer is displayed

7) Quick save. Carefully check your work against **model answer EX12D** which has been saved on the disk that accompanies this book. Print one copy and clear the screen

PRACTISE ROUTING COPIES

Exercise 10d

Routing copies was covered in the first section of this book (see Lesson 6, page 71). However, extra exercises are provided here because in one of the Stage II word processing examination tasks you will almost certainly be requested to send extra copies.

1)   Type in the following text:

Typist – double line spacing with justified right margin, unless indicated

EXTRA COPIES OF TYPED WORK

Sometimes it is necessary to produce more than one copy of a document. The extra copies are often given to other people concerned. In the case of a letter or memorandum the names of these recipients are usually typed in a list at the foot of the letter or memo. The first name is preceded by the initials "cc ...." (carbon copies).

Single line spacing

At work the words "Distributed to.........." or "Copy for............" are sometimes used instead of ~~the~~ "cc". For example, let us say that a letter enclosing a report has been sent to a Mr John Brown and in that letter Mr Brown is told that a copy of the report has been sent to Mrs June Stock and Miss Sally Green. At the foot of the letter after the word "Enc" the typist would add: -

Emphasise →

cc Mrs June Stock
   Miss Sally Green   *single line spacing*
   File

single line spacing, justified to the left

The ~~4th~~ *original* copy would be sent to Mr Brown and none of the names at the foot of the letter would, in that case, be ticked, **but Mr Brown would know that the people named had also been sent a copy.**

The typist would then produce 4 copies of the original letter and would tick one name on each copy, that copy then being sent to the person ticked.

---

2)   Carefully check your work and correct any mistakes found. Spell-check

3)   Print preview and print one copy. Save your file as **COPIES.** Clear the screen

4)   Carefully check your work against **model answer EX10D** which has been saved on the disk that accompanies this book

AMEND HEADERS AND FOOTERS

Exercise 12d

1)   Type in the following text:

Insert COPIER/LASER LABELS to appear as a header on every page.

PRODUCT INFORMATION ← embolden / emphasise

All our labels are available in Super white and White — emphasise and all are supplied in packs with carrying handles for greater convenience. For your information we have set out product descriptions below:

Laser and Ink jet labels ← embolden all should headings + centre

These labels are designed to withstand heat and align with the character spacing of Most modern desk top printers. Label sheets feed automatically into the printer and are guaranteed not to melt or peel-off inside the laser printer.

✱ Start a new page here

Continuous labels

Sprocket loaded and fanfolded for trouble free use. These are specifically designed for high speed printers.

✱ Start a new page here

Plain reel address labels

Specially designed for use with a typewriter, the flexible backing sheet makes for easy feeding. No ~~sprocked~~ sprocket holes are used with these labels.

---

2)   Carefully check your work and spell-check. Save your file as **LABELS**

3)   Leave the document on screen

PRACTISE ROUTING COPIES

Exercise 10e

TARGET TIME 10 MINUTES

1) Key in the following text. Remember to time yourself and fill in your target time sheet

MEMO
To Jason Downend, Overseas Sales Section
From Chris O'Connell, Personnel Department
Ref CO/--
I have today received confirmation from the ~~secretary~~ organiser
of "SALES 2000" for Daniel Butler, Tracy Edmunds and
you to attend the weekend seminar from Friday,
29 April to Sunday, 1 May 19--. Accommodation
is at the Grand ~~Hotel~~ Hotel and I will let
you have full details in due course.
Typist: Top + 3 copies please. One for Daniel, one for Tracy + file copy. Indicate routing.

2) Carefully check your work against the following correct copy

3) Spell-check and save your file with a name of your choice

4) Print 4 copies and indicate routing as instructed

5) Clear the screen

MEMORANDUM

TO   Jason Downend, Overseas Sales Section
FROM   Chris O'Connell, Personnel Department
DATE   Today's date
REF   CO/your initials

I have today received confirmation from the organisers of "SALES 2000" for Daniel Butler, Tracy Edmunds and you to attend the weekend seminar from Friday, 29 April to Sunday, 1 May 19—. Accommodation is at the Grand Hotel and I will let you have full details in due course.

cc Daniel Butler
   Tracy Edmunds
   File

**An instruction to "INDICATE ROUTING" would require you to add these details
and then print 4 copies. One name should be ticked on each copy. The original copy
which would not be ticked would be for the addressee (Jason Downend)**

PRACTISE INSERTING HEADERS AND FOOTERS

Exercise 12c

1) Retrieve the following document saved as **XMAS**

2) Immediately rename the file **XMAS2** Amend as indicated

Insert CHRISTMAS CATALOGUE to appear as a header on every page, and SECTION 3-CARDS as a footer on every page. Change to double line spacing & use a justified right margin. NO page numbers please. Amend as shown

centre CHRISTMAS CARDS

Overprinted cards

The cards illustrated below are available only as overprinted versions. The minimum quantity is ~~500~~ 250 of each version. The price is 55p per card for "Christmas Greeting", and 58p for "Joyful tidings". Postage and package is extra and typesetting costs will depend upon the number of words required, *but to give you some idea of costs a simple message such as "Best wishes from Zena and John" would cost an extra 9p per card.*

Robin Bumper Pack *(start a new page here)*

One of our lines Christmas
~~Our~~ most popular ~~line~~ last ~~Xmas~~. The greeting inside these traditionally illustrated cards is "Merry Christmas and a Happy New Year". Packs of 12 cards, all of which are printed on quality card.

(start a new page here)

Father Christmas

must
A ~~most~~ for small children. These *tiny* cards are just the right size for ~~small~~ hands. Your ✓ children will delight in giving these to their friends ~~at school~~. The greeting inside these appealing cards is "Happy Christmas". Packs of 10 or 20 are available; the larger size is more cost effective as can be seen below:

(start a new page here)
THE THREE KINGS/MADONNA AND CHILD ← *change all shoulder headings to look like this.*

The biblical painting*s* printed on these card captures the true meaning of Christmas. The message inside reads "Best wishes for a Happy and Peaceful Christmas". Each pack of 8 cards contains 4 of each variety. *To give the true meaning of ~~card~~ Christmas a card such as this should be chosen.*

---

3) Carefully check your work and quick save your document. Use **Print Preview** to check placement of headers and footers. Print one copy and clear the screen

4) Carefully check your work against **model answer EX12C** which has been saved on the disk that accompanies this book

PRACTISE ROUTING COPIES

Exercise 10f

1)   Type in the following text:

KC/BM
Miss C Shahin
98 Groundswell Avenue, Leicester, LEI 8TH
Dear Miss Shahin
LLB LAW WITH FRENCH
I am very pleased to be able to confirm that we have decided to make you an offer for entry to the Law with French course. [As you know we were one of the 19 Law Schools offered the award of Excellent in the recent independent Higher Education Funding Council for England Survey of Teaching in Law Departments. For your information I enclose the Council's Report. [a copy of

I know that you have confirmed acceptance of the above by telephone but can you now please confirm as soon as possible in writing that you will be accepting this place. As requested a copy of this letter has ✓ been sent to Mr R Tompkins at The Department of Social Security, Leicester.

We look forward to welcoming you to the University.
Yours sincerely
Keith Charles
Tutor for Admissions

(Top & 2 please, one for Mr Tompkins & one for file. Routing needs indicating.)

2)   Carefully check your work. Spell-check and save your file as **UNIV**

3)   Clear the screen

4)   Carefully check your work against **model answer EX10F** which has been saved on the disk that accompanies this book

5) There will be a flashing **I** beam in the rectangular **Footer** box

6) Type in capital letters the words THIS IS MY FOOTER

7) Click on [Close] . You will see the words you have typed in faint outline at the bottom of the document if you are working in **Page Layout View**

8) Check footers in **Print Preview**. Quick save your document and print one copy before closing your file. Each of the 3 pages printed should now have a header and a footer as **model answer EX12A** which has been saved on the disk that accompanies this book

PRACTISE INSERTING A HEADER

Exercise 12b

1) Using Page Layout View type in the following text. Use a font of your choice. The font used here is [Albertus Medium] sized [11]

2) Carefully check and spell-check your work. Save as **PLYMTH**. Print preview before printing one copy. Look especially at the headers and check that they can be seen before printing one copy

3) Carefully check your work against **model answer EX12B** which has been saved on the disk that accompanies this book. Clear the screen

ALLOCATION OF VERTICAL SPACE

In the examination you will be requested to leave vertical space within a document. It is easier

to leave accurate space if using a font such as `Courier`. However the examination board does not stipulate that you should use a specific font and the choice is up to you. In the following exercises you will practise leaving space within retrieved and new documents,

using both `Courier` and `Times New Roman` fonts.

Exercise 10g

INSERTING SPACE WITHIN NEW TEXT – USING `Courier` FONT

1)   Change the font to `Courier` size `12` .

2)   Type in the following text:

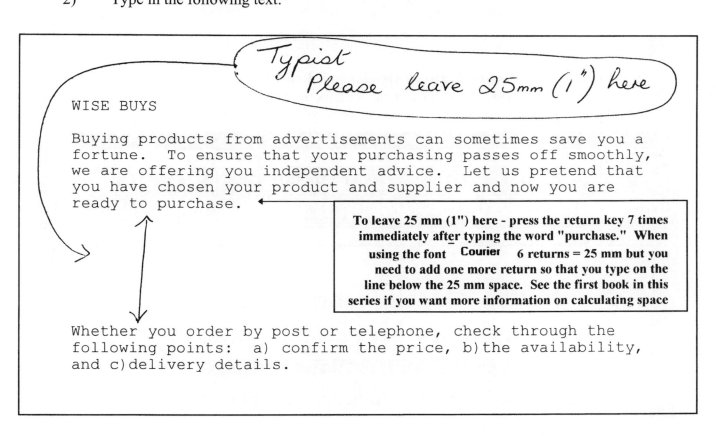

```
WISE BUYS

Buying products from advertisements can sometimes save you a
fortune.  To ensure that your purchasing passes off smoothly,
we are offering you independent advice.  Let us pretend that
you have chosen your product and supplier and now you are
ready to purchase.
```

Typist
Please leave 25mm (1") here

To leave 25 mm (1") here - press the return key 7 times immediately after typing the word "purchase." When using the font `Courier` 6 returns = 25 mm but you need to add one more return so that you type on the line below the 25 mm space. See the first book in this series if you want more information on calculating space

```
Whether you order by post or telephone, check through the
following points:  a) confirm the price, b) the availability,
and c) delivery details.
```

3)   Carefully check your work and correct any mistakes found

4)   Save your file as **WISEBUY** and leave on screen

INSERTING A FOOTER

1) Click on **View** on the **Menu Bar**

2) From the drop-down menu click on **Header and Footer**

3) The following toolbar and rectangular **Header** box will appear (this time the header you typed previously will be shown)

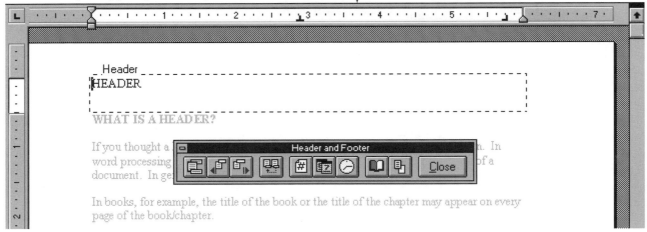

4) Click on the **Switch Between Header and Footer** icon on the toolbar. Word moves you to the bottom of your document. The footer margin is now displayed, together with the Footer toolbar which is placed on top of your document

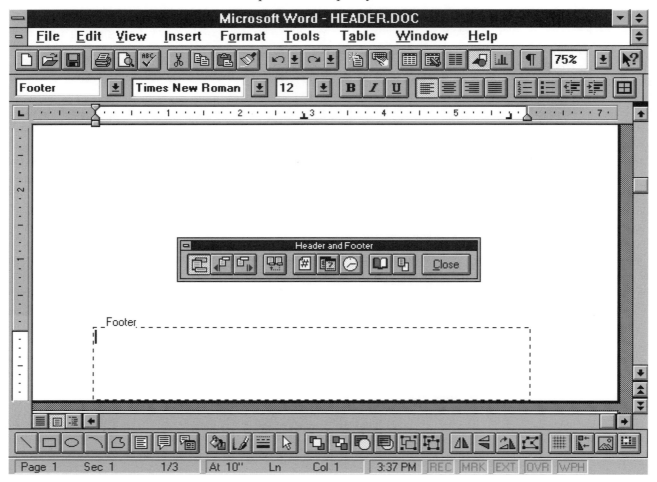

Checking against the vertical ruler bar

It is possible to check the space in the above task against the vertical ruler bar on screen. To do this:

1)   Click once on **Page Layout View** icon at the bottom left of your screen

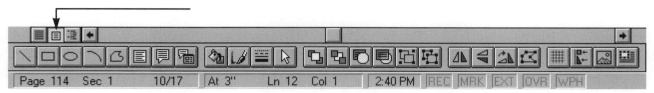

2)   Down the left hand side of the screen a vertical ruler bar will appear (this will show inches or centimetres depending upon which measurement system you have chosen). See the first book in this series for details on changing measurements

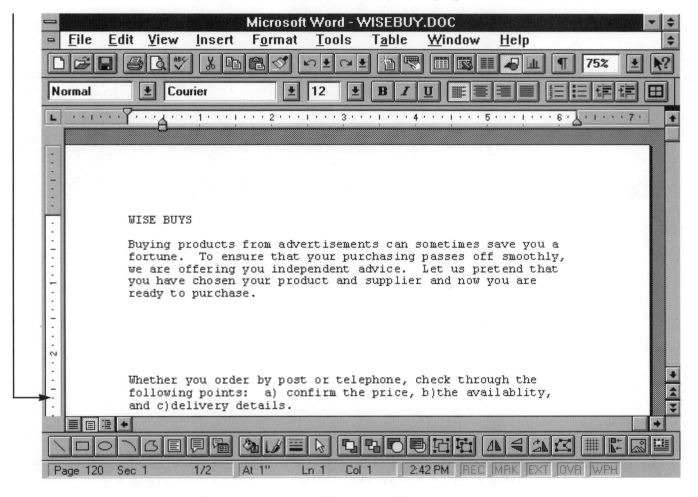

3)   If you compare the space on screen against the vertical ruler bar you will get some idea as to whether you have inserted the required space

Remember it is <u>very unlikely</u> that you will be requested to leave an exact measurement, the examination paper usually says "at least" 25 mm (1").

For a quicker way to measure space see the next page.

7)   There will be a flashing **I** beam in the rectangular **Header** box

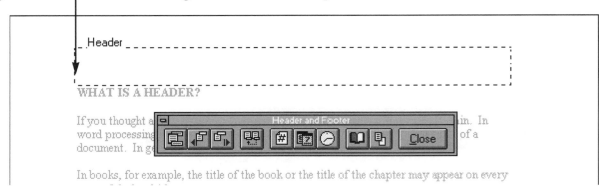

8)   Type in capital letters the word

                          HEADER

9)   Click on Close

10)   You will see the word HEADER as a faint outline at the top of the document if you are working in **Page Layout View**. If you are working in **Normal View** headers and/or footers will not show. When inserting headers or footers it would be advisable to change to this view by clicking on the icon at the bottom left of your screen

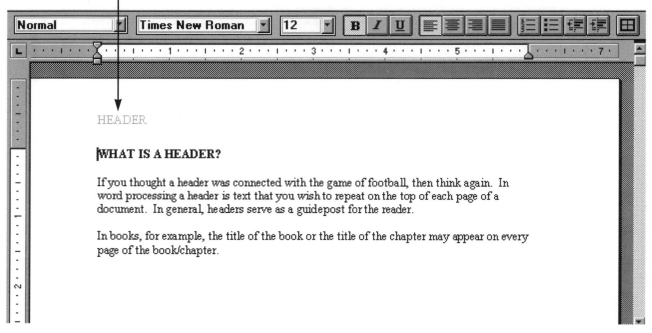

11)   **Print Preview** your document to check that the header appears on each page. **IF YOUR HEADER IS NOT SHOWING WHEN IN PRINT PREVIEW** adjust your top margin and header measurements on **Page Setup (File menu)**. This problem is similar to the one in Lesson 4 when page numbers did not appear when in Print Preview

12)   Quick save your document and print one copy. Each of the 3 pages printed should have the word HEADER on the top left

13)   Leave your document on screen

SHOW/HIDE ICON

1)   You can quickly see how many returns you have pressed by clicking on the **Show/Hide** icon on the **Standard toolbar**

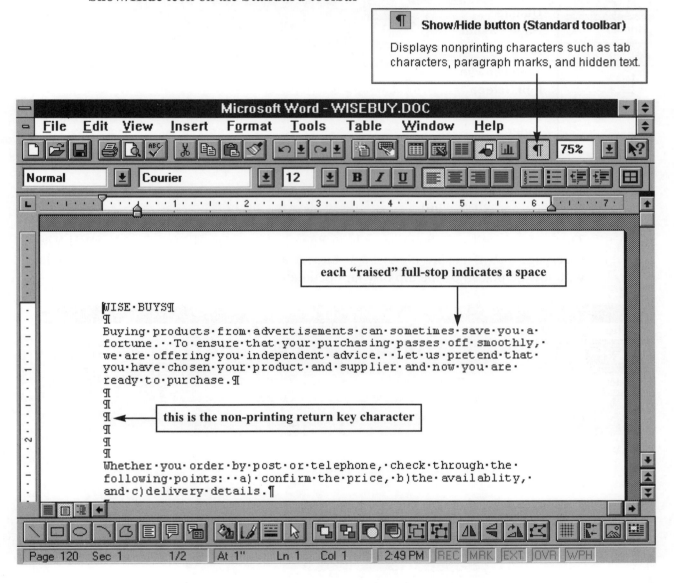

2)   Pressing this icon reveals on screen the special (non-printing) characters. In this exercise as well as the return key character you can see the number of spaces you have left between words (shown as a raised full stop)

3)   Check the size of the space you have left. Amend if necessary and print one copy of the document. Leave on the screen

INSERTING A HEADER

4) Click on **View** on the **Menu Bar**

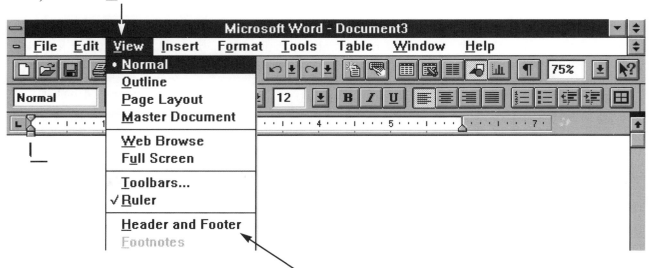

5) From the drop-down menu click on **Header and Footer**

6)   The program will switch temporarily to **Page Layout view** if you are in **Normal View**. (See page 116 if unsure about Page Layout and Normal View.) The Header toolbar will now be placed on the top of your document

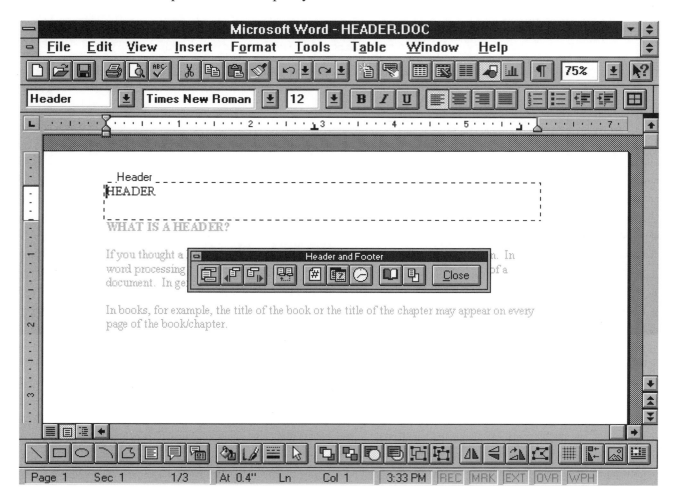

NORMAL VIEW AND PAGE LAYOUT VIEW

Most functions work equally in **Normal View** and **Page Layout View**. There are slight differences which you might find interesting.

Normal View   As the name implies, Normal is the view most people normally use for most of their work. It is generally considered to be a WYSIWYG (What you see is what you get) because what you see on the screen is a close approximation of what you'll get on the printed page. By default normal view will show you all character and paragraph formatting, line breaks, tab stops and page breaks (shown as a dotted line across the screen page).

It does not show headers and footers (covered in Lesson 12), footnotes, top and bottom margins on a page, ruler bar, etc. Normal View will let you see the text at the bottom of one page and the top of another at the same time – you may find this facility useful. It is also faster working in Normal View than working in Page Layout View.

With the **WISEBUY** document on screen look at Normal View now.

1)   To set your screen for Normal View click on the **Normal View** icon at the bottom left of your screen

2)   Look at your screen, perhaps put a hard return (see Lesson 5) between the 2 paragraphs to see the page break detail

Page Layout View   One of the advantages of Page Layout View is that it shows headers and footers, and footnotes as they will appear on the printed page. It also displays snaking columns side by side and shows how text will wrap around fixed-position objects (covered in the third and advanced book in this series). However Page Layout View requires Word to work much harder – making complex calculations to determine the line and page formatting. As a result you will find that your computer works slower than in Normal View.

If you scroll around your document in Page Layout View, Word displays top and bottom margins of each page as well as the top and bottom edges of the pages. You can also see the left and right edges of the page when you scroll horizontally. When you are viewing the bottom of one page and the top of the next in Page Layout View your page margins take up much of the available screen space.

With the **WISEBUY** document on screen look at Page Layout View now.

3)   Click once on **Page Layout View** icon at the bottom left of your screen

4)   When you have finished looking at Page Layout View clear the screen

LESSON 12	HEADERS AND FOOTERS
	INSERTING A HEADER
	INSERTING A FOOTER
	PRACTISE INSERTING A HEADER
	PRACTISE INSERTING HEADERS AND FOOTERS
	AMEND HEADERS AND FOOTERS
	INSERT PAGE NUMBERS WITHIN A FOOTER
	DELETE OR AMEND EXISTING HEADER OR FOOTER
	INSERTING HEADERS/FOOTERS AND PAGE NUMBERING THE SECOND AND SUBSEQUENT DOCUMENT PAGES
	CONSOLIDATION (combined with Lesson 13)

HEADERS AND FOOTERS

Exercise 12a

> **TARGET TIME 18 MINUTES – keying in time only**

1) Remember to time yourself and fill in your target time sheet. Type in the following text:

All shoulder headings in CAPS

What is a header?

If you thought a header was connected with the game of football, then think again. In word processing a header is text that you wish to repeat on the top of each page of a document. In general, headers serve as a guidepost for the reader.

In books, for example, the title of the book or the title of the chapter may appear on every page of the book/chapter.

← *start a new page here (insert a hard page break –)*
(hold down Ctrl. + press return)

What is a footer?

A footer is similar in function to a header except instead of being placed at the top of the page it is placed at the bottom. The words contained in the footer can be centred to the page or aligned to the left or right as desired.

← *start a new page*

Page numbering

 required

If ~~desired~~ page numbering can be inserted at the same time as a header or footer. If a header is needed on a multi-page document some people prefer to add the page number at the same time to save a separate task later.

2) Carefully check your work and correct any mistakes found. Spell-check

3) Save your file as **HEADER**. Leave the document on screen

PRACTISE OPENING AND RENAMING AN EXISTING DOCUMENT AND INSERTING SPACE WITHIN RETRIEVED TEXT – USING [Courier] **FONT**

Exercise 10h

TARGET TIME 20 MINUTES

---

1) Retrieve the following document saved as **BIKINI.** Immediately rename the file **BIKINI2**. Amend as indicated. Remember to time yourself and fill in your target time sheet

---

A MESSAGE FOR WOMEN *(Justify right margin)*

WHAT TO WEAR IN WINTER ← *(bold)*

It's cold outside, in fact ~~water~~ *ice* is freezing on the pavements. The weather man forecasts freezing rain and you are so glad to be snug and warm in your centrally heated ~~house~~ *rooms*. As you put your feet up, mug of hot coffee in hand, ready to read the newspaper, give a thought for the glamour model draping herself decorously against some cold iron railing on a seaside pier. She is modelling ~~next~~ the new designer swim range for next summer, but ~~of course~~ in order to meet the advertising and marketing plan the photographs have to be taken in chilly January. *(Leave at least 25mm (1") here)* ↕

In the following July as you bask in the heatwave, ice-cold drink in hand, ~~and carefully painted toe nails curling in the sand,~~ spare these poor long-suffering women another thought. Think about them wrapped in fake fur wearing long black skirts which have material as thick as blankets. *t*hink of them *(siting)* under the ~~ark~~ *arc* lights in a stuffy studio, or walking up and down the promenade under the glaring sun so that just the right image can be captured on film. ∥ Think of them and smile ...... be glad that you are not 6 feet tall, with a figure like Popeye's girlfriend and a smile like a dentist advertisement. You are allowed to be slovenly and laze in the sun or curl up by the fire whenever you please!

Did you think that these poor ~~skinny~~ models would be whisked away to warmer climates? The internationally famous variety are very likely to be modelling bikinis in Kuwait but their 'bread and butter' sisters whose new season trends are likely to ~~be photographed~~ *appear* in the local catalogue will be suffering a very different fate. *(or somewhere equally as hot)*

who, at that very minute, is

Move last paragraph underneath space

---

2) Carefully check your work and correct any mistakes found. Spell-check

3) Quick save your file, print preview and print one copy. Measure the space for accuracy

4) Carefully check your work against **model answer EX10H** which has been saved on the disk that accompanies this book. Clear the screen

CONSOLIDATION EXERCISE FOR LESSON 11

Exercise 11g

TARGET TIME 15 MINUTES

Practise what you have learnt so far by following the instructions below:

1)   Remember to time yourself and fill in your target time sheet. Retrieve the following document saved as **CLIENT**. Immediately rename the file **CLIENT1**. Amend as indicated

Change to double line spacing, unless indicated, and use a justified right margin. Adjust line length to either (a) 12.5cm(5") or (b) 50 characters.

CLIENT VERSUS CUSTOMER ← *emphasise*

Please add pg. no's

When a young man visits the ~~barber~~ *hairdresser* to buy a new hair style ~~at the~~ does the ~~hairdresser~~ *barber* refer ✓ to him as a client or a customer? Is there a difference in approach in the unisex or ladies hairdressers? [The word "client" is increasing in popularity and before long ~~buying~~ a sticky bun at the local bakers ~~will enable the~~ *no doubt you will hear the* shop assistant to call out "next client please". *when you*

Not so long ago the 2 words had separate and distinct meanings. Everyone was a customer, whether they were visiting the hairdressers or waiting for a train.

A client was someone who used someone else's professional services: perhaps it is the demise of the description of 'profession' which has brought about the dual use of the words client and customer. In the 15th century very few people were thought of as being employed in a profession - lawyers were one of the few professions at that time, and they most certainly had 'clients'.

inset 25mm (1") from left margin.

Those misled into thinking that being called 'client' is rather classy and a mark of respect should always remember that the word has its Roman origins in an ancient protection racket. In return for a patron's protection the 'client' would pay 'over the odds'. Does anything ever change?

Today if you look through your local newspaper you will find that the marketing people rather like the term 'client'. It is used *by* those who employ the services of insurance brokers, public relations people, estate agents, midwives, *and* social workers, to name but a few.

emphasise in some way and inset in

Leave at least 50mm (2")here ↕

For information the dictionary definition of client is "employer of a lawyer; employer of any professional man" and the definition of customer is "a buyer; a person to deal with."

This last paragraph in single line spacing

2)   Carefully check and spell-check your work. Quick save your file. Print preview before printing one copy. Clear the screen

3)   Carefully check your work against **model answer CONSOL11** which has been saved on the disk that accompanies this book

INSERTING SPACE WITHIN NEW TEXT – USING Times New Roman FONT

Exercise 10i

TARGET TIME 20 MINUTES

1) Change the font to Times New Roman size 12

2) Type in the following text. Remember to time yourself and fill in your target time sheet

(Justify right margin + double line spacing, unless specified.)

THE SPORT OF KINGS? ← centre

WINTER IN THE GULF ← (change layout to look like second sub-heading)

The time may be ~~close~~ near when no horse owner hoping to win a Classic or a Group race ~~can~~ will be able to afford not to give their horses the edge that wintering abroad can provide. English winters, it seems, do not improve winning techniques as much as winters in Dubai. Recently horses whose owners have been able to afford to send them to winter in the sunshine have been extending their advantage over those left in England.

↕ ← (Please leave at least 50mm (2") here)

Showmanship

(Single line spacing)

Modernisation of the ~~restuarants~~ restaurants and bars at racing grounds is a matter the British Horseracing Board is giving serious consideration this summer. France-Galop the equivalent of the B........... H.............. B................ have already realised that they need to work at enticing holidaymakers and upgrading facilities have been high on their list in order to satisfy an ever-demanding audience. In Deauville a total of £4.2 million has recently been spent on upgrading facilities. Some French people believe that this is too much, but if compared with the betting turnover on the Tierce in France, then it is not.

3) Carefully check your work and correct any mistakes found. Spell-check

4) Save your file as **HORSE**, print preview and print one copy. Measure the space for accuracy

5) Carefully check your work against **model answer EX10(I)** which has been saved on the disk that accompanies this book

PRACTISE SETTING LINE LENGTHS WITH RETRIEVED TEXT

Exercise 11f

> ## TARGET TIME 10 MINUTES

1) Remember to time yourself and fill in your target time sheet. Retrieve the following document saved as **RETIRE.** Immediately rename the file **RETIRE.** Amend as indicated

Adjust line length to 11.5CM (4½"), use a justified right margin

RETIREMENT

Leaving work can be a major threat to the identity of a person if it is not carefully planned. Commencing a new job can be stressful but also may be a ~~very~~ positive move for various reasons - promotion, moving house or seeking a different environment ~~in~~ *working* ~~which to work~~ can all have beneficial effects. Retirement can also enrich life providing the individual has prepared for change. A recent Department of Social Security survey found that most people expected to retire before state pension age. However, ~~very~~ few people plan for their retirement and it becomes a challenging moment ~~in people's lives~~.

in their lives. Attending a pre-retirement course can help people adjust to the idea beforehand and also help them plan their short and long term objectives.

2) Carefully check your work, especially against the following correct copy. Quick save your document and clear the screen

RETIREMENT

Leaving work can be a major threat to the identity of a person if it is not carefully planned. Commencing a new job can be stressful but also may be a positive move for various reasons - promotion, moving house or seeking a different **working** environment can all have beneficial effects.

Retirement can also enrich life providing the individual has prepared for change. A recent Department of Social Security survey found that most people expected to retire before state pension age. However, **very** few people plan for their retirement and it becomes a challenging moment **in their lives**. Attending a pre-retirement course can help people adjust to the idea beforehand and also help them plan their **long and short** term objectives.

INSERTING SPACE WITHIN RETRIEVED TEXT – USING Times New Roman FONT

Exercise 10j

1) Retrieve the following document saved as **MEASURE**

2) Immediately rename the file **MEASURE1**. Amend as indicated. See page 220 for instructions on how to insert fractions if you are unsure.

MEASUREMENT AND CENTRING ← *centre and bold*

MEASUREMENT OF VERTICAL SPACE ← *bold*

You will be required to leave vertical space within one document in the examination. It is *indeed* very unlikely that the space you leave will have to be exactly measured. You are more likely to be asked to leave "at least" 25 mm (1") at a certain point in the document.

The measurement of the space requested is also likely not to be an exact conversion from inches to millimetres. For example 25.4 mm = 1" but the examination paper will probably ask for a 25 mm (1") space.

For your information exact conversion figures are given below:

1"	= 2.54 cm or 25.4 mm
1½ "	= 3.81 cm or 38.1 mm
2"	= 5.08 cm or 50.8 mm
2 ½"	= 6.35 cm or 63.5 mm
3"	= 7.62 cm or 76.2 mm
3½	= 8.89 cm or 88.9 mm

emphasize all figures here

Leave 1½" (38mm) here

CENTRING ← *bold*

The performance criteria for this examination also states that the candidate should know how to *centre* over the typing line. This means that you should know how to able to centre *be* a heading in existing and new text. This was dealt with in detail in the first book in this series but if you have forgotten how to do this, it is simply a matter of clicking on the "**Center**" (spelt the American way!) icon on the *formatting* toolbar before typing in new text. If the text already exists highlight it first and then click on the "**Center**" icon.
place the cursor anywhere within the text

---

3) Carefully check your work against the following correct copy. Spell-check

4) Quick save your file, print preview and print one copy. Measure the space you have left for accuracy

5) Carefully check your work against **model answer EX10J** which has been saved on the disk that accompanies this book. Clear the screen

PRACTISE SETTING LINE LENGTHS

Exercise 11e

1)   Set the left and right margins at 1.39″ (3.52 cm). This will give you a line length of 5½″ (13.97 cm). Type in the following text:

SETTING LINE LENGTHS ← *centre*

If you need to adjust the line length of your entire document it is better to set new margins before you begin typing. If you wish to amend the line length of a completed document after input, ~~highlight all the text concerned and~~ set the margins using **File and Page Set̲u̲p̲** from the Menu Bar. ^*new*

Justify text
The right margin will need to be justified (fully) in order to display the line length to its full advantage. This can be chosen before commencing input or ~~if preferred~~ by highlighting *all* the text and clicking on the **Justify** icon on the Formatting Toolbar.

Line lengths   *set out below*
(✓)(✓) To obtain line lengths ~~indicated below~~ set the margins as ~~advised~~:

3½ inch (8.89 cm) line length set left and right margin at 2.39 inches (6.06 cm)
4 inch (10.16 cm) line length set left and right margin at 2.14 inches (5.42 cm)
4½ inch (11.43 cm) line length set left and right margin at 1.89 inches (4.79 cm)
5 inch (12.7 cm) line length set left and right margin at 1.64 inches (4.15 cm)
5½ inch (13.97 cm) line length set left and right margin at 1.39 inches (3.52 cm)
6 inch (15.24) line length set left and right margin at 1.14 inches (2.88 cm)
6½ inch (16.51) line length set left and right margin at 0.89 inches (2.25 cm)

↕ *Leave at least 25 mm (1″) here*
REMINDER ← *(lower case + underlined)*

Double line spacing

if you prefer you can do this at the end

(a) In the examination all measurements are likely to be rounded up or down as appropriate. For example a line length of 5½ inches would be expressed as 14 cm.

room
(b) You are allowed to take into the examination ~~to have~~ a copy of the margin settings needed for various line lengths.

— *Inset this section 13mm (½″) from leftmargin*

---

2)   Carefully check your work against **model answer EX11E** which has been saved on the disk that accompanies this book. **Take extra care checking the figures in this case**

3)   Spell-check and save your file as **LINELNTH**. Print preview before you print one copy and **KEEP FOR FUTURE REFERENCE**. Clear the screen

CONSOLIDATION EXERCISE FOR LESSON 10

> **TARGET TIME 17 MINUTES**

Practise what you have learnt so far by following the instructions below. Remember to time yourself and fill in your target time sheet

1) Retrieve the following document saved as **CHARITY**

2) Immediately rename the file **CHARITY2**. Amend as indicated

---

CI/BB

Mrs S Grundy
The Rose and Crown Inn
Meadow View
Tunbridge Wells
Kent TN3 3RY

Justify right margin

Dear Mrs Grundy

ACTION FOR ANIMALS CHARITY ← *centre*

On behalf of the above charity I would like to thank you and your customers for the generous donation of £83.14. The valuable work we do would come to a standstill if it were not for ~~your~~ *your* the kindness and support ~~of people such as you.~~

~~Our charity is solely supported~~ by voluntary contributions and we rely upon ~~our vital~~ *the generous* ~~campaigns~~ to help animals in distress. *support of the public*

I am enclosing a dated receipt and a second copy of this letter *as requested* to enable you to ~~display a copy in both bars~~ *give a copy to Mr Johnson for the skittles Team.*

It will be our annual ACTION FOR ANIMALS DAY from 4 - 10 October and I am arranging to send to you under separate cover ~~the ANIMAL'S DAY~~ *our special* pack. This contains peel-off button stickers which are quite eye-catching (see below), posters and ideas for fund-raising, etc. I hope it will be of interest to you.

Yours sincerely ↕ ← *Leave 1½" (38mm) here for peel-off button to be placed at least*

Stephen Iles
ACTION FOR ANIMALS CHARITY

---

3) Carefully check your work and correct any mistakes found. Spell-check and quick save your file. Print preview and print one copy and clear the screen

4) Carefully check your work against **model answer EX10J** which has been saved on the disk that accompanies this book

MARGINS – CHANGING LINE LENGTHS

The RSA Word Processing 2 Part 2 examination will request that you format the line length to a certain width. For example you might be instructed to adjust the line length to either (a) 14 cm (5½″) or (b) 55 characters. If you are using proportional spacing you need to choose (a). You will also need to format to a justified right margin. **This has been fully explained in the first book of this series if you need detailed instructions on working out your own line lengths**

Exercise 11d

1) Choose a proportional font such as **Times New Roman.** Size **12**

2) Fully justify the page (ie left and right margins both aligned straight).

3) A4 size paper is approximately 21 cms (8¼″ wide). The default margin setting (ie the size the computer chooses automatically unless you change it) is normally 3.81 cm (1½″) each side.

   Set the left and right margin at 6.06 cm (2.39″). This will give you a line length of 9 cm (3½″).

4) Type in the following text:

SHENANDOAH ← emphasise

As we paid our 5$ to enter the Shenandoah National Park in America my mind wandered back to my childhood when as a junior school pupil I learnt the old folk song "Shenandoah". I always thought it was a love song but I could never quite make sense of the words - now it all fell into place.

Shenandoah encompasses 195,000 acres of woodland and meadows straddling the Blue Ridge section of the Appalachian Mountains. It is a sanctuary for more than 100 varieties of trees, 200 species of birds and over 1,00 flowering plants. It is 1,000 so beautiful it is breathtaking. So It is no wonder that the words of the folk song said "Oh Shenandoah, I love your daughter" because I learnt as I entered the Park that Shenandoah means "daughter of the stars".

5) Check your document and clear the screen without saving

LESSON 11	WORKING WITH RETRIEVED TEXT
	INDENTING TEXT FROM LEFT MARGIN
	RULER BAR METHOD
	AUTO-INDENT METHOD
	TO UNDO AUTO-INDENT
	PRACTISE INDENTATION OF PARAGRAPHS IN
	RETRIEVED WORK
	MARGINS – CHANGING LINE LENGTHS
	PRACTISE SETTING LINE LENGTHS
	PRACTISE SETTING LINE LENGTHS WITH
	RETRIEVED TEXT
	CONSOLIDATION

WORKING WITH RETRIEVED TEXT

Exercise 11a

TARGET TIME 20 MINUTES

1)   Retrieve the following document saved as **SHOOT.** Remember to time yourself and fill
       in your target time sheet. Immediately rename the file **SHOOT2**. Amend as indicated

CRUELTY TO CLAY PIGEONS! ← *centre + bold*

Justify right margin please. Add page numbering bottom right to both pages

I had heard the old tales of the origins of organised shooting in England, but could I really
believe that some ingenious old soul actually put a pigeon under his top hat and then
promptly announced to the world that he would straightaway release the bird, replace his
hat - and then shoot the pigeon! *If this were true there would have been some very yukky sticky hair styles in the early 1800's.*

The next part of the story conjures up hilarious visions of a field full of little hats with tiny
little pigeon legs running beneath.

little

I can believe the *next* part of the story as it seems immensely more sensible to put the pigeons on
the ground beneath old hats with a string attached. When the string was "PULLed" - the hat
released and the sportsman shot as it. *This* ←
↳the bird   at

run on

When the string was pulled a *can* pigeon would have jumped back quickly under the safety *← ca*
of the hat and made a quick bee-line for the hedge. Who wants to be shot at? With all this in
mind I ventured to a Shooting Beginners day in the Mendip Hills. As a complete beginner I
approached this day with some trepidation - I was not going to be very good at this sport, I

PRACTISE INDENTATION OF PARAGRAPHS IN RETRIEVED WORK

Exercise 11c

TARGET TIME 15 MINUTES

1) Remember to time yourself and fill in your target time sheet. Retrieve the following document saved as **CAR**

2) Immediately rename the file **CAR1**. Amend as indicated. Choose a different font for this work

---

SPECIFICATIONS ← *centre heading & embolden*

← *leave at least 25 m/m (1") here*

All our new cars are fitted with high safety equipment as standard. The basic models all contain:

Electronic anti-lock brakes
Driver's full size airbag
Front/rear fog lamps
Side impact protection bars
Halogen head lamps with levelling control

indent this section 38 mn (1½") from left margin

For your comfort and convenience all basic models contain power assisted steering and a height adjustable steering column plus a stereo radio/cassette. The 2.0 CDXi models have many extras including tinted glass, adjustable height seats, folder rear seats *and electric front and rear windows.*

Special Note

Double line spacing

We are constantly always seeking ways to improve specification, design and production of our vehicles and alterations take place continually. Whilst every effort is made to produce up-to-date current literature this should not be regarded as an infallible guide to current specifications. However we are sure you would be delighted with any changes made.

---

3) Spell-check and carefully check your work. Print preview before printing one copy

4) Carefully check your work against **model answer EX11C** which has been saved on the disk that accompanies this book. Clear the screen

have terrible hand-eye co-ordination I told myself, (why! I can't ~~reach~~ hit a slow moving
badminton shuttle cock) and beside which my balance isn't good either. I can't even balance
on one rollerskate, let alone trusting my wobbly legs to 2. Still, I couldn't be the coward in
the family could I, _especially with 2 teenagers eagerly watching?_

> need   dressed   astronaut

I imagined I would really ~~have to~~ be ~~kitted out~~ rather like an ~~astronaught~~ in order to be let
loose with a gun. You know the kind of outfit I mean - helmet, goggles, sponge inner ear
plugs with sound-protection ear muffs on top, bullet proof vest (you never know who might

> mosquitoes

miss their aim), shooting vest, protective leggings (in case of rain, ~~mosquitos~~ or just pigeons
bent on getting their own back).

> Surprisingly

~~Suprising~~ no, when I arrived all I needed (was) ear muffs and my sunglasses would suffice as
goggles. They trusted me just as I was - 10 our of 10 so far.

> Insert (A) here   (this will be given to you later)

The tutor seemed very confident as he led our little party of 4 onto the riffle range - but the
fun had yet to begin!

> (leave at least 25mm (1") here
> (after insert (A)))   ↑ emphasise
>   the words
>   underlined

2)   Carefully check your work and correct any mistakes found. Spell-check

3)   Quick save your file. Leave the document on screen and add the paragraph below as
        indicated

> (A) (to be inserted in the above document where indicated)
>
> ~~On arrival~~ The tutor assured us of the safety of
> shotgun shooting. 'That was before we arrived'
> I thought. The one golden rule that we should
> remember above all else we were told   ← emphase
> was "never point your gun at something you
> are unwilling to destroy". My chance had come,
> a little gleam appeared in my eyes as I
> looked at my family - this could be goodbye to
> mounds of washing + ironing, endless cooking, ~~waiting~~
> up staying awake until 3am to make sure someone
> arrived home safely and above all _I would no longer have_ ~~having~~ to listen to
> loud noisy music permeating every corner of the house.

4)   Quick save your work once more and print one copy

5)   Carefully check your work against **model answer EX11A** which has been saved on
        the disk that accompanies this book

2) Click once on the **auto-indent increase icon** on the formatting toolbar

3) Look at your text – it will have indent 1.25 cm (½ inch). Indent this text by 50 cm (2 inches) by clicking on the auto-indent increase icon 3 more times

4) Click on the **Print Preview** icon to view your work. The third paragraph should now be indented as below:

DIAMONDS

If someone mentions the name Africa, do you immediately think of Nelson Mandela? or

perhaps you are a rugby fan and your mind turns to sport. On the **other hand** it may

remind you of very hot **sunshine** and drought. If you deal in international financial

transactions on the stock exchange it will, no doubt, be diamonds that spring to mind.

Africa has been one of the principal diamond-producing countries in the world since
1866 when a child playing on the bank of the Orange River in South Africa picked up a
pretty pebble that was identified as a diamond.

> Natural diamonds are formed when pieces of carbon come
> under enormous pressures and temperatures deep in the
> earth. However, only 20% of rough diamonds are suitable
> for **jewellery**, the remainder being used for industrial
> purposes.

> Certain diamonds have become famous, One of the oldest, the Koh-i-Noor
> (Mount of Light) was so coveted by Asian rulers that wars were fought over it. It
> is now among the crown jewels of Great Britain. The **2 largest** are the Star of
> Africa (530 carats) and the Cullinan II (317 carats). The Cullinan diamond, found
> in the Transvaal in 1905, was presented to Edward VII and after cutting yielded 9
> principal gems.

5) Return to Normal View or Page Layout View (whichever you prefer to work in – see page 116). Quick save your document

TO UNDO AUTO-INDENT

1) Place cursor anywhere within the third paragraph once again

2) Click on the **Decrease indent** icon (to the left of the **Auto-indent increase icon**) 4 times

3) Each time you clicked on the **Decrease icon** the third paragraph text will have moved 1.25 cm (½ inch) towards the left margin. Clear the screen without saving again

INDENTING TEXT FROM LEFT MARGIN (RULER BAR AND AUTO-INDENT METHODS)

Exercise 11b

1)   Type in the following text:

Diamonds ← CAPS + CENTRED

If someone mentions the name Africa, do you immediately think of Nelson Mandela? Or perhaps you are a rugby fan and your mind turns to sport. On the other hand it may remind you of very hot sunshine and drought.

Double line spacing

If you deal in international financial transactions on the stock exchange it will, no doubt, be diamonds that spring to mind.

Natural diamonds are formed when pieces of carbon come under enormous pressures and temperatures deep in the earth. However, only 20% of rough diamonds are suitable for jewellery; the remainder being used for industrial purposes.

decorative purposes

Africa has been one of the principal diamond-producing countries in the world since 1866 when a child playing on the bank of the Orange River in South Africa picked up a pretty pebble that was quickly identified as a diamond.

Certain diamonds have become famous, One of the oldest, the Koh-i-Noor (Mount of Light) was so coveted by Asian rulers that wars were fought over it. It is now among the crown jewels of Great Britain. The largest 2 are the Star of Africa (530 carats) and the Cullinan II (317 carats).

The Cullinan diamond, found in the Transvaal in 1905, was presented to Edward VII and after cutting yielded nine principal gems.

---

2)   Spell-check and save your file as **DIAMOND.** Print preview your document

3)   Carefully check your work against **model answer EX11B** which has been saved on the disk that accompanies this book

4)   Leave your document on screen

(B) Auto-indent method of indenting text

A far quicker way to indent text is to use the auto-indent icon. If this icon is clicked once it will indent text to the first default tab stop. Default tabs are set at 1.25 cm (½ inch) intervals (see the first book in this series if you would like more information on tabulation and tab setting). Each time the icon is clicked it will indent to the next tab setting, ie click 4 times and the paragraph would indent 50 mm (2 inches):

$$4 \times 1.25 \text{ cm} = 50 \text{ mm}/4 \times \tfrac{1}{2} \text{ inch} = 2''$$

If you wish to indent a measurement other than a multiple of 1.25 cm [½ inch] then you must insert a tab setting first.

Follow the instructions below to indent the third paragraph using the auto-indent icon:

1)   Place the cursor anywhere within in the third paragraph

international financial transactions on the stock exchange it will, no doubt, be diamonds that spring to mind.

Africa has been one of the principal diamond-producing countries in the world since 1866 when a child playing on the bank of the Orange River in South Africa picked up a pretty pebble that was identified as a diamond.

Natural diamonds are formed when pieces of carbon come under enormous pressures and temperatures deep in the earth. However, only 20% of rough diamonds are suitable for **jewellery**; the remainder being used for industrial purposes.

Certain diamonds have become famous, One of the oldest, the Koh-i-Noor (Mount of Light) was so coveted by Asian rulers that wars were fought over it. It is now among the crown jewels of Great Britain. The **2 largest** are the Star of Africa (530 carats) and the Cullinan II (317 carats). The Cullinan diamond, found in the Transvaal in 1905, was presented to Edward VII and after cutting yielded **9** principal gems.

INDENTING TEXT FROM LEFT MARGIN (continued)

In the examination you will be requested to indent a specific section of text. There are several methods that you could use to do this. To indent paragraphs of the **DIAMOND** text (**EX11B**) follow the instructions below.

(A)   Ruler bar method of indenting text

1)   Place the cursor in the last paragraph of text

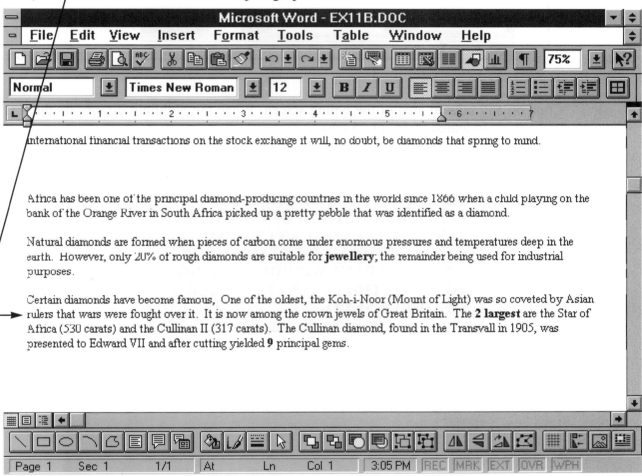

2)   Point into the small rectangular box immediately underneath the bottom triangle